ANDREW MARVELL AND EDMUND WALLER

ANDREW MARVELL
AND
EDMUND WALLER

Seventeenth-Century Praise
and
Restoration Satire

A. B. Chambers

THE PENNSYLVANIA STATE UNIVERSITY PRESS
University Park and London

Library of Congress Cataloging-in-Publication Data

Chambers, A. B. (Alexander B.)
    Andrew Marvell and Edmund Waller : seventeenth-century praise and
restoration satire / by A.B. Chambers.
        p.   cm.
    ISBN 0-271-00703-6 (alk. paper)
    1. English poetry—Early modern, 1500–1700—History and criticism.
2. Marvell, Andrew, 1621–1678—Criticism and interpretation.
3. Waller, Edmund, 1606–1687—Criticism and interpretation.
4. Laudatory poetry, English—History and criticism. 5. Verse
satire, English—History and criticism. 6. Praise in literature.
I. Title.
PR541.C48   1991
821'.409—dc20   89–71031

It is the policy of The Pennsylvania State University Press to use acid-free
paper for the first printing of all clothbound books. Publications on
uncoated stock satisfy the minimum requirements of American National
Standard for Information Sciences—Permanence of Paper for Printed
Library Materials, ANSI Z39.48-1984.

Contents

Old Waller, trumpet-gen'ral, swore he'd write
This combat truer than the naval fight.
                    —Marvell's "Last Instructions"

Preface

Strange though it seems, in 1660, the year of the Restoration, Edmund Waller actually was an eminent poet whose claims to fame rivaled those of even his most illustrious predecessors, and Andrew Marvell can have had scarcely any poetic reputation at all. Today, of course, that situation has completely reversed itself. Waller, it is true, continues to be mentioned in literary histories because he simply cannot be totally ignored. After all, he did anticipate the style, especially the versification and diction, which largely prevailed from Dryden through Pope. It is Marvell, however, who now occupies a position which Waller, along with many another writer, might earlier have envied.

The modern assessment of these two authors is more accurate, surely, than the earlier one, but it seems to me that Marvell is not always praised for all of the right reasons and that Waller, whatever the reasons, has fallen on undeservedly hard times. "To his Coy Mistress," to begin to be specific, is both broader and deeper in its implications than has been thought by even the most ardent of Marvell's admirers. This in itself is a point worth establishing, but also important is that Marvell's "Last Instructions to a Painter" has received considerably less recognition than a mock epic of such astonishing vigor and virtuosity merits. Further, Marvell quite literally could not have penned his satire had Waller not preceded him by instructing an artist how to paint a picture of glowing praise, and that poem also was and is worth reading. Waller was attempting to educate his monarch, as well as an imaginary painter, about what Restoration England could and should become, a lesson he earlier attempted to convey—unsuccessfully, as it turned out—in "On St. James's Park As Lately Improved by His Majesty." And since Waller also had high praise for ladies, whether coy or not, he and Marvell approach one another more closely than might be supposed from either the older or the newer evaluations of their work.

Marvell and Waller, I therefore suggest, are mutually illuminating in more ways than one and are so in poems of substantial intrinsic interest. I take this to be true even though the relationships between these writers are sometimes oblique rather than straightforward. The conceptual and poetic problems encountered by both authors were, moreover, by no means simplistic, and the strategies they evolved in addressing comparable needs are often subtly complex. In the chapters which follow I particularize these generalizations with various materials which may seem to have a complexity of their own because of their relative unfamiliarity to some readers today, but the final point is not at all opaque or indirect: The door through which Dryden made his entrance to become the dominant literary figure of the Restoration was pried open earlier by both of the authors considered here.

I am very grateful to The Pennsylvania State University Press, specifically to Philip Winsor, Senior Editor, for supporting this project, and I must not end this preface without acknowledging a long-standing debt of staggering proportions to the Department of English of the University of Wisconsin—Madison.

1

Marvell and Waller

Andrew Marvell was fifty-seven in 1678, the year of his death, and surely did not anticipate dying "from medical treatment prescribed for a tertian ague."[1] He did not necessarily intend, therefore, that his last work be a polemic in prose: *An Account of the Growth of Popery and Arbitrary Government in England* (1677). Edmund Waller, born in 1606, was fifteen years older than Marvell and outlived the younger man by nine years. He chose, deliberately and explicitly, to end his writing career piously with "divine poems" on the grounds that "When we for age could neither read, nor write, / The subject made us able to indite" (*Works*, 201).[2] Marvell's prose is grimly precise: The texts of parliamentary bills are given, speeches are quoted, statistical documentation is amassed; apparently no stone that Marvell could think of was left unturned to fulfill the aim, baldly announced, of showing quite conclusively that lawful government was being subverted into absolute tyranny and true religion being displaced by downright popery. Waller's intent, equally overt, was to urge, "Could we forbear dispute, and practice love, / We should agree, as Angels do above" ("Of Divine

---

1. *The Oxford Companion to English Literature*, 5th ed., ed. Margaret Drabble (Oxford and New York, 1985), 625.
2. The References give bibliographical information about works frequently cited and the system used in citing them.

Love," 3). Waller could scarcely pretend ignorance of factional dispute; indeed, his couplet acknowledges and laments its existence. His vision, however, was so broad (or, if one prefers, so hazy) that he looked far beyond the boundaries of denominations and/or countries and even beyond those of the Christian religion itself. Divine Love, if responded to, could "make inward peace, / And foreign strife among the nations cease."

> No martial trumpet should disturb our rest,
> Nor Princes arm, tho' to subdue the east;
> Where, for the Tomb, so many Heroes (taught
> By those that guided their devotion) fought.
> Thrice happy we, could we like ardor have
> To gain his love, as they to win his grave!
> Love as he lov'd! A love so unconfin'd,
> With arms extended, would embrace mankind.

Since Waller clearly supposes that those who guided the devotion of the crusaders were themselves misguided, one of the medieval goals of the Church Militant, the winning of Jerusalem, is devalued into a manifestation of narrow-minded wrongheadedness. From this point of view, merely local fights between papists and Protestants (and, by extension, among Protestants themselves) begin to look about as seemly as a neighborhood tavern brawl.

Whatever the merits of these dichotomous positions may be, Marvell's and Waller's articulations of them will win few admirers. "When we for age," it is true, has joined hands in what might be called an ecumenical way with "Go lovely rose" as one of the few poems by Waller to be anthologized with some regularity, and the opening lines of the last verse paragraph are quite splendid in a macabre sort of way: "The soul's dark cottage, batter'd, and decay'd, / Lets in new light, thro' chinks that time has made." Versified platitude, however, is the better phrase to characterize "Of Divine Love" and "Of Divine Fear," not to mention "Some Reflections of His upon" the Lord's Prayer. Marvell's prose, as its title proclaims, is openly a tract for the times in which, as Chernaik points out, "Marvell strives for unembellished truth." "Such a work," he adds, "with its raw data, minimally selected and arranged, . . . represents a total, desperate renunciation of art."[3]

Interest in these works, insofar as it exists, probably is aroused not

---

3. Warren L. Chernaik, *The Poet's Time: Politics and Religion in the Work of Andrew Marvell* (Cambridge, 1983), 86.

by subject matter, therefore, but by the characteristic methodology or approach to the material which the writers adopt. Marvell unquestionably was a person of general principles intensely upheld; the tract itself evidences this fact. Despite or possibly because of it, in this work and elsewhere, he consistently examined particular cases with extraordinarily meticulous care, whether a parliamentary bill and speech or "The Nymph Complaining for the Death of Her Faun." "The Definition of Love" is a prototypical title in the sense that one of the principles Marvell evidently felt most strongly about was that imprecise thinking and writing could serve no useful purpose. He refers to himself as an "easy philosopher" in "Upon Appleton House" (561), but he is an uncommonly difficult poet, and one of the important reasons is that he seldom trusts the easy generalization. Another is that he regularly ransacked anything he could lay hands on in an effort to scrutinize whatever the subject might be from as fully informed a position as possible. His method very often is that of comparative analysis and is not unlike that of the Talmudic scholar: The sacred immutability of the Torah or Law is never in question and can sometimes even be taken for granted; what often needs to be done is not to discover and/or identify Truth Itself but rather to examine every significant detail of the particular case in its relationship to all other relevant particulars. Since "Puritan" appears to be one of the few labels for Marvell that have not come unglued almost as soon as put on, the preceding analogy probably looks odd. Yet I have little doubt that if Marvell himself thought the comparison could possibly be appropriate (and worth worrying about), he would have mentally reviewed exegetical technique—and probably not as exegesis was practiced by some ill-defined rabbinical group but as exemplified by Rashi, Kimchi, and other quite specific writers. Time permitting, he would have brushed up his Hebrew if need be, perhaps sent round to his bookseller, and settled in for some sedulous research.

Waller, until age slowed him down, usually would have paid a social call or written a polite poem instead. He very frequently gives the illusion of being at least as interested as Marvell in concrete detail—perhaps more so, in fact—since poem after poem is "occasional" work in the strict sense. King Charles I repairs St. Paul's Cathedral or is brought the news of Buckingham's death; Waller has been visiting at Penshurst or has encountered an acquaintance of some eminence at the Louvre in Paris; an author has published a book; a death or a wedding has occurred; tea has been commended by Her Majesty; or a lady named Isabella is playing the lute. It sometimes seems that any

and every occasion, however momentous or trivial, is the perfect
occasion for a poem. Usually, however, Waller merely appears to examine the particular situation. Or rather, he notices only those details
which are useful in enunciating a preconceived "message" which the
occasion can be seen to convey and embody in some way or other.
Elijah Fenton, Waller's idolatrous eighteenth-century editor, began
annotating "Upon the death of my Lady Rich" with the remark, "In all
Mr. *Waller*'s collection of Beauties, no one appears more amiable in all
lights than she whose untimely death is deplor'd in this excellent
elegy" (lxxv). Fenton cites firsthand information from Sidney Godol-
phin (the royalist poet and friend of Suckling) and from Dr. John
Gauden (to whom the pseudonymous *Eikon Basilike* of Charles I is
sometimes attributed) to show that Waller's high opinion was not
fanciful. Indeed, the lady's "accomplishments were in every kind so
extraordinary, that they seem to have transcended even [Waller's]
genius to delineate them as they deserv'd" (lxxvi).

These comments tell more, perhaps, than Fenton intended them to.
Lady Rich is part of a collection of Beauties, and if no one of them
appears more amiable than she, it also is true that no one of them
appears notably less so. Not many of her extraordinary accomplishments in every kind are sharply delineated in the poem, as they are in
Fenton's note, because Waller is concerned instead with resolute ac-
ceptance of Death itself and with the firm bases of consolation for the
bereaved. A latitudinarian aesthetic is not necessarily inimical to
respectable art, and this poem is not in fact a bad one, but the immediate point is that here, as often, Waller starts from the specific simply
because there is no other good place to begin.

The poem for Lady Rich is, moreover, an exceptionally useful example to cite for my purposes because Marvell wrote a comparable
poem for an untimely death, in this case of "the Lord Hastings."
Since Marvell's poem, like Waller's, is respectable but cannot stake a
claim to major status, no serious injustice will be done, I think, by
using both of them here to indicate—fairly briefly but also rather
concretely—the seventeenth-century context which they share and
the backgrounds which underlie their very different effects. Lady
Rich died in 1638 at the age of twenty-seven, Hastings in 1649 at the
age of nineteen. Waller was thirty-three, and Marvell twenty-eight.
For purposes of comparison, one can add that "Lycidas" was first
published in 1638, when Milton was thirty, and that Dryden, himself
nineteen, contributed a poem for the same memorial volume for
Hastings in which Marvell's lines first appeared. These dates and
ages are worth noticing, partly to keep a sense of literary history

firmly in mind, partly to keep one's sense of proportion. All of these poems are timely, but one of them, after all, is much more than that. "Lycidas" sets a standard that few poems of any age, including Milton's other funeral verse, can scarcely measure up to. In looking at Marvell and Waller, one will have to settle for less, and since that is so, a chronology not dependent on seventeenth-century dates may be helpful here.

Death itself seldom seems timely, of course, no matter at what age it arrives, but the poetic problems, and possibly emotional ones as well, are clearly different when lamenting an infant and mourning someone advanced in years. "Youth" and "prime of life" are stretchable terms but unmistakably fall somewhere in between the very young and very old. It is not unreasonable, therefore, to set to one side (to mention a famous and lengthy example) the ceremonies honoring the death of Anchises as celebrated by Aeneas and described by Virgil in his fifth book. With equal reasonableness, one may set to the other side Jonson's epigram (22) for Mary, his six-month-old daughter, and Milton's "On the Death of a Fair Infant." Among classical standards to cite for medial situations would be the poem by Statius (*Silvae*, 2.1) and the double poem by Martial (6.28 and 6.29) for the death of Glaucias, not quite thirteen when he died but old enough, as both authors assure us, to have given ample evidence of pure morals, simple modesty, a quick mind, rare beauty, and thus, to paraphrase Fenton, to have been amiable in nearly every kind.

Statius (vv. 124–25) makes the point that the youth's "rising years," as the Loeb translation puts it, "though infancy still was near, had begun to draw level with the toils of Hercules." "Young as he was," he had "early surpassed his peers in pride of step and countenance, and had far outstripped his years" (108–9; more literally—"multumque reliquerat annos"—had left the years much behind). This death is stern proof that "our race is of the mortal kind" (212), that "doomed are we all, ay, doomed" (218–19). The first consolation is that "gods and men hath he escaped, and doubtful chance and the dangers of our dark life" (220–22). The second, a startling one for which the only preparation that I can see is the remarkable worth of the youth, is that Glaucias is to speak from beyond the grave to comfort those yet living: "Come hither, Glaucias, who alone canst obtain all thou dost ask" (228–29); "soothe" ("mulce," 230), "tell . . . thou art not dead" ("periise nega," 233), "commend thy unhappy parents and thy sister left forlorn" (233–34). Since funeral verse deals with life and death, a doubleness would seem intrinsic to it, but in Statius there is a double reversal: Because doom is universal, only the dead have truly escaped; at the conclusion, instead of having the living weep for the dead, Statius has the now freed Glaucias soothe those still doomed to be alive.

Martial's verse for Glaucias is explicitly a double poem, and for several good reasons. The most obvious one, beyond the antithesis of life-death itself, is that 6.28 is appropriate for the funeral monument (Glaucias, we are told, reposes beneath this marble sepulcher), but 6.29 is not. A second point arises from the fact that the parents of Glaucias were slaves, but Glaucias himself had been freed. Martial thus works with the double freedom, an ironic kind, of a freed youth who leaves behind the slavish bondage of life. A third reason for doubleness is that two complementary conclusions can be given, one of them admonitory. 6.28 ends with the apparently unrealistic hope that the traveler who passes by the tomb will never have a greater loss to lament. 6.29 explains why those traveling onward (down the Flaminian Way or, implicitly, through the corridors of time) should not be excessively grieved by any other death, not even their own: Whatever it is you love, desire that you not have been pleased by it too much ("Quidquid ames, cupias non placuisse nimis").

As it happens, of course, 6.29 was an overt model for Jonson's epigram 45, "Farewell, thou child of my right hand, and joy," and Statius is probably in the background too.[4] Jonson begins, however, with antitheses which are biblical in origin. The first "Benjamin" had originally been named "Benoni," "son of sorrow," by his dying mother Rachel (Genesis 35.18) and renamed by Jacob, his father, to signify "son of the right hand" and thus to balance gain against loss. In Jonson, the sorrow of "Farewell" is set off by "joy," each word in emphatic position; the words bracket "child," one not yet named in the title or in this first line, and "of the right hand," a translation of what the name not mentioned means. This young son, who is both a Ben-oni and a Ben-jamin as the poem begins, died at the age of seven. Little more than half as old as Glaucias, and already half-free at birth, he nonetheless was neither too young nor too undoomed by life to teach some of the same lessons as his Roman predecessor.

> For why
> Will man lament the state he should envy?
> To have so soon 'scap'd world's, and flesh's rage,
> And, if no other misery, yet age?

4. Jonson is quoted in *Poems*, ed. Ian Donaldson (London, Oxford, and New York; 1975) (Oxford Standard Authors).

With a reversal of customary roles, not unexpected in a Glaucias-like poem, the living, especially the father, are to be spoken to and instructed by the dead son. The biblical foundation also allows the father to omit the original suffixes of Ben-oni and Ben-jamin and to substitute the suffix "jonson" instead. It is Martial, however, not the Bible, who contributes the final line.

> Rest in soft peace, and, ask'd, say here doth lie
> Ben Jonson his best piece of poetry;
> For whose sake, henceforth, all his vows be such,
> As what he loves may never like too much.

Glaucias was transitionally placed between slavery and freedom but also between infancy and full maturity. Jonson could reduce in one direction for a child of seven, and Marvell could expand in the other for a young man of nineteen. To do so he picks up the "haste" of his subject's name and thereby can add something that Jonson necessarily left out. Short is the life, Martial had said, of those unusually gifted, and rarely do they attain old age ("Immodicis brevis est aetas, et rara senectus"). Statius had remarked that Glaucias had left his own years behind him. "Alas," Marvell writes, Hastings' "virtues did his death presage: / Needs must he die, that doth out-run his age" (9–10). The race of life, explicit in Statius and implied by the Flaminian Way in Martial, is here timed in a double way so that Hastings overtakes and outruns himself. In the opening verse paragraph Marvell had already interposed human "tears" between "early showers" and the "flowers" on which the merely natural moisture of "morning" should "fall." Next he envisages the ancient image of "Time's wheel" (12), but here it is also a kind of ship; the "phlegmatic and slow" (11) person "sticks" to it, like a "remora" (12), the "sucking fish" which "was believed to stay the course of a ship to which it had attached itself" (Donno's note). Time is being measured, moreover, not simply in terms of the relative fast or slow experiencing of it but by the proportional ratios of "the geometric year" (18).

With a shift to biblical metaphors, both trees from the Garden of Eden are mentioned, but having "made a feast" (20) on the Tree of Knowledge, Hastings cannot partake of the Tree of Life. That superlative achievement is denied because "democratic stars" (25), balanced against and within Time's wheel, "did ostracize" it (26). A prisoner of state supplies the analogies which immediately follow, but evidently Hastings, like Glaucias and young Ben, was imprisoned before death, not afterwards; in "the crystal palace" (33) in the realm on high he "re-creates" (with double meaning) "his active mind" (32) even though he is there "confined" (31). The gods, also above, are pleased for the most part, but there are two exceptions: "Hymeneus" (43) and "Aesculapius" (47), deities of marriage and medicine. Here below, one of their counterparts is Dr. "Mayern" (52), the king's physician and father of the bride whom Hastings was to have married the day following his death; the second counterpart is the bride herself.

These various doublets are capped by the one which constitutes the poem's final line: "And art indeed is long, but life is short." The general principle is a truism, but here it has the ring of a hard, specific truth because of the particulars which have preceded and prepared for it.

Waller's poem for Lady Rich, née Anne Cavendish, comes in at 88 lines as compared to Marvell's 60.[5] Both are brief in absolute terms and closer to Martial in this respect than Statius, but Waller's is a third again longer, and one reason is that Waller is trying to dilate and thus dilute the grief of an unexpected as well as an untimely death. The grief is not Waller's own, or at least not primarily, nor even that of Lady Rich's husband and young child. The sorrow of Lady Rich's mother, "the heroic dame whose womb she blest" (26), is great, but the principal lamentation is Sacharissa's or (to name her, though Waller does not) Lady Sidney's. As represented by the poem, the two ladies were quite close in friendship, beauty, virtue, honor, and evidently much else besides, but since they both were more divine than human, precise knowledge is totally unnecessary. The death of Lady Rich is as terrifying to contemplate (21–24) as the wounding of Aphrodite on the windy plains of Troy (*Iliad*, 5.330); alternatively the Lady was a latterday Astraea forsaking the earth for her heavenly home (69–70). "Essexian plains" are already "curst" (1) as a place of "hasty death" (2), a phrase that Marvell could afford to omit because it was everywhere implied by "Hastings" itself. Waller can afford to suppress "riches" and "richness" for much the same reason, as when he is momentarily outraged "That Death should license have to rage among / The fair, the wise, the virtuous, and the young!" (19–20). In life, Lady Rich was "gracious to all" (39), but to those she loved, she was

> So fast, so faithful, loyal, and so true,
> That a bold hand as soon might hope to force
> The rowling lights of heav'n, as change her course.
> (40–42)

5. Waller's poem, reproduced from Fenton's edition, is given in Appendix I.

Waller is as astronomical as Marvell, but to compare rolling lights with stars which democratically ostracize is to see a significant disparity. The two are closer when Marvell imagines that a post-mortal Hastings "doth the Eternal Book behold, / On which the happy names do stand enrolled" (37–38). Waller, delaying what Lady Rich herself is to say, would have "Some happy Angel, that beholds her there, / Instruct us to record what she was here!" (43–44). That angelic assistance, temporarily substituting for the angelic lady now gone, would enable due praise here below; as for heaven above, "there the Muse shall raise / Eternal monuments of louder praise" (49-50).

The emphasis has been on praise for Lady Rich through line 50, the one just quoted. In lines 51–52, however, it is heaven and Lady Rich who "shall have occasion to recite" the name of "Fair SACHARISSA." The poem is thus doubly occasional since it anticipates an answering work of praise directed not from the living to the dead but from heaven back down to earth. With this modulation, the two ladies become approximately equal in value for the remainder of the poem, a structure artfully designed to reflect the mutual friendship treasured when both were alive and the endurance of it even though the original basis for it no longer seems to exist. "To sacred friendship we'll an altar rear" (54), Waller promises. It is to be "Such as the ROMANS did erect of old" (55), and as with Martial's poem for the sepulcher, the altar has two forms: "a marble pillar" (56) and the poem itself. Sacharissa is herself a living monument: "Consent in virtue [did] knit your hearts so fast, / That still the knot, in spight of death, doth last" (71–72). Death has altered the face of things, therefore, but not much more, especially since earth and heaven become temporal and atemporal images of one another. "Such was the sweet converse 'twixt her and you, / As that she holds with her associates now" (63–64). "Well chosen love is never taught to die / But with our nobler part invades the sky" (79–80). "So, all we know of what they do above, / Is, that they happy are, and that they love" (75–76). Waller is carefully unraveling the knot of death by means of the unseverable knitting of love, and the terrors of mortality are being softened so as to be dissolved into tears which then disappear. In the final lines, appearance and reality, as perceived in corporeal terms, reverse or rather invert themselves to become interchanged in value so that each actually is what the other seemed to be.

> Then grieve no more, that one so heav'nly shap'd
> The crooked hand of trembling age escap'd.
> Rather, since we beheld her not decay,

> But that she vanish'd so entire away,
> Her wond'rous beauty, and her goodness, merit
> We should suppose, that some propitious spirit
> In that coelestial form frequented here;
> And is not dead, but ceases to appear.
>
> (81–88)

Beneath the surface, but only slightly, is a serious pun which cannot easily be paraphrased without coarsening it. That Lady Rich's physical richness ceases to appear is immaterial; her worth is no less apparent now than before; and the system of values which she helped to call into existence and of which she continues to be a treasured contributor both was and is intangible and invisible and nonetheless quite luminously real.

Waller's poem cannot possibly be helped and would be damaged, in fact, by the inclusion of chiseled details such as the remora or the geometric year. Marvell, moreover, is far less consoling—though not less resolute—than Waller is. Art is long, the Eternal Book is infinitely longer, but there remain some unblinkable temporal facts which do *not* cease to appear. I elided most of Marvell's conclusion to point up a contrast with Waller and should make up that omission here. Dr. Mayern, though the physician of the king, on this medical case could do nothing.

> But what could he, good man, although he bruised
> All herbs, and them a thousand ways infused?
> All he had tried, but all in vain, he saw,
> And wept, as we, without redress or law.
> For man (alas) is but the heaven's sport;
> And art indeed is long, but life is short.

This conclusion is extremely untypical, not necessarily of classical funeral verse, but of Christian adaptations wherein the consolation of heaven is ready to be seized. We find ourselves back in the world of Statius ("doomed, ay doomed") and in the wilds, not Essexian but Kentish, with Gloucester: "As flies to wanton boys are we to the gods; / They kill us for their sport" (*Lear*, 4.1.36–37). Even Gloucester, however, having lost one son ultimately found another, and his heart burst smilingly. Marvell, scrutinizing this particular death at this particular time in these particular circumstances, simply will not permit himself to arrive at the standard Christian conclusion, no matter how comforting it might be. Here, quite explicitly, no redress is visible at the end despite the Eternal Book which Hastings earlier beheld.

Waller's poem, with all its self-conscious artifice, may be the more humane of the two if the prime consideration is the commonly perceived emotional need of survivors. In this respect it is closer to Statius than to Martial. With Marvell, however, the situation is reversed since his poem, like Martial's, is uncompromising in its bleak minimalization of soothing remarks when consolation can only be false not only to appearances but, perhaps more importantly, to this specific reality and truth.

Waller himself was not blind to everyday realities, but Lady Rich and Sacharissa illustrate two closely related problems which are symptomatic of and probably endemic to the kind of poetry he most often writes. First, his portraits, any one or two of which may be quite touchingly done, tend to be so unrelievedly similar that they are numerically distinct but otherwise not always easy to tell apart. In this poem, Sacharissa and Lady Rich were nearly interchangeable, a potential weakness which Waller converts to a strength since it underlines the mutuality and equality of their shared friendship and love. Such a strategy, however, would lose its utility if regularly exploited, even if it were more or less literally true. Waller's output was not large, especially if one considers that he apparently wrote poetry on a fairly regular basis for more than sixty years. Fenton cites evidence, necessarily secondhand, that far from being "the parent of those swarms of Insect-Wits who affect to be thought *easy writers*," Waller in fact "bestow'd much time, and care, on his Poems, before he ventur'd them out of his hands" (cliii). He may have been polishing his versification to achieve the smoothness which Dryden and Pope so much admired, but if so, he also smoothed out most of the marks of imperfection which distinguish one person from another. The second problem arises because Waller regularly discounted distinctive detail for the sake of generalized truth and often seems not to have distinguished between momentous occasions and merely momentary ones. The eminently reasonable presumption is that Waller, from a Marvellian point of view, is always superficial. If one picks up Waller at all, one expects to find "the rhymer of a court gazette," as Douglas Bush contemptuously called him, or a polisher of what can only be called platitudes, whatever their abstract or even emotional value may be.[6]

6. Bush made the statement in *English Literature in the Earlier Seventeenth Century 1600–1660*, 2d ed. (Oxford, 1962), 177, repeating verbatim from the 1st ed. of 1945.

There were at least two occasions, however, when Waller departed from his normal procedure in order to address present realities of immediately urgent significance. "On St. James's Park" and "Instructions to a Painter" are quite as glossy as Waller's other poems, but Waller subordinates hyperbole and praise—even though both are highly prominent—to the service of exhortation, which he thought imperative to give and for King Charles II to hear. Neither one of these poems has the stature and weight to elbow Milton and Virgil aside, but they hold up quite well against most competitive standards, and the claim made by Earl Miner, that "On St. James's Park" "stands as one of the significant seventeenth-century poems,"[7] is not, as I see it, in any way exaggerated. Except by the very highest standards, and whatever one's preconceptions may be, these poems are not minor work.

That point finally brings me to where and how this study began. Miner's statement has not become the prevalent view and has been implicitly though not overtly dismissed as eccentric. I thought it worthwhile to reargue the case for a belief that anyone willing to confer value on poems such as Jonson's "To Penshurst," Denham's "Cooper's Hill," or Pope's "Windsor Forest" ought not to shortchange Waller's topographical verse. It also seemed to me that if two Waller poems could be looked at in fairly close proximity, then each could supply hearsay evidence, as it were, for the credibility of the other. The obvious choice appeared to be "Instructions to a Painter"; while designed in terms of a different structural metaphor and principle, this poem also ought to be more than merely the backdrop, briefly acknowledged, for the painter poems—especially Marvell's "Last Instructions to a Painter"—which Waller's poem led to. Marvell may or may not have written "The Second Advice to a Painter" and "The Third." This is an issue to come back to, but the author(s) of those poems read Waller with considerable care, and the satiric inversions of Waller's materials often illuminate, retrospectively, Waller's uninverted originals. One supposes that the proper place for "The Last Instructions" surely ought to be a study of Marvell, but any effort to examine that poem apart from its predecessors necessarily begins with, though it may recover from, a false start since the poem explicitly derives from earlier work, including Waller's own. The poem is an especially forceful illustration of a proposition set forth earlier, that Marvell is normally involved, perhaps inextricably, with the minutest of details and their internal relationships even when he confronts

7. *The Cavalier Mode from Jonson to Cotton* (Princeton, 1971), 37.

issues of very wide dimensions. Much bruising might be saved in the argumentation over what label to affix to Marvell if it were conceded that labels often are generic and not always suitable for specific applications. I earlier suggested the analogy with Talmudic exegesis, among other reasons because no one could possibly take it as more than an unliteral comparison.

This proposition, like the one on Waller, seemed worth advancing, and it further was obvious that it, too, could benefit from some hearsay evidence from another work. In this case, however, the other work almost necessarily had to be one of Marvell's lyrics. Citing another political poem, so far as I can tell, would be merely duplicative and thus of no use at all. Comparison of Waller's and Marvell's poems to Cromwell may therefore seem a curious omission, but my purposes cannot be helped by that material and would in fact be hindered because Waller, in the "Panegyric" and the funeral poem for the Lord Protector, probably *is* too much concerned with Truth to take truths into much account. The lyric best suited to my needs is Marvell's most famous poem. Everyone admires "To his Coy Mistress," but it contains one very precise detail which many people refuse to believe is there. I realize that putting this poem in will seem as strange as leaving the Cromwell poems out, but I doubt a better way exists for showing how very Talmudic Marvell at times could be than by doing some ransacking of my own to try to show that in this context it is glue, meaning glue and not something else, which is the specificity that Marvell wanted for his elegant poem.

I have ended up with more pages on Marvell than on Waller, but if small things to great may be compared, I found myself where Brahms once was: A work intended to be in the key of D kept sliding up to E flat, he said, until finally he decided to leave it there. It also has not seemed sensible to follow in the pages below the convoluted process outlined above but to proceed with the straightforwardness of chronology. "To his Coy Mistress" is thus placed first; "On St. James's Park," second; and the painter poems, third. This arrangement, as it happens, also is appropriate because of the necessarily different strategies of argument and their differing backgrounds. Biblical commentary and Roman verse were enormously useful materials for the lyric and the topographical poem, and classical materials continued to be closely relevant for the painter poems. Even so, Waller's "Instructions" became the unmistakable literary background for the author(s) of subsequent poems based upon it, and these poems necessarily have an inherent internal cohesiveness because of that fact. The last lines of Marvell's "Last Instructions," for obvious reasons, really ought to be final, but I want to return to some of the issues raised introductorily here in the hope of clarifying and extending them after particular cases have been examined. Evidently, if any substantial claims about these two authors are to have any chance at all of looking plausible, then many details—some of them very small indeed—will have to be looked at first.

2

Glue and Marvell's Mistress

Most of Marvell's poems, including the lyrics for which he now is chiefly famous, were not published in his lifetime. An additional fact, at least as important and very possibly more so, is that they did not circulate widely in manuscript. Donne, after all, was famous as a poet even though very little of his poetry was actually printed until after his death, and large numbers of manuscript copies still survive. Not so with Marvell. His contemporary reputation, such as it was, depended on his public role as parliamentary member from Hull and the reputed author of satires —"prudently published anonymously," to quote the Oxford *Companion*—on the governmental regime and its policies.[1] The *Companion* offers the view that "even when his poems were published in 1681, they were greeted by two centuries of neglect" and further asserts that latter-day compensation has been more than abundant.

> In the second half of the 20th cent. his small body of lyrics has been subjected to more exegetical effort than the work of any other metaphysical poet. His oblique, ironic, and finally enigmatic way of treating quite conventional poetic materials (as in 'The Nymph Complaining for the death of her Faun' or 'To his Coy Mistress') has especially intrigued the modern mind.

1. *The Oxford Companion to English Literature*, 5th ed., ed. Margaret Drabble (Oxford and New York, 1985), 625.

I have no statistical counts ready at hand whereby to test one of these statements, and a second, concerning the poet's enigmatic way and the modern mind's intrigue, is not susceptible to numerical verification in any case. The "neglect" of Marvell, however, is a little exaggerated. There must have been some presupposed market in 1726, when Captain Thomas Cooke brought out *The Works* in two volumes, again in 1772 when a reissue appeared, and in 1776 when Edward Thompson thought it worthwhile to offer a new edition in three volumes. A. B. Grosart's four-volume edition of 1872–75 also ought to be mentioned if for no other reason than the fact that it continues to be the collection of Marvell's prose works that one has to use. The contrast between Marvell's modest fame in 1681 and his current prestige nonetheless is extraordinary. Marvell's star has risen at least as much, in fact, as Waller's has fallen.

The modernity of the enormous attention given to Marvell, an editorial tradition which nevertheless dates from 1726, along with the fame of "To his Coy Mistress," combine to make it impossible, so far as I can tell, to approach the points of interest to me in a simple way. This lyric oscillates between gestures toward the vast and nearly illimitable on the one hand and, on the other, an inclusion of precisely located detail. The word *glue* is one of the details, and a very nice one, but at a time prior to 1726, when Cooke decided to delete it, this specificity may not have seemed very much more precise than some of the others, and it certainly was not outré or grotesque in any way. The word represented, in fact, a quite lovely compliment to the lady, and was probably selected because earlier writers had found it useful in considering approximately the same remarkably broad contexts in terms of which Marvell chose to scrutinize this particular affair.

Part of the evidence given below might be considered abstruse in some circles (mine, for example) since it draws on various sources which are not in everyday use in reading Marvell, including the physiology of human skin as understood in scholastic philosophy and the philology of Hebrew, Greek, and Latin words as interpreted in widely scattered biblical passages. There is nothing especially difficult about most of the background materials, however, except for their unfamiliarity, and that problem is the kind that can be remedied. Two problems that cannot be ignored or successfully evaded are that the history of the text is itself complicated and that while the modern mind may be intrigued by Marvell and his enigmatic way, modern taste is usually offended by his glue. As a result, matters of text and taste have become involved so convolutedly that it is not always easy to separate them into their theoretically distinct roles. Sometimes glue is completely thrown out, but sometimes careful explanation shows that glue actually means glow. The commentary which has clustered itself around this poem is not, moreover, merely voluminous. Much of it is quite subtle and highly informative even when based on a foundation which I take to be as unhistoric as Marvell's own modern reputation is. A big difference here, of course, is that we have the poems and Marvell's contemporaries did not. It can be argued, however, that they had a perspective on certain words which we now lack. At least one result of literary history and the tides of taste is factitious, strictly speaking, but nonetheless possessed of its own kind of reality: The two lines in which glue does (or, as some maintain, does not) appear are a focal lens through which to look at the lyric as a whole and at Marvell's allusive techniques and strategies. Since this is Marvell's most famous poem today, though it was scarcely known at one time in the past, these strategies are—or at least presumably ought to be—characteristic of Marvell when at the very top of his form.

An account of editorial evidence and practice should be scrupulous about detail and objective insofar as possible; Chernaik therefore decided to place in an appendix his remarks on "Manuscript evidence for the canon of Marvell's poems," and I want to do the same for most of the intricacies of argument over Marvell's couplet.[2] The story has a specialized kind of fascination as one watches two mutually exclusive positions being derived from the same initial starting point or, at times, a convergence on the same editorial choice for contradictory reasons. What I need here, however, is the result rather than the process. And to place the result in the poem, one needs to recall that Marvell's verbal signposts suggest the structure of a syllogism, the first two parts of which take the form of hypothesis and minor premise. Textbook examples normally start with "If," but Marvell inverts his word order so that the first two verse paragraphs, reduced to the skeletons of their opening lines, look like this:

> Had we but world enough and time,
> This coyness, Lady, were no crime.
>
> But at my back I always hear
> Times winged charriot hovering near.

---

2. Warren Chernaik, *The Poet's Time: Politics and Religion in the Work of Andrew Marvell* (Cambridge, 1983), 206–14; see also the review of problems and evidence in Appendix II.

At this point and not before, one is ready for the concluding "therefore." The beginning of the third and final verse paragraph at present exists in three alternate versions.

Either: Now therefore, while the youthful hew
          Sits on thy skin like morning glew.

Or: Now therefore, while the youthful glew
          Sits on thy skin like morning dew.

Or: Now therefore, while the youthful hew
          Sits on thy skin like morning dew.

A very basic way of formulating the problem here is to say that three words are competing for the two spaces available. A very basic solution is to suppose that the words don't really matter and thus to argue, "We need not worry about whether Marvell originally wrote 'glew' for 'hew' or 'dew.' The speaker's sense is that the youthful appearance of the lady is transitory and will eventually pass."[3] This statement, however, reduces Marvell to a level of bland generality to which even Waller would have taken vigorous exception; "Go lovely rose," after all, differs enormously from "Go some youthful and transitory thing or other." I propose to go to what may be the other extreme by looking at Marvell's words as carefully as I can, partly for themselves and partly for some contexts in which they appear and which they help to establish. This procedure may eliminate a few of the questions about "this much debated couplet," as Donno puts it, on the grounds that they probably need not be asked, but the editorial crux as such clearly cannot be solved in this way. To do that, one would have to discover fresh textual evidence from some hitherto unsuspected source—preferably, of course, a holograph copy or perhaps a letter in which Marvell (quite uncharacteristically) commented on his own compositional process. On the evidence now available, it seems likely to me that Marvell experimented with all three words in varying combinations in an effort to see which ones were best not only for the couplet but also for his larger purposes. No certainty at present can exist on that point either, but the words themselves are suggestive and the patterns of thought are indicative, I think, of one of the ways that Marvell's mind seems to have worked.

3. Bruce King, *Marvell's Allegorical Poetry* (New York and Cambridge, 1977), 71.

I

"Hew" is the word to look at first because it does not appear to present as many difficulties as the other two. Those who comment on the word obviously assume that it means "color." Martz, in fact, is quite explicit on this matter: "The speaker is talking about a *hue*, a color."[4] The *OED* entry for "hue" indicates that this meaning had become largely lost well before Marvell's time, at least for prose: "Down to the 16th c. app. exactly synonymous with 'colour'; but it appears to have become archaic in prose use about 1600." Nothing is said about poetry, however, and for a reason shortly to be given, it seems probable that Marvell, archaically or not, does have the older sense in mind. If, however, color is to be suppressed, then we should understand "external appearance of the face and skin," as in this example from 1600: "The women . . . contenting themselves only with their naturall hiew"—without, one assumes, the otiose addition of cosmetics. In any case, the point which probably should be stressed is that color, tint, complexion, and the like are *developed* senses which refer to the external appearance of *skin*. The etymology of "hue" goes back, via Middle and Old English, to Germanic and, ultimately, Sanskrit forms with the root meaning of "hide." The sense was available in the past from the alliterative collocation of "hide and (or) hue," as in examples from 1549, "ye ar so haill of hew and hyd," and 1535, "Of hyde and hew baith plesand wes and fair" (*OED*, "Hide"). The phrase became obsolete, and hide itself, when applied to people, became merely "contemptuous" or "jocular" (*OED*, quoting, for example, from Milton's *Colasterion*: "hide of a varlet"). Hidebound, however, despite figurative use, retained its literal sense with all seriousness: "having the skin tight and incapable of extension." The *OED* illustrates with Quarles (1634): "My bones are hide-bound." Also worth noting is a quotation for "hide" from 1536: "He was fairer of visage and hide, than wes ony lady of the world." "Hew," whether or not it means "color," has primary reference to the physical properties of the lady's "skin," the place where "youthful hew" is said by Marvell to "sit."

This fact may be important because keeping firm hold on the idea of the *physical* condition, as distinct from youthfulness, rosiness, and so on, is a potential help in understanding "dew," a word of which Marvell was especially fond. Thompson, in 1776, thought it should

---

4. The References give bibliographical information about works frequently cited and the system used in citing them.

appear (in place of "new," the customary reading) in "The First Anniversary" (325–26):

> So when first man did through the morning *dew* (*new*)
> See the bright sun his shining race pursue.

I cite this example because of the "morning dew" in the disputed couplet, but it is a dubious case, and others are less close but more certain. In "Upon Appleton House," each flower "yet dank with dew, / . . . fills its flask with odours new" (295–96). Weepers such as the Magdalene, "to preserve their sight more true, / Bathe still their eyes in their own dew" ("Eyes and Tears," 27–28). "On me," Damon says, "the morn her dew distills / Before her darling daffodils" ("Damon the Mower," 43–44); less than ten lines earlier, he brings "chameleons, changing hue, / And oak leaves tipped with honey dew" (37–38). This example is particularly interesting not only because of the rhyming of "hue" with "dew" but also because "hue" itself in this case *does* appear to refer specifically to changes of color. Elsewhere in "Upon Appleton House" (406–8), "Rails" are the birds which ironically substitute for the "quails" miraculously received by the Jews in the Exodus journey; "dew," presumably, is ironic as well:

> He call'd us Israelites;
> But now, to make his saying true,
> Rails rain for quails, for manna, dew.

And yet Marvell surely intended no irony, or not of the sardonic kind, in the last lines of "On a Drop of Dew":

> Such did the manna's sacred dew distil,
> White and entire, though congealed and chill,
> Congealed on Earth: but does, dissolving, run
> Into the glories of th' almighty sun.

The remainder of the poem and "Ros," the Latin version, further indicate how interested in this subject Marvell at times could be.

These images generate strong internal resonance, especially when reference is also made to the mysterious manna since it too was fragile and of short duration: "they gathered it every morning . . . and when the sun waxed hot, it melted" (Exodus 16.21). Evidently the background passages have a reverberance of their own, a fact from which two problems arise of a superficially contradictory kind, those of hearing too much and/or too little. Clayton (368) was reminded of one of the psalms and, quite understandably, thought the verbal similarity worth citing.

> I must emphasize that the positive, strictly semantic, claims of "dew" are so strong and obvious as to require little comment, although note might be taken of Psalm 110.3, which seems pertinent whatever the resolution of the crux: "Thy people shall be willing in the day of thy power, in the beauties of holiness from the womb of the morning: thou hast the dew of thy youth."

Clayton was extraordinarily unlucky, however, in hitting on this particular text. He might have chosen from thirty-three other places in the Authorized Version of the Old Testament where "dew" occurs, in each case translating the Hebrew "tal." Some of these speak of morning dew, in Hebrew as well as in translation, and one of them, Hosea 6.4–5, even brings "dew" and "hew" together, although in this passage the latter word is understood to mean "cleave" in the sense of "shape": "Your goodness is as a morning cloud, and as the early dew it goeth away. Therefore have I hewed them by the prophets." Whether or not one chooses to mention Hosea and so on, Psalm 110.3 is in any case exactly the reference to avoid, the reason being that this verse itself is a crux of formidable complexity. A footnote in The Revised Standard Version indicates that it cannot, in fact, be solved: "The meaning of the second sentence can no longer be recovered with certainty." This remark, while uncontestably modern, is neither irrelevant nor even anachronistic. Seventeenth-century authorities were more sanguine about the matter but not notably so.

Cardinal Bellarmine gives a comparative exposition of the Hebrew and Septuagint texts in order to explain, not necessarily to justify, the version in the Vulgate; as translated in the Douai, the same verse is almost unrecognizably different: "With thee is the principality in the day of thy strength: in the brightness of the saints: from the womb before the day star I begot thee." Poole comments that no place in Psalms is more obscure than this one. ("Locus hic difficilis est, quo non arbitror ullam in Psalmis obscuriorem esse.") He reports several mutually exclusive explanations handed down in rabbinic and patristic tradition. According to one of them—it has to do with "the womb of the morning"—one should understand that by an "eleganti translatione" the meaning of tal-ros-dew is "semen." ("*Roris* nomine semen eleganti translatione appellant Hebraei.") In a parallel passage in his

English commentary, with a different audience in mind, Poole writes that "the words are diversly rendered and understood," but the possibility of ros-semen-seed is quietly suppressed along with untransliterated Hebrew and untranslated Greek. To comment on Marvell's crux by referring to an even worse biblical crux seems imprudent at best.

One might be better off in noticing—at least at first—an altogether different Hebrew word and the two biblical places where it occurs since these can lead back to ros-dew as the terminology is used in some physiological contexts. The word is "leshad," translatable as "moisture," and one of the texts is Psalm 32.4: "My moisture is turned into the drought of summer." The commentators explain that the psalmist here laments literal and spiritual dessication when, as he says, "my bones waxed old" (v. 3). In Poole's paraphrase, for example, "My very radical moisture was in a manner dried up, and wasted." Ainsworth reports that "the Hebrew *Leshad*, is the best oily moisture in mans body, *Psal*. 32.4," yet his remark is appended not to the psalm but to his commentary on Numbers 11, where the word occurs with seemingly different meaning:

> 6 But now our soul is dried away: there is nothing at all, besides this manna, before our eyes. . . .
> 8 And the people went about, and gathered it, and ground it in mills, or beat it in a mortar, and baked it in pans and made cakes of it: and the taste of it was as the taste of fresh oil [leshad].
> 9 And when the dew [tal] fell upon the camp in the night, the manna fell upon it.

Ainsworth reconciles the two passages by comparing the idea of "best oily moisture" in the psalm to the idea that "so here it is the best sweet moisture of oyle." No opinion is offered as to which meaning is primary, perhaps because no significant distinction should be made. Leigh suggests this may be the case by collocating the two passages in one entry with minimal differentiation in meaning between the two occurrences of the same word:

> [Hebrew characters for *leshad*] Humor, Succus, *Num*. 11.8. *Psal*. 32.4. *moisture*, the *chief sap*, or *radical moisture*, which is an airy and oily substance, dispersed thorow the body, whereby the life is fostered, and which being spent, death ensueth. It is used only there [the psalm, i.e.] and in *Num*. 11.8. where it is

applied to the *best moisture* (or *cream*) of *oyl*. . . . Humidum Radicale, in quo vita est hominis. [Radical humidity in which human "vita" ("health," "vitality") consists.]

Two of Leigh's Latin words need some attention here because he is coming to a point possibly relevant for Marvell in two different ways. The first is "suc(c)us," defined in the *Oxford Latin Dictionary* as "the vital fluid in trees, plants (essential to their vigour and healthy appearance), the sap." The *OLD* also notes that "sucus" is "credited to human beings, animals," citing Terence's *Eunuch*. In the Roman farce, Chaerea has glimpsed a girl more beautiful than he earlier thought imaginable; a veritable blossom or flower ("flos ipsum"), as the slave Parmeno puts it (v. 318), she is sixteen years of age, with "color verus, corpus solidum et suci plenum" (a natural complexion and a plump body full of "sap"). Spenser's Priamond, Diamond, and Triamond might also be mentioned in this connection for an English, albeit masculine, version. They are "Like three faire branches budding faire and wyde, / That from one roote deriu'd their vitall sap" (*FQ*, 4.2.43).[5] Worth quoting also is a comment by Sir Thomas Browne on premature aging and death: "Though the radicall humour containe in it sufficient oyle for seventie, yet I perceive in some it gives no light past thirtie."

This "radicall humour," the "humidum radicale" referred to in Leigh's definition of "leshad," is the second term on which to pause. The noun itself is variable: Humour, humidity, moisture, sap, or—as in Walton's account of Donne's death—even heat: "this desire of glory . . . like our radical heat . . . will both live and dye with us."[6] In all these phrases, however, the adjective "radical" is technical: "In mediaeval philosophy, the humour or moisture naturally inherent in all plants and animals, its presence being a necessary condition of their vitality" (*OED*, "Radical," A1). Behind this definition is the discussion in scholasticism of physical fluids as they occur in human bodies with relationship to theoretically perfect form. The topic seems a strange one for theological discussion, but the philosophers

5. Spenser is quoted from *The Works*, ed. Edwin Greenlaw et al. (Baltimore, 1932–57). The quotation from Browne given next is from *Religio Medici*, 1.43, ed. J. J. Denounain (Cambridge, 1955), 56.

6. Isaak Walton, *The Lives* (Oxford, 1927; rpt. 1966), 77 (The World's Classics edition). Cf. George Wither, "A Hymn encouraging sicke persons to be willing to dye," in *Haleluiah*, rpt. Spenser Society (1879), 26.109: "My moisture and my vitall heat, / In me, do now begin to cease."

believed themselves to be confronted with a physiological oxymoron of spiritual significance. Perfection necessarily has the prerequisite of immutability, but the body, including its *serum*, is in the flux of continual change. Yet the example of Christ has already shown in the past and the general resurrection is to prove in the future that perfect bodies can exist. It follows that "fluids" at some point can attain a momentary stage of perfection, and that this stage, subsequent to growth but prior to corruption, in at least some instances can be preserved inalterably. In arguing these matters, Saint Bonaventure first establishes several preliminary points.[7] Perfect bodies should be approximately the same age as the resurrected Christ—about twice the age of Terence's girl, therefore. They should have hair, as evidenced by Luke 21.18: "There shall not an hair of your head perish. (It is worth noting that Lapide, in commenting on this verse, refers to the discussion of Bonaventure I am summarizing and also to the one of Aquinas very shortly to be quoted.) Sexual organs also shall be retained, although not, of course, for generative use. Physical details of this kind lead to a consideration of fluids. Relying to some extent on Avicenna, Bonaventure distinguishes several kinds of "humours" for which he finds it necessary to employ and explain three terms. One is "cambium," which signifies fluid in the process of transformation, but serves my purposes only in the context of the other two. "Rosdew" is the first. The second is "gluten-glue."

Since the closely parallel explanation of Aquinas already exists in translation, I give it here, in outline form and with some abridgment.[8] "There is," Aquinas says, "a threefold humidity in man":

1. One which occurs as receding from the perfection of the individual,—either because it is on the way to corruption, and is voided by nature, for instance urine, . . . or because it is directed by nature to the preservation of the species . . . as seed . . . as milk . . .

2. One that has not yet reached its ultimate perfection:
   a. has a definite form and is contained among the parts of the body, for instance the blood

---

7. Bonaventure, *In IV Sent.*, dist. 44, Art. 1, Q. 1, Conclusio, in *Opera omnia*, ed. A. C. Peltier (Paris, 1866), 6.476–77.

8. *The Summa Theologica*, trans. Fathers of the Dominican Province (London, 1921), 20.173–74. The passage is *ST*, 3 (Supplement), Q. 80, Art. 3c; for the Latin, see, e.g., the *Summa* (New York, 1875), 7.708–9.

  b. is in transition from form to form, namely from the form
     of humour to the form of a member
       1. either . . . at the beginning of its transformation, and
          thus it is called *ros*
       2. or . . . in the course of transformation and already be-
          ginning to undergo alteration, and thus it is called
          cambium

  3. That which has already reached its ultimate perfection that
     nature intends in the body of the individual, and has already
     undergone transformation and become incorporate with the
     members. This is called *gluten*.

It might be difficult to work "cambium" into a poem, but since
physiology is the context for ros-gluten in Scholasticism and for dew-
glew in Marvell, the presumption would appear to be strong that
there ought to be some kind of connection. Lying in the way, however,
are two stumbling blocks that must be moved for the assumption to
be tenable. First is the fact that the Dominican Fathers do not translate "gluten"; had they thought "glue" an appropriate English substitute, they would surely have used it. Indeed, it seems reasonable to
believe that no English suggested itself to them as sufficiently accurate for any of the technical terms since "cambium" and "ros" also
remain untranslated. A second difficulty is presented by the Aquinas
Lexicon, not because it omits translations but precisely because it
does give them, and "glue" is not mentioned even as a possibility.
Citing the passage quoted above and also the parallel in the commentary by Aquinas on the *Sentences*, the *Lexicon* defines "gluten" as "an
albuminoid or protein compound substance found in animal matter,
coagulable lymph," and "(2) *transf.* a bond, *connecting tie*." I also
should quote the definition for *ros*, and not merely for the sake of
completeness: "(1) *dew*, (2) of *blood*, ros, the humidity found in the
smaller veins."[9] The latter part of what is said about "ros" is unquestionably true of scholastic usage since both Bonaventure and Aquinas
specifically refer to "foraminibus parvarum venarum" (apertures of
the small veins). "Coagulable lymph," moreover, is not an innovative
term borrowed by the *Lexicon* from modern biology. It appears, under "lymph," in Chambers's eighteenth-century *Cyclopaedia*—at one
time, after all, a popular work—as a translation for "gluten": "this

---

9. Roy J. Deferrari, *A Lexicon of St. Thomas Aquinas* (Baltimore, 1948–49),
s.v. "cambium," "gluten," and "ros."

coagulable *lymph*, which some have called the fibrous part of the blood or the gluten, ought not to be confounded with the SERUM of the blood, . . ."[10] With all respect to the *Lexicon*, however, I do not see how "bond" can be a transferred meaning unless the transfer is being made not from "coagulable lymph" but from the customary sense of "gluten" as used from classical times down through the eighteenth century. The *Cyclopaedia* itself continues,

> It appears . . . that sizy blood coagulates much more slowly than other blood; that inflammation actually lessens the disposition of that fluid to coagulate; and, that in inflammatory disorders, where this whitish crust or size appears, the blood, or at least the coagulable *lymph*, which constitutes this inflammatory size is nearly attenuated.

"Sizy" and "size" are here approximately the same as "gluey" and "glue," as one can tell from another entry in the work: "There are divers kinds of glues made use of in the divers arts; as the *common glue, glove glue, parchment glue*: but the two last are more properly called SIZE." The heading, moreover, under which this statement appears is "GLUE, GLUTEN." Young's dictionary is a quick way to confirm the general point since it supplies the same information from both of the possible sides: to find "gluten" one looks up "glue" or to find "glue" one looks up "gluten."

The usage of Cardinal Bellarmine and Lapide is also worth noting, especially because the contexts in which the word appears will be useful in establishing a pattern of thought where the force of "gluten" as a metaphor supplements literal and physiological levels. In Psalm 133.3 there occurs one of the appearances of tal-ros-dew mentioned earlier ("As the dew of Hermon, and as the dew that descended upon the mountains of Zion"). Bellarmine's explanation includes a reference to "glutino charitatis," the glue of love. Romans 11.26, "And so all Israel shall be saved," is one of the passages which mentions the ultimate conversion of the Jews, a concept Marvell also alluded to: "And you should, if you please, refuse / Till the Conversion of the Jews."[11] Lapide includes a brief homily to the effect that if even Israel

10. E. Chambers, *Cyclopaedia: Or, An Universal Dictionary . . . with the Supplement . . . by Abraham Reese*, 4 vols. (London, 1791).

11. The wording of Donno's note is probably misleading, however unintentionally: "Though Biblical historians and millenarians could supply dates in the remote past and in the distant future for these two events [the second is

is to be saved, then it is of paramount importance that Christian Gentiles "take heed" (Romans 11.21) lest they be "cut off" (v. 22) from the "olive tree" (24) onto which they have been engrafted. Gentiles, he says, have special need for the "gluten" of faith.

Comparable transfers of meaning are visible in English as well as Latin. On the one hand, the *OED* supplies two quotations which probably refer to the meaning of, though not actually the term, coagulable lymph: from 1398, "In the fyrste joyninge of the bones is a maner of glewy and glemy moysture" ("Gluey"); and from 1594, "The fourth [humour] is called Gluten ("Gluten," 2). On the other hand, metaphoric use is illustrated from 1639: "The love of virtue (which was the cement, or gluten of their friendship)" ("Gluten," 1). Close also is a citation from Henry More (1664) under "agglutinate:" "That Mystery which was . . . intended for the most enduring and agglutinating Cement of all those that are called in his Name." Under "glutinous" one finds "the glutinous bond of true love" from Jonson's *Sejanus*, an idea not remote from Donne's statement—for obvious reasons not given in the *OED*, at least not here—that "Likeness glues love" (Elegy 3, "Change," 23).[12]

At this point, surely, one begins to see how highly favorable the connotations of glue-gluten can be when speaking of ideal conditions in ideal circumstances or times. A few details can usefully be added, however, partly because "dew" also comes under seriatim consideration. It is not accidental that Bellarmine should mention "gluten" when commenting on the "ros" of Psalm 133. He is explicating the force of two

---

the Flood] they fall within the literary convention of the catalogue of impossibilities (*adunata*). Roger Sharrock (*TLS* 31 October 1958; 16 January 1959) and E. E. Duncan-Jones (*TLS* 5 December 1958) suggest possible dates for the poem on the basis of these allusions." One may doubt that dates of biblical chronology can be a convincing basis for dating the poem, but there was widespread certainty that the events alluded to were in no sense "impossibilities." Cf. Legouis (1.332–33), commenting on "The First Anniversary" ("But Indians whom they should convert, subdue; / Nor teach, but traffique with, or burn the Jew"): "The reign of God was to be preceded by the in-gathering of the nations (l. 115) and in particular of the Jews. It might be noted that during the winter of 1655–6 proposals were discussed for re-admitting the Jews into England." Legouis quotes from Henry Fletcher, *The Perfect Politician* (London, 1680), for Cromwell's support of these proposals; he neglects to add, however, that Fletcher's work is hostile: The title is sardonic, and Cromwell is alleged to have been promised a bribe of £200,000.

12. Donne is quoted from *The Elegies and The Songs and Sonnets*, ed. Helen Gardner (Oxford, 1965).

similes as they apply to the binding together of brothers ("fratres," "friars") in fraternal unity. His observations are keyed, of course, to the Vulgate, but in this case the Douai's English is close enough.

> Behold how good and how pleasant it is for brethren to dwell together in unity: Like the precious ointment on the head, that ran down upon the beard, the beard of Aaron, Which ran down to the skirt of his garment: as the dew of Hermon, which descendeth upon mount Sion.

Bellarmine points out that the ointment could scarcely flow from the head to the beard nor from the beard to the vestments were the beard itself cut off. The dew, he says, is beneficent because, unlike rain, it does not flow away. The beard "adheres" to the head ("nisi enim barba capiti adhaereret . . ."), and the dew "sticks" ("ros autem haeret"). So the "fratres" need to be bonded in unity by the "gluten" of "charitas" ("nisi fratres habitarent in unam & inter se glutino charitatis coniuncti essent . . ."). Bellarmine may have been influenced here, however surprisingly at first glance, by the example of Cicero; "conglutinatio," as Lewis and Short point out in their entry for the word, was "a favorite trope" for that author when he spoke of "cementing" concord and friendship. Alternatively, since Bellarmine often adopts the traditional practice of interpreting Psalms proleptically from a New Testament perspective, he may have taken a hint from Acts 17. Many Athenians completely rejected or at least were skeptical of Saint Paul's teaching of the resurrection, but "certain men clave unto him, and believed" (v. 34). They were joined, as Poole puts it, "in more than ordinary friendship; they were as glued to him." Leigh, whose comments on "leshad" were quoted earlier, also makes this point. Explaining the Greek "kollaomai" ("cleave"), giving "adhaero" and "adjungo" as Latin translations, and citing this verse, he says that "there is not a word in all the Greek language that signifieth a nearer conjunction than this word, used for *cleaving*, or *gluing*."

One of the passages cited by Leigh in addition to Acts 17 is Acts 8.29, wherein Philip is urged by the Spirit to "join thyself to this chariot." The vehicle is an Ethiopian's, and Philip's timely action results in the immediate conversion of that Gentile. Because of Marvell's chariot ("Times winged charriot hurrying near"), one would like to perceive in the poem an inverted parallel for purposes of amorous haste. I temporarily delay that point, however, to notice that cleaving to the chariot is a step toward gathering a Gentile into the fold and that Lapide quite understandably makes his own kind of inversion by referring to the "gluten" of faith when commenting on the ultimate ingathering of the Jews. Like Bellarmine, Lapide is unfolding a biblical image, in this case the metaphor of the olive tree. The stock was and is Israel, God's chosen seed. But with the coming of Christ, many of the Jews were lopped off, separated from the stock because of their unbelief, whereas many Gentiles have been grafted in. As "ros" led Bellarmine to think of the "gluten" of love, so the integral incorporation of new branches leads Lapide to think of the "gluten" of faith, especially since many Gentiles have been excised and many Jews ultimately are to be restored.

The commentators, including Lapide, regularly compare the final ingathering to the return of the Jews from their Babylonian captivity, an event to which Isaiah is said metaphorically to allude: "Thy dead men shall live, together with my dead body shall they arise. Awake and sing, ye that dwell in dust: for thy dew is as the dew of herbs, and the earth shall cast out the dead" (26.19). Under "dew," Wilson gives the following simile:

> That as the dew of heaven bringeth forth hearbs & fruit, out of the seed corrupted in the earth: so the liues & soules of the Iewes should be quickened of God wonderfully; wch was fulfilled at the deliverance both from the *Babylonians*, and shall be also in their restoring by the Gospell, where their raising vp shall bee as life from the dead. Esay 26, 19. *Thy dew shall be as the dew of hearbs*. Rom. 11, 15.

Wilson ends the "definition" with a reference to Romans 11.15 because the rhetorical question asked there—"For . . . what shall the receiving of them be, but life from the dead"—has already supplied the metaphoric language of his own preceding sentence. Poole reports that this imagery of resurrection as used by Saint Paul is "a proverbial speech, to signify a great change for the better." "The conversion of that people and nation," he says, "will strengthen the things that are languishing and like to die in the Christian church." For Poole, therefore, the shift is not particularly abrupt when the imagery of verse 15 is replaced by metaphors of the "first fruit," "root," and "branches" of verse 16 and then by the olive tree of verse 17, which elicited Lapide's reference to glue. One more detail needs to be added before a general point can be made. Lapide indicates that "all Israel" cannot be interpreted literally but must be understood to mean "almost all" ("pene omnes"). His belief is based on the idea that the tribe of Dan, for example, has been irretrievably lopped off, as indicated by the passage in Apocalypse or Revelation 7.4–8, which lists the other tribes but not that one. Poole, commenting on the same passage in Revelation cited by Lapide, also observes that "the tribe of Dan is here left out" and refers to "the Gentiles, who are now God's Israel ingrafted into the true olive."

I venture no opinion as to whether or not the olive tree of Saint Paul actually should be associated with imagery from Isaiah's prophecies and/or a vision of Saint John in which no apparently comparable metaphor occurs until four chapters later: "These are the two olive trees" (11.4). It would seem safe to say, however, that to the commentators the tree was a comprehensive symbol with implications for human history spanning a time period all the way from at least as early as the Babylonian captivity up until, as Poole puts it in commenting on Romans 11.15, "the end of the world, at the resurrection of the dead." It also seems clear that dew and glue, though in one sense unimportant in so vast a context, were thought helpful by writers coming to the larger issues from different directions and for varying purposes: Bonaventure and Aquinas on ideal physiology, Bellarmine on the paradigm for a religious community, Lapide and Wilson and Poole on a perfected world at a perfected time. There is a circle of ideas here, or perhaps it would be better to say a kind of ellipse since that construct has more than one focal point. While two foci of Marvell's poem could be thought of as "World enough, and Time," it would be difficult, for the amateur at least, even to suggest what those of the pattern in the background might be, but they certainly are not dew and glue. The words, however, are among the small arcs without which the shapes as a whole would not exist. The same statements hold true for the elliptical shape described next, but the size of this one is bigger and therefore dependent on more component parts. Since a number of them will seem of no consequence at all to Marvell without some prior indication of possible relevance, it may be helpful to list in advance some of the bits and pieces which, not coincidentally, are to be noticed: proud and exalted ladies, dusty tombs, deserts of vast eternity, carnal inversions of the exigencies of spiritual time, unnatural solar movements, winged chariots, and the need for dew and glue.

II

In biblical chronology the duration of the Babylonian captivity was a period of seventy years and therefore, as Leigh puts it in a note

shortly to be quoted at greater length, "the whole time of mans life."
It seemed, moreover, interminably longer. Isaiah refers to post-
Babylonian rebuilding as happening in places which have long lain
desolate. "They shall build the old wastes, they shall raise up the
former desolations . . . the desolations of many generations" (61.4).
"They . . . shall build the old waste places" (58.12). "Waste places"
here translates "chorbah"; the Vulgate has "deserta"; for the same
Hebrew word in Isaiah 48.21, the Authorized Version gives "deserts":
"And they thirsted not when he led them through the deserts." "*Old*
wastes" and "*old* waste places" translate "olam," a word which occurs
with considerable frequency, most often translated as "ever" (more
than 250 instances) but also as "evermore," "everlasting," "perpetual," and so on. Despite so many occurrences, it is not completely
arbitrary to notice that the word, again translated with "old," appears in Isaiah 63.9: "In all their affliction he . . . bare them, and
carried them all the days of old." Poole at this point gives information
in the English commentary of a kind normally reserved for the more
scholarly *Synopsis*: "he is said to do it *of old*, to remember his ancient
kindness for many generations past; *olam* signifies an eternity, or a
long time past, as well as to come." In Isaiah 60.15, "olam" is in fact
translated not with "old" but with "eternal": "I will make thee an
eternal excellence, a joy of many generations." Poole comments: "*eternal*, i.e. for a great while; it being a hyperbolic expression, frequent
among the Hebrews, who express a long time by eternity." The expression "old waste places" in Isaiah 58.12 is similarly hyperbolic, as
Poole also notes: "*The old waste places*, Heb. *wastes of eternity*." Marvell's phrase, "deserts of vast eternity," is reverberating in my mind at
this point, but in a biblical context Poole's information helps to clarify an observation Leigh made in his entry for "olam," that "Interpret-
ers sometimes render" the Hebrew with "*aeternum*, sometimes *perpetuum*, sometimes *seculum*." Depending on context, the word means
any one of the three:

> An absolute perpetuity, eternity, when it is affirmed of God . . .
> [2] A Periodicall or circumscribed perpetuity . . . when it is
> affirmed of things mutable in their own nature . . . it signifieth
> the whole time of mans life . . . [and, 3] a long indefinite time,
> though not infinite [in the sense of being] without beginning.

Long duration is also signified by a Hebrew radical, *ayin daleth*.
"Ad" is now a usual transliteration, but, for technical reasons not
relevant here, in the seventeenth century "Ghned" was sometimes

used.[13] Leigh, translating with "AEternitas" in his entry for the radical, comments that "the Hebrew Ghned is added to Eternity or Ever to increase the durance of it and to note all Eternities." Ainsworth, explaining Psalm 9 (v. 5: "for ever and ever"), also observes that "*Ghned, yet,* is added to *eternity . . .* to note all eternities." The temporarily important point is that if either *olam* or *ad* alone is hyperbolic when applied to human affairs, then "ad olam" is doubly so. And yet this is exactly the phrase that Babylon applied to herself in self-exaltation. Anticipating neither the end of Jewish captivity nor her own ruin, she boasted, "I shall be a lady for ever" (Isaiah 47.7; Hebrew: "ad olam"; Vulgate: "in sempiternum"). The presumption was, of course, ill-founded. Her own *olam* was to be the one prophesied for her in Jeremiah 51.26: "Thou shalt be desolate for ever" (Vulgate: "perdita in aeternum eris"); she was to face, as the marginal translation puts it, "everlasting desolations." This is the more immediately important point, as Matthew Henry, commenting on Isaiah 47.7, makes clear:

> Thus the New Testament Babylon says, *I sit as a queen, and shall see no sorrow*, Rev. xviii.7. Those ladies mistake themselves, and consider not their bitter end, who think they shall be ladies for ever; for death will shortly lay their honour with them in the dust.

I am reminded, of course, of the evanescent glory of Marvell's "Lady," of the turning of her quaint honor to dust, but Henry himself is remembering the apocalyptic Babylon and also echoes the way the chapter in Isaiah begins: "Come down, and sit in the dust, O virgin daughter of Babylon . . . for thou shalt no more be called tender and delicate" (v. 1). Lapide paraphrases the boast of Babylon so as to refer to the transitory beauties of this world, and—quite unlike Marvell both in tone and attitude—he takes considerable satisfaction in noting that she will be forced to "bare the leg, uncover the thigh" (v. 2). Lapide also includes a brief sermon against carnal glory which concludes with an admonition to ponder eternity: AETERNITATEM COGITA.

Pursued in a different direction, these materials lead to the story of Hezekiah, most directly because Isaiah prophesied of the Babylonian

13. Part of the explanation has to do with "rough" and "smooth" breathing. Somewhat similarly, the name of the city usually referred to as "*Gaza*" in fact begins with *ayin*, not *gimel*. Cf. Milton's usage in *Samson Agonistes*: "Eyeless in Gaza" (41) but also "Gates of Azza" (147). (Milton is quoted from *Complete Poems and Major Prose*, ed. Merritt Y. Hughes [New York, 1957]).

captivity to that king so that he might be rebuked. The sequence of events is given briefly in 2 Chronicles 32: Hezekiah's illness and return to health, a recovery attested to by a sign from God; subsequent ingratitude and the threat of God's wrath; a welcoming of envoys from Babylon; a humbling of the king; and the postponement of the captivity for some years. Most of the interesting details of this story appear in the fuller versions given in the parallel accounts of Isaiah 38 and 2 Kings 20. One might notice, for example, that Hezekiah came perilously close to "the gates of the grave" (Isaiah 38.10) and thus became intensely aware that "the grave cannot praise . . . death cannot celebrate" (v. 18). We are never told the lady's reaction to a soundless marble tomb wherein no song echoes, but Hezekiah vowed thanks for health: "the Lord was ready to save me: therefore we will sing my songs . . . all the days of our life" (20). Yet having been delivered "from the pit of corruption" (17), the king soon turned again to "his precious things, the silver, and the gold, and the spices, and the precious ointment, and all the house of his armour, and all that was found in his treasures" (2 Kings 20.13), and he took pride in displaying these goods to Babylon's ambassadors.

This was the occasion of Isaiah's rebuke and prophecy: "that which thy fathers have laid up in store unto this day, shall be carried into Babylon; nothing shall be left" (v. 17). The biblical accounts certainly appear to stress the magnificence of Hezekiah, his "goodness" (2 Chronicles 32.32), his "acts . . . and all his might" (2 Kings 20.20), and the idea that "there shall be peace and truth in my days" (Isaiah 39.8). But one of the things that impressed the commentators was his foolish vainglory. Not only had his life been lengthened unexpectedly, but the sign of it was a miraculous change in solar movement. Marvell hopes to make the sun run since he cannot expect to make it stand still, and in a manuscript version (discussed in Appendix II below), he thinks he "cannot make the Sun / Goe backe." In Hezekiah's case, however, that is precisely what the sun was made to do. The report in 2 Chronicles 32 states only that "the Lord . . . gave him a sign" (v. 24) and that "the princes of Babylon . . . sent unto him to enquire of the wonder that was done in the land" (31). As usual, the other two accounts are more explicit. "And Hezekiah said unto Isaiah, What shall be the sign that the Lord will heal me" (2 Kings 20.8). Given a choice of seeing the sun move unnaturally either forward or back, the king chose the latter, and "so the sun returned ten degrees, by which degrees it was gone down" (Isaiah 38.8). "Duplex," as Lapide points out in commenting on the passage, was this "miraculum": that the sun should have gone back and that health should have been restored to a king despairing and ill ("quòd sol regrederetur; . . . quòd regi desperatae valetudinis adderetur vita"). He adds that Hezekiah ought indeed to have vowed songs of praise, for in the grave they could never be sung: "hoc autem facere nequit mortuus" (this, however, he who is dead is unable to do). And yet Hezekiah forgot. Poole places this ingratitude in the context of the many worldly honors bestowed upon the king. The comment is appended to 2 Chronicles 32.25, "his heart was lifted up":

> *His heart was lifted up*, for that prodigious victory over the Assyrians, above, ver. 21, and for his miraculous restoration from sickness, and the confirmation of that work by a strange and supernatural motion of the sun, and by the honour since done him by an embassy from the great and potent king of Babylon; all which probably raised in him too great an opinion of himself, . . . And . . . he took the honour to himself, and vaingloriously showed his riches and precious treasures to the Babylonish ambassadors, 2 Kings xx.12, &c.

Lapide, commenting on Isaiah 38.7–8, also emphasizes the great favor shown to Hezekiah by God. "Nota," he says, "haec tria miracula." Each requires the subservience of the sun itself: at Isaiah's command, its going back; at Joshua's (Joshua 10), its holding back ("was not the sun stopped . . . and one day made as two?" [Douai Ecclesiasticus 46.5]); at the Passion of Christ, its eclipse.[14] These com-

---

14. Craze (323–24) refers to Hezekiah and Joshua and quotes from Psalm 19: "in them hath he set a tabernacle for the sun: which cometh forth as a bridegroom out of his chamber and rejoiceth as a giant to run his course" (translation unspecified; because of "giant" and "course," where the Authorized Version has "strong man" and "race," it could be the one in the Book of Common Prayer). Craze also quotes from Bishop Joseph Hall and Edward Benlowes to show that "the three suns were coalesced at least twice by contemporaries of Marvell," but he may be overconfident in stating that the poem's "final line unquestionably derives from" these "three Old Testament books." Commentaries on Joshua and Hezekiah regularly mention Psalm 19 in passing, but the eclipse is specifically cited as the third solar miracle. Donno calls attention to a reference to Joshua's command in Marvell's poem on the death of Cromwell, 191–92. Spenser presumably had Joshua and Hezekiah in mind in a comment on Fidelia (*FQ*, 1.10.20):

> And when she list poure out her larger spright,
>   She would commaund the hastie Sunne to stay,
> Or backward turne his course from heauens hight.

parisons are made to Hezekiah's disadvantage, however, and the biblical accounts apparently do indicate that in some ways he emulated the proud folly of Babylon herself in not pondering eternity, despite the imperatives to do so. Matthew Henry, commenting on Isaiah, draws out the various morals of this tale. Hezekiah prayed to the Lord, "Come between me and the gates of the grave, to which . . . I am hurried," and the prayer was miraculously granted. "The sun is a faithful measurer of time, . . . but he that set a clock a going can set it back when he pleases, and make it to return." "A mortifying message is sent to Hezekiah, that he might be humbled for the pride of his heart, and be convinced of the folly of it." Hezekiah said, "thou hast cast all my sins behind thy back" (Isaiah 38.17), and it was true, but "when we cast our sins behind our back, and take no care to repent of them, God sets them before his face." "It concerns us to prepare when we see death approaching." "It is just with God to take that from us which we make the matter of our pride, and on which we build a carnal confidence." All of this Hezekiah had good reason to know. The warnings were numerous, and such was the force of them that "the impressions, one would think, should never have worn off, and yet, it seems, they did." For the sad fact remains:

> It is a hard matter to keep the spirit low in the midst of great advancements. Hezekiah is an instance of it: he was a wise and good man, but, when one miracle after another was wrought in his favour, he found it hard to keep his heart from being lifted up, nay, a little thing then drew him into the snare of pride.

This story, however, has a happy ending, at least for a moralist. Hezekiah himself, having at last learned his lesson, "slept with his fathers" (2 Kings 20.21), and "we must reckon it a favour to . . . be gathered to the grave in peace."

There may seem to be small room for amorous desire in so moral a tale, but in actual fact the possibility of carnal inversion of spiritual needs was explicitly recognized in the commentaries. In both the *Synopsis* and the English adaptation, Poole assumes that since the day became literally longer for Hezekiah, the night elsewhere must have been correspondingly extended. Commenting on 2 Kings 20.11, he speculates that there may be a corrupted reference in "what the poets fabled of Jupiter's making the night twice as long as it should have been, that he might enjoy Alcmena longer." Chapman may have been turning this idea upside down when he amplified his source by having the gods lengthen the day unnaturally to postpone Leander's last and fatal crossing of the Hellespont to Hero: "Day doubles her accustomd date," as he summarizes in "The Argument of the Fift Sestyad."[15] Lapide, at any rate, refers to those poets who took over from this narrative their myth of the sun's chariot being driven backwards ("Denique ex hac historiae poetae fabulam sumpserunt de Solis curru retroacto"). Evidently he supposes that everyone knows the fable and that Ovid is one of those who refer to it. Without retelling the one or naming the other, he casually quotes, or rather misquotes, a line from the *Tristia* (2.391–92). The couplet as a whole normally takes this form:

> Si non Aëropen frater sceleratus amasset,
> aversos Solis non legerimus equos.

(*Equos*, "horses," probably means "chariot," as indicated by Lewis and Short, s.v. "equus:" "In *plur.*"—"like [*hippoi*] in Homer"—"*a chariot*"; the lines thus say, "Had that accursed brother not loved Aerope, we would not read of the chariot of Sol turned back.")

Lapide's version—"aversos Solis dum [while] regerimus [we would throw back] equos"—may be a double misprint or the result of faulty memory or even an adaptation for his own purposes, but in any case the infamous fable itself was a part of the equally infamous story of Atreus and Thyestes.

The pertinent detail of the sun occurs in two forms—either or both of which Ovid could have had in mind—as the *Oxford Classical Dictionary* (s.v. "Atreus") points out:

> Atreus served up to Thyestes the flesh of the latter's own children, at which the sun turned back on its course in horror. . . . In another version . . . Atreus . . . offers to let Thyestes, who has seized the throne, keep it till the sun turns back; Thyestes agrees, and Zeus immediately turns the sun backwards.

Of the various sources mentioned by the *OCD*, Seneca's *Thyestes* (782ff.) is the noteworthy one. The rhetorical tone is not unlike that adopted toward Hezekiah by Isaiah, but more to the point may be the fact that this is the play whence—not quite four hundred verses ear-

---

15. Quoted from *Elizabethan Minor Epics*, ed. Elizabeth Story Donno (New York and London, 1963; rpt. 1967). No counterpart is given in Chapman's translation of Musaeus (also in Donno's edition).

lier than the reference to the sun—Marvell derives his poem, "The Second Chorus from *Seneca's* Tragedy *Thyestes*": "Stet quicunque volet potens" in Seneca (398ff.), and "Climb at *Court* for me that will" in Marvell. In the Loeb translation, the passage about the sun is this:

> In the midst of these thy woes, Thyestes, this only good remains, that thou knowest not thy woes. But even this will perish. Though Titan himself should turn his chariot back, taking the opposite course ["verterit currus licet / sibi ipse Titan obvium ducens iter"]; though heavy night, rising at dawn and at another's [Loeb's note: *i.e.* the day's] time, with strange shadows should bury this ghastly deed, still it must out. There is no sin but it shall be revealed.

The *OCD*, perhaps unsurprisingly, does not mention Plato's allusion to this myth, but I think it deserves a reference here. In the *Politicus* (268E), the Eliatic Stranger reminds Socrates of "the portent connected with the tale of the quarrel between Atreus and Thyestes." There can be no doubt about what portent is meant since it serves as a pretext, in both senses of the word, for—as the Loeb puts it—Plato's own "long mythical tale of the reversed motion of the world." Abandoning the chariot, Plato here substituted the image of a ship: "Then the helmsman of the universe dropped the tiller . . . and innate desire made the earth turn backwards . . . and . . . the universe was turned back" (272E). In the *Phaedrus* (246E), however, the chariot of heaven is restored: "Now the great leader in heaven, Zeus, driving a winged chariot ["elaunon ptenon harma"], goes first." These metaphors, at least to some extent, may be symbolic equivalents, as suggested by the fact that they have sometimes been combined with no sense of incongruity. Philo Judaeus, referring to Moses, writes that "as a philosopher and interpreter of God he . . . envisaged a someone who is borne on the universe like a charioteer or pilot. He steers the common bark ["skaphos"] of the world . . . He guides that winged chariot ["ptenon harma"]."[16] William Drummond of Hawthornden, in "An Hymne of the Fairest Faire" (71–76), makes a comparable synthesis:

16. *Quis rerum divinarum heres*, 60 (301). The quotation from Drummond which appears next is from *Poems and Prose*, ed. Robert H. Macdonald (Edinburgh and London, 1976). Michael J. B. Allen includes seven passages from Ficino (some of them extensive), in Latin and translation, "that deal," as he puts it (26), "with the charioteer myth in some detail"; see *Marcilio Ficino and the Phaedran Charioteer* (Berkeley and Los Angeles, 1981).

> Thy *Providence* at once which generall Things
> And singulare doth rule, as Empires Kings;
> Without whose care this world (lost) would remaine,
> A Shippe without a Maister in the Maine,
> As Chariot alone, as Bodies prove
> Depriv'd of Soules by which they bee, live, move.

It was the Platonic chariot, however, and not the ship, that interested Lapide because he thought it another instance of how pagans
distorted biblical truth. For him, the accurate version was the Cheru-
bic, winged chariot of God envisioned by Ezekiel in the fifth year of
his Babylonian captivity.[17] Citing the "alatum currum" of the *Phaedrus* in particular (953B) and "aemulati Poëtae" in general (951A),
Lapide explains that the right conception is of God himself who, like a
charioteer, directs the course of everything by means of his will (953A,
"Deus, quasi auriga, pro voluntate omnia regit") and that the entire
universe is, as it were, a chariot (955A, "Totus enim mundus quasi
currus"). God's chariot, however, moves irresistibly forward, never
back, for the motion of God is immutable and cannot be reversed
(941A, ". . . motum Dei immutabilem esse, ac retractari non possit").
This may not always appear to be so, but the truth, as Matthew Henry
observes, commenting on Ezekiel 1.1–14, is that God's work "is going
on even when it seems to us to be going backward." Poole, explaining
1.21, mentions this idea in connection with "the profane thoughts of
atheists and epicures," and he notes in connection with 1.13 that since
"God only is an unmoved mover," all else necessarily is in motion.
Lapide, with special reference to Ecclesiastes (1.5, "The sun also
ariseth, and the sun goeth down, and hasteth [margin: "panteth"] to
his place where he arose"), remarks that nothing in human affairs
(961B, "nihil in rebus humanis") is either "stabile aut perpetuum."
The questions, therefore, concern what lies behind and what before
and what one hears as the impelling force. Marvell hears time's
winged chariot hovering at his back. Ezekiel heard the noise of Cheru-
bic wings. Henry, commenting on 1.24, observes that the "sound of
God's alarms" serves "to awaken the attention," and Poole remarks
that "though some of God's judgments are executed with silence, . . .
yet here is an alarm, and they may be heard." Those who are deaf or
who mishear are also inevitably forced forward, but as Lapide (942B),

---

17. Since Lapide's commentary on Ezekiel 1 runs to twenty double-column
pages, in what follows I insert parenthetical references; 953B in the next
sentence, e.g., indicates *not* Plato but the folio and column in Lapide.

quoting Gregory the Great, points out, it is the "impetus carnis," the driving force of the flesh, which impels the "reprobos" toward a gluttonous palate ("ad gulam") and such things as "rixas" or—as Marvell has it—"strife."

In explaining Ezekiel 3.14, Poole cites the example of Saint Philip and the chariot of the converted Ethiopian, an event which I mentioned earlier, and on 1.1 refers to "proto-martyr Stephen," who "saw the glory of God, and . . . said, Behold, I see the heavens opened" (Acts 7.55–56). Lapide also refers to Saint Stephen (941A), but especially advocates that one follow the path of Saint Paul (941B). Writing to the Philippians (3.13), Paul emphasized "this one thing I do," the doing of which was in two parts: "forgetting those things which are behind, and reaching forth unto those things which are before, I press toward the mark for the prize" (3.13–14). He was emulating, in part, the Cherubim, who "turned not" but "went every one straight forward" (Ezekiel 1.9), who "looked not back," as Poole paraphrases, and "gave not over till they had completed their course." What Paul was "forgetting," therefore, was by no means God's prior motions but rather, as Poole says of Philippians 3.13, "how much he had run of his Christian race" thus far. In reaching forth, Poole continues, Paul was "straining forward, as it were, with all his force and skill, . . . so running that he might obtain (1 Cor. 9.24 [the allusion is to "So run, that ye may obtain"]) all and the whole." "He did not look back." He "did follow hard, with an eager pursuit, . . . maugre all difficulties." In the ellipsis of the preceding sentence, Poole indicates that the "difficulties" can be severe; he cites, without quoting, Matthew 11.12: "the kingdom of heaven suffereth violence"—or, as the margin translates, "is gotten by force"—"and the violent take it by force." Poole, commenting on this passage, explains that "great ardour and heat, . . . zeal, and fervour" are necessities, for "they are not lazy wishes or cold endeavors that will bring men to heaven." The sermon with which Lapide concludes his remarks on Philippians 3.14 makes a similar point quite extensively, but the summary advice is this:

> Manè ergo cùm surgis, cogita cum S. Antonio: Hodie coepi currere, hodie coepi Deo servire, hodie forsan & finiam. Sic vivam ergo, quasi hodie moriturus; sic curram, quasi hodie cursum consummaturus. Itaque curram velociter, quia currendi tempus breve est, & grandis mihi restat via in caelum.

"When, therefore, in the morning you arise, take thought with St. Anthony: Today I begin to run, today I begin to be bonded to God, today also perhaps I may stop. May I so live as if today I were to die; so run as if today I were to finish the race. And thus may I run swiftly because the time of running is short, and of weighty import for me is the way to heaven that remains."

Lapide further urges close attention to the advice given by Saint Paul himself at the beginning of the next chapter: "Stand fast in the Lord" (4.1). This does not mean motionlessness, of course, since almost nothing can be made to stand still. It has to do with what Lapide calls perseverance, with *holding* fast to the Lord or perhaps, as Henry points out in commenting on Philippians 3.12, not only "of our keeping hold of Christ, but his keeping hold of us." Lapide has this to say: "Stat ergo in Domino" (he, therefore, stands fast in the Lord), "qui verè . . . dicere potest" (who truly can say): "Mihi autem adhaerere (graecè ['proskollaothai'], id est agglutinari) Deo bonum est, *psal.* 72.28" (yet for me it is good to adhere—in Greek, "to be glued," that is [in Latin], to be glued—to God). In the Hebrew text of the psalm here cited, the word being translated with "adhaerere," "agglutinari" and, in Greek, "proskollaothai" is a form of the verb "qarab" ("join"). The word appears also in Ezekiel 37.17, "join them one to another into one." Poole, denying that in Ezekiel this joining was "done miraculously," says that "it was enough if glued together." Gluing is quite enough in the passages of the psalm and of Philippians as well, a point made by Lapide in this way: By what glue, he asks, may we be glued to God? ("Quo glutino agglutinabimur Deo?") According to Saint Bernard, he replies, while metaphoric binding ropes and iron nails make for strong ties, the "gluten" of "charitas" works best. It is by glue, that is by love, that one truly may be glued to God, cleaving to him ("verò glutine ei conglutinatur, id est caritate, . . . adhaerens Deo").

Psalm 63 and its attendant commentaries supply a means whereby to illustrate, in brief, the repetitive sequence in which many of the motifs I have been describing recur. This may be the place to state very firmly that I have not been and am not now leading up to the proposition that Marvell's amorous lyric is an allegorically disguised version of this psalm or of any other biblical text(s). The poem is a song, not a canticle.[18] I am noticing instead a context of verbal usage

18. Except for editorial commentary on the crux itself, controversies about the interpretation of Marvell's poem have been deliberately sidestepped throughout this discussion. Margarita Stocker, however, deploys material which is sometimes quite similar to my own in general substance though not in specific detail, and it therefore is sensible to give a reference in this particu-

which in this case is sacred but, as already noticed from time to time, quite applicable and often applied to secular situations. Not all of the imagery hitherto noticed can be discovered in this one psalm nor, I think, in any other single place. This is a point to be returned to in the section that follows, but for the moment I want to call attention to some close associations of important metaphors in a rather tightly delimited context which seems relevant to me despite the great difference in purpose behind the words.

According to the headnote, this is "A Psalm of David, when he was in the wilderness" (Vulgate: "in deserto"), where his soul "thirsteth for" the Lord "in a dry and thirsty land" (v. 1; Vulgate: "in terra deserta . . . et inaquosa"). Longing for "lovingkindness," which "is better than life" (v. 3), David says that his "soul followeth hard after" God (8). Poole explains that a more literal translation would be, "My soul and spirit cleaveth to thee, as this verb signifies." Leigh, defining "dabaq" ("cleave"), remarks that in this verse the word is a metaphor fetched from things joined together by glue ("metaphora petita à rebus glutine . . . conjunctis"). Bellarmine mentions the psalmist's need that God sprinkle dew upon him from heaven ("rorem de caelo aspergit") and adds that David began to be bedewed and taste manna ("irrorari coepit, & manna gustare"), that he cleaved after the footprints of the Lord with the glue of love ("glutino . . . charitatis *post te*, idest vestigiis tuis inhaesit"). Ainsworth translates with "My soule cleaveth after thee" and gives a cross-reference to 1 Corinthians 6.17, "he that is joined unto the Lord," a passage cited by Wilson in defining "cleave": "to be glued unto one, or ioyned together most straightly." In the *Synopsis* Poole refers to David's need for moisture by mentioning radical humidity and cites Proverbs 17.22, "a broken spirit drieth the bones"—that is, as he paraphrases in the English commentary, "wasteth . . . the moisture and strength of the body." Lapide unfolds that proverb with references to Galen and Theophrastus on the one hand and to Aquinas and Cajetan on the other for ideas about "humor vitalis" and vital "sap" ("succum"). He further mentions the need for "pinguedinem . . . charitatis." Young's dictionary defines "pinguedo" as "fat" and specifies that "pingue" is "the fat betwixt the skin and the flesh." One of Lapide's quotations is Psalm 32.4. That verse is a place where "leshad" occurs in the Hebrew text

---

lar case despite the fact that my approach differs greatly from hers. See *Apocalyptic Marvell: The Second Coming in Seventeenth-Century Poetry* (Athens, Ohio, 1986), esp. 202–34.

and is the one Poole paraphrases with "My very radical moisture was in a manner dried up and wasted."

III

Following the trail of citations and explications thus leads back once again to words and images first mentioned much earlier. For the most part, this statement is factual, not interpretive, since the cross-references and their attendant glosses are being given in the commentaries themselves. Even so, since reporting them necessarily introduces an artificial element, some indication ought to be given of the kind of thing my account leaves out, especially because an awareness of what I have not included may well affect the reaction to what I have. Deliberately omitted here are several matters of considerable importance to the commentators as well as particularities of interpretation which look to be idiosyncratic. Poole conveniently illustrates both halves of this point. Perhaps because of his meticulous scholarship, Poole seldom finds occasion to be prejudicially partisan, but like many English divines of the time, he tends to see Rome as well as red when the subject of Babylon and her scarlet attire comes up. This antipapacy theme could easily be pursued from passage to passage, but there seems no need. Commenting on Ezekiel 1.17, Poole remarks that "such a wheel will readily be turned to all points of the compass, as a ball on a billiard table." This beguiling analogy is not, I think, a standard comparison. Many similar items, some from a shared tradition and others not, have definite places in the background literature but are passed over here. Also, of course, some of the items prominent in Marvell's poem have no apparent place in the background at all. Poole's billiard ball has made me cautious about ruling out possibilities in advance, but Hull's river, the Humber, is not mentioned in what I have read, nor would I expect to find it in what I have not.

These instances of mutually exclusive interests are mentioned because they can lead to areas in which a larger common ground might be expected than in fact appears to exist. Two examples illustrate this situation, both of them dependent on materials not unlike Marvell's. Consider first the praise of an ideal woman in the twenty-two verses with which the book of Proverbs ends (31.10–31). The climactic positioning of this encomium is worth noticing in itself, but the hyperbole takes a number of other forms, one of them not readily evident in translation. In the Hebrew, each successive verse begins with each successive letter of the alphabet from first to last so that the praise runs from *aleph* to *taw* or, in our terms, from *A* to *Z*. The compositional technique, as Poole points out, "is used in some, and but in a few places of Scripture"—Poole does not mention them, but Lamentations and Psalm 119 are two other most impressive instances—"to oblige us to the more diligent consideration and careful rememberance of them, as things of more than ordinary importance." Since the ideal is but rarely encountered, its value is not easily estimated: "Who can find a virtuous woman? for her price is far above rubies" (31.10). In Lapide's opinion, this paragon should be sought after even unto the remote ends of the earth ("in ultimis terrae finibus sit inquirenda"); to her there should be brought riches from the farthest lands of the inhabitants of India ("de ultimis Indorum terris"), for there is nothing in our own country, however so precious ("nihil enim quantumvis pretiosum in terra nostra est"), which may match the worth ("quod pretium . . . adaequet") of a "mulieris fortis" who is beyond all price ("omne pretium superat"). Within this frame are several details which might have served Marvell's purposes quite well: "Her clothing is silk and purple" (v. 22); "she shall rejoice in time to come" (25); "many daughters have done virtuously, but thou excellest them all" (29). And since this praise, though high indeed, remains inadequate, this lady is best praised indirectly by herself; hence *Taw*, the concluding verse: "Give her the fruit of her hands; and let her own works praise her in the gates."

This encomium at one time was of sufficient importance to give rise to elaborate expansion. Lapide, not himself a concise writer, has great admiration for the "ingentem librum," the huge book, in which Albertus Magnus developed an entire chapter from each of the verses. In 1614 an English exposition of them running to seventy-eight pages was published as a separate volume; in 1632 they were the text for *The Incomparable Jewell*, a work "wherein also is displayed," to quote the title page, "the hatefull company and hellish condition of a vicious ———."[19] In *Amoretti* 15, Spenser advises "tradefull Merchants"

---

19. *Bathshebaes Instructions . . . containing a fruitfull and plaine Exposition of the last chapter of the Proverbs* (London, 1614). (The work has been attributed to Robert Cleaver [*The New CBEL*, 1.1866], but the preface is "signed" John Dod and William Hinde.) W. L., *The Incomparable Jewell, Shewed in a Sermon* [on Prov. 31.10–31] (London, 1632). The encomiastic use has continued in some circles; cf. the "dedication" in Frederick W. Danker, *Multipurpose Tools for Bible Study* (St. Louis, 1960): "To the best commentary on Proverbs 31.10–31."

who "do seeke most precious things," that they need not venture "so farre" as the "Indies" for "treasures" such as "Saphyres" and "Rubies": "For loe my loue doth in her selfe containe all this worlds riches that may farre be found." Juliet asks, "By whose direction foundst thou out this place"; Romeo replies, "By love," and adds, "wert thou as far / As that vast shore wash'd with the farthest sea, / I should adventure for such merchandise" (2.2.79–84). Donne's song, "Goe, and catch a falling starre," includes the ironic directive, "Ride ten thousand daies and nights" in vain search for "a woman true, and faire." Marvell may well have known these texts and, in any case, was surely acquainted with the eulogy in Proverbs. Yet the only possible signs of his awareness in this poem that I can see are the spatial immensity of a "World enough" to supply fit praise and the details of the Ganges and its gorgeous gems: "Thou by the *Indian Ganges* side / Should'st Rubies find." Rubies, however, are also found elsewhere in Proverbs, notably in estimating the value of wisdom: "For wisdom is better than rubies" (8.11), "is more precious than rubies" (3.5). And to quote such passages probably ought to evoke Job's rhetorical question, not about where to find an ideal woman, but "where shall wisdom be found?" (28.12). This is a hard question too, of course, and in answering it, "No mention shall be made of coral, or of pearls: for the price of wisdom is above rubies" (v. 18). Commenting on this chapter of Job, Matthew Henry found space for "Holy Mr. Herbert" and "his poem called *Avarice*," but the ladies of Proverbs and Marvell have disappeared.

As for the Ganges, since it is not a biblical river, at least not by that name, Marvell's source—if he needed one—may be the exotic Orientalism sometimes employed by Roman writers who had heard of India in a vague sort of way. There are some references scattered in Ovid and in Seneca, for example, including the *Oedipus*, where a Gangean tiger briefly appears (458, "tigris . . . Gangetico"), along with the *Thyestes*— though not the chorus translated by Marvell—with its "Indians of the nearer sun" (602, "Phoebi proprioris Indus"). Virgil (*Georgics*, 2.136ff.) might also be mentioned. In what one editor refers to as "this famous panegyric on Italy," Virgil asserts that neither the beautiful Ganges ("nec pulcher Ganges") nor India nor any other foreign place can vie with his homeland in praise ("laudibus Italiae certent"). He thought there was no need to ride anywhere to seek the ideal.

> But neither *Median* Woods (a plenteous Land,)
> Fair *Ganges*, *Hermus* rolling Golden Sand,
> Nor *Bactria*, nor the richer *Indian* Fields,
> Nor all the Gummy Stores *Arabia* yields;

Nor any foreign Earth of greater Name,
Can with sweet *Italy* contend in Fame.
(Dryden's translation, 187–92)[20]

It might be difficult to cite examples of much greater historical significance than Virgil's *Georgics* and the book of Proverbs for expressions of two themes important in Marvell's poem. It also is difficult to know whether these particular echoes ring true or false. Much earlier I mentioned the problem of hearing too much and/or too little, but the difficulty needs to be reconsidered. Part of my own argument obviously depends on probability or improbability; when two distinguishable bodies of material share significant features and are both internally coherent in terms of those features, the likelihood of coincidental similarity is reduced. Scattered parallels from varying sources, clearly, are a very different kind of thing. One way to address this issue is to consider the images which present Marvell's own echoing song in connection with a dusty grave, the improbability in such a place of any kind of embrace, and an irruption through the iron gates of life.

Donno, following Leishman, offers a partial analogue from the *Greek Anthology*, "The joys of love are in the land of the living, but in Acheron, dear virgin, we shall lie dust and ashes." The citation may be a good one, but Propertius may be even closer and probably was more widely known. In 1.18, scorned by an arrogant Cynthia, the poet retires to a landscape of barren rock and empty groves, there to lament—as the Loeb has it—with "Ah! how oft do my passionate words echo ('resonant') beneath your delicate shades, how oft is Cynthia's name carved upon your bark!" Carving is an inane practice, as Orlando demonstrates in *As You Like It* and as Marvell himself observed in "The Garden": "Fond lovers"—foolish, that is, but perhaps affectionate as

20. The editor referred to is T. E. Page, *P. Virgili Maronis Bucolica et Georgica* (London, 1898; rpt. 1957), 256. Dryden's translation is quoted from *The Poems*, ed. James Kinsley, 4 vols. (Oxford, 1958). For Ovid, see *Fasti*, 3.729 ("Gange totoque Oriente subacto," the Ganges and all the East, i.e., "India," having been subjugated); *Amores*, 1.2.47 ("Gangetide terra," Gangean land); and esp. *Met.*, 5.46–47 ("Erat Indus Athis, quem flumine Gange edita Limnace vitreis peperisse sub undis," there was an Indian named Athis to whom Limnace, daughter of the river Ganges, is said to have given birth beneath the glittering waves. The spelling of the proper names varies from edition to edition, perhaps because they were not well known from other writers: Ovid is the only major source for this myth.)

well—"Cut in these Trees their Mistress name" (19–20). In Propertius this kind of inscription is particularly self-defeating since in consequence the woods themselves—again, quoting the Loeb—"re-echo" ("resonant") with "Cynthia," nor do "these lone crags have rest from the sound of thy name" ("nec deserta tuo nomine saxa vacent").

In the poem which immediately follows, 1.19, the situation is both better and worse. "To Cynthia, not to Forget Him in the Grave" is the title supplied, aptly enough, by Ronald Musker. His translation, more readable than the Loeb's, in part is this:

> The gloomy world where the dead abide, my Cynthia,
> Now holds no fears, nor the doom the pyre fulfils.
> But in the grave to be without your love!
> . . . .
> In the realm of darkness, Protesilaus, the hero
> Of Thessaly, could not forget the wife he loved.
> Still eager with spectral hands to clasp his joy,
> He returned, though only a shadow now,
> To his ancient home.
> There, ghost, or whatever else, I shall still be yours:
> Great love leaps over the very shores of death.
> . . . .
> If, while you live, I am ashes, may you feel
> The same for me: then death were nowhere bitter.
> . . . .
> So, while we may, let us love and rejoice together:
> Love, though it had the whole of time,
> Would be all too short.[21]

"Non satis est ullo tempore longus amor"; the Loeb translation is worth quoting too: "Eternity itself is all too brief for love." In Virgil it is the lady herself—this is the glamorous Circe, daughter of the Sun—

---

21. *The Poems of Propertius* (London, 1972). Propertius was intermittently fond of imagining his own death and also Cynthia's exequies for him. Cf. 1.17; 2.13.35–36 (an inscription for his own future tomb; QVI NVNC IACET HORRIDA PVLVIS, / VNIVS HIC QVONDAM SERVVS AMORIS ERAT, he who now lies here as grim dust once was the servant of one love only) and 57–58 (the poem's final couplet: "sed frustra mutos revocabis, Cynthia, Manes: nam mea qui poterunt ossa minuta loqui?"—but vainly, Cynthia, shall you call back my mute ghost, for what might all my pulverized bones be able to speak?); and 2.24.35–36.

who causes groves to echo with continual song (*Aeneid*, 7.11–12, "ubi Solis filia lucos / adsiduo resonat cantu"). Propertius and Virgil may not have wanted their readers to hear a mocking version of echoing song, but Marvell just conceivably might. If so, then Horace has a relevant passage in his famous defense of satire. He says that some poets, oblivious to whether it is the wrong place or the wrong time, are so inconsiderate as to declaim their lines in the public baths where the enclosed space "echoes" with an ironically "melodious" voice (*Sermones*, 1.4.76, "suave locus voci resonat conclusus").

The example of Horace leads to a related problem caused by echoes, the possibility of some of them drowning out others. Donno's discussion of Marvell's gates is a striking example of this point and is so, among other reasons, precisely because it so oddly contrasts to the manifest excellence of the commentary which she characteristically supplies. Donno chooses to print "grates" (her authority being the Bodleian volume referred to below in the References), partly because "the traditional figurative phrase was 'gates of death' (*mortis januae*), not 'gates of life' "; "the one literary example I know that specifies a 'gate' into life (as well as death) is found in Spenser's account of the Garden of Adonis." In fact, however, as the quotations from Spenser clearly show and as Donno herself next points out, that account merely implies a gate of life and does not actually specify one. Donno further supports "grates" with the argument, "The adjectives most commonly associated with gates are *horn* and *ivory*, whereas *iron* is commonly used with *grates* (see *OED*)." The phrase "gates of death" is unquestionably well known, but evidently what has happened here is that its volume level has been turned up too high.

Consider first the fact that Jones's dictionary of classical quotations and Stevenson's *The Home Book of Quotations* both include an entry for "Mors janua vitae" (death [is] the gate of life), in one case without attribution, in the other citing Saint Bernard. Stevenson's book perhaps was old-fashioned even when it first appeared in 1934 and thus may have been intended for roughly the same sort of reader John Buchan had in mind in 1915. At any rate, the first chapter ("The Man Who Died") of *The Thirty-Nine Steps* has this exchange:

> "But I thought you were dead," I put in.
> "*Mors janua vitae*," he smiled. (I recognized the quotation: it was about all the Latin I knew.)[22]

22. Hugh Percy Jones, *Dictionary of Foreign Phrases and Classical Quotations* (Edinburgh, 1929; rpt. 1963); *The Home Book of Quotations*, ed. Burton

Buchan and Bernard aside, a tremendously important part of what Milton's Adam learns from Michael in the last book of *Paradise Lost* is that "suffering . . . / Is fortitude to highest victory, / And to the faithful Death the Gate of Life" (12.569–71). Since, moreover, this gate leads to life eternal, there is a close connection to the "Kingly Palace Gate" (3.505) of Heaven from which depend "Stairs . . . such as . . . *Jacob* saw" (3.510) when the mysterious ladder caused Jacob to exclaim, "This is none other but the house of God, and this is the gate of heaven" (Genesis 18.17). Donne once told his congregation that "the dust of great persons graves is speechlesse . . . it sayes nothing, it distinguishes nothing."[23] But on another occasion he said that the dead

> shall awake as *Jacob* did, and say . . . *this is . . . the gate of heaven*. And into that gate they shall enter, and in that house they shall dwell where there shall be . . . no noyse nor silence, but one equall musick . . . no ends nor beginnings, but one equall eternity.

Since, however, these descriptions say nothing of iron, it may be desirable to notice some that do. The example I want to emphasize is the "iron gate" mentioned in Acts 12.10, but I need to lay some groundwork first. The gates of Milton's Hell, strictly speaking, are "Adamantine" (2.893), but in unlocking them, Sin "in the key-hole turns / Th' intricate wards, and every Bolt and Bar / Of massy Iron or solid Rock with ease / Unfast'ns" (876–79). The broad allusion is, of course, to the commission entrusted to Peter by Christ: "Upon this rock I will build my Church; and the gates of hell shall not prevail against it. And I will give unto thee the keys of the kingdom of heaven" (Matthew 16.18).

Stevenson, 9th ed. (New York, 1964), 377, #18 (the entire section concerns death and life). Buchan is quoted from a reprint (Boston, 1943), 6. The concluding sentence of Bacon's essay "Of Death" is worth noting: "Death hath this also, That it openeth the gate to good fame, and extinguisheth envy" (*A Selection of His Works*, ed. Sidney Warhaft [New York, 1965], 50). Further afield are biblical references such as John 10.9 ("I am the door: by me if any man enter in, he shall be saved") as well as Herbert's line, "On Sunday heaven's gate stands ope" ("Sunday," 33, in *The Works*, ed. F. E. Hutchinson [Oxford, 1941], 76).

23. *The Sermons*, ed. George R. Potter and Evelyn M. Simpson, 10 vols. (Berkeley and Los Angeles, 1953–62), 4.52–53. The quotation which follows is from 8.191.

Since Milton is inverting Matthew, he may be inverting Isaiah as well: "Thus saith the Lord to his anointed, to Cyrus . . . I will . . . break in pieces the gates of brass, and cut in sunder the bars of iron" (45.1–2). The result is breaking into Babylon and laying it waste. One of the points here is that Hell and Babylon are symbolic prisons. Satan breaks out of one; Cyrus breaks into the other. This leads to the prison in Jerusalem. Imprisoned and condemned to death, Peter was visited and freed by an angel: "When they were past the first and the second ward, they came unto the iron gate that leadeth to the city; which opened to them of his own accord" (Acts 12.10). The Douai has "the iron gate . . . which of itself opened to them," translating "por tam ferream . . . quae ultro aperta est eis." The Greek has a form of "sìderios," "iron," elsewhere used for the "rod of iron," as in, for example, Revelation or Apocalypse 2.27, "he shall rule them with a rod of iron." The apocalyptic text echoes Psalm 2.9, "thou shalt break them with a rod of iron," where the Hebrew is "barzel," as in Isaiah 45.2, the "bars of iron" (the ones Cyrus cuts in sunder), and Ezekiel 4.3: "set it for a wall of iron between thee and the city: and set thy face against it, and it shall be besieged, and thou shalt lay siege against it." Iron obviously clangs in various biblical passages both earlier and later than Acts. When the iron gate for Peter opened, he immediately went "to the house of Mary" and "knocked at the door of the gates" (12–13). Those within "were astonished" (16) because they were unaware that "the Lord had brought" Peter "out of the prison" (17).

Peter's gates had, of course, an intrinsic importance of their own, but one of the reasons for their fame was that the narrative details inevitably reminded the commentators of an event recorded concerning the resurrected Christ. Risen from the tomb, he came to the house of his disciples and "the doors were shut." Yet suddenly he "stood in the midst" (John 20.19). The parallels are obvious enough: two prisons, though one is the grave, two freeings, two shut doors, two sets of astonished people, and so on. The next things to notice are that the second narrative was a "proof" text in doctrinal controversy and that some of the details of the second account were read back into the first. How did the risen Christ pass through doors that were closed? Poole's report, much shortened, is this:

> Here is a great question betwixt the Lutherans and the Calvinists, how Christ came in amongst them when the doors were shut? whether he went through the doors remaining shut? which the Lutherans stiffly maintain, as a strong proof of the possibility of the real presence of the body of Christ, in, with, or

under the elements of the Lord's supper; . . . the Lutherans object, . . . The Calvinists on the other side object, . . . In the Lutherans' reason . . .

The same kind of controversy, though in quite different terms, spills
over into explanations of the freeing of Peter. The biblical account
explicitly states that the iron gate opened itself, but what of those
inner wards through which he first passed? Lapide at this point is
unconcerned with Lutherans or Calvinists, but he reports the opinion
that the inner gates of the prison were shut and that Saint Peter passed
through them by means of divine force, even as Christ after the resurrection went through closed doors to his disciples. ("Consent, intima
ostia carceris fuisse clausa, ac proinde S. Petrum ea vi divina pene-
trasse, sicut Christus ea penetravit post resurrectionem iis clausis in-
travit ad discipulos"). Lapide is dubious on the grounds that there was
no need for such a miracle in Peter's case; if the iron gate could be
opened for him, then so could the first and second wards. In any case,
he adds, the important point is that the bonds of the prison and of
death were loosed. Mystically, as Bede says, the iron gate is that which
leads to the celestial Jerusalem ("Mysticè Beda: ferrea porta quae
ducit ad Ierusalem caelestem").

Lapide cited an Ovidian "corruption" in commenting on Hezekiah;
in this case he omits the gates in *Amores*, 1.6, but the poem was not
obscure. It recounts a mock siege upon the "janitor" and the "janua"
intervening between the poet and his mistress. The hours of the night,
moist with crystalline dew ("vitreoque madentia rore") are fast slip-
ping past, the gates themselves are moist from the lover's tears ("uda
sit ut lacrimis janua facta meis"), Ovid threatens an attack with iron
and fire ("ferroque ignique"), a refrain ("excute poste seram") insistently demands that the way be unbarred, but the keeper himself is
hard-heartedly "ferreus," "iron," and the doors of delight remain
closed. A literary descendant of this "janitor," Gardner notes, is
Donne's "grim eight-foot-high iron-bound serving-man" who "to barre
the first gate doth as wide / As the great Rhodian Colossus stride" (Elegy 4, "The Perfume," 31ff.). An erotic kind of heaven and a sexual death
might be experienced, no doubt, if only the gates could be entered, but
not, alas, with this doorman in the way: "Which, if in hell no other
paines there were, / Makes mee feare hell, because he must be there."

These things, finally, might also be mentioned: that "chalkeos"
(referring to a metal, often "brass") is an epithet in Homer (*Iliad*,
11.241) for "Sleep," the phrase as a whole meaning "death"; that
"chalkeos" becomes "ferreus," "iron," in Virgil's imitation (*Aeneid*,

10.745, "ferreus . . . Somnus"); that Lapide cites and quotes the Virgilian version in commenting on "umbram mortis" (shadow of death),
in Jeremiah 13: "Be not proud . . . you shall look for light," and the
Lord "will turn it into the shadow of death. . . . Say to the king, and
to the queen: Humble yourselves, sit down: for the crown of glory is
come down from your head" (Douai, 13.15–18); that in verse 11,
Jeremiah quotes Yahweh himself as saying that "as the girdle sticketh
close" (Douai, translating "adhaeret") "so have I brought" Israel
"close to me" (translating "agglutinavi"); that the Authorized Version
has "as the girdle cleaveth . . . so have I caused to cleave unto me";
and that the Hebrew for both verbs gives forms of "dabaq," the
radical which Leigh translates as "glue."

The texts quoted in the last few paragraphs are, I hope, appropriately reminiscent of themes in Marvell's poem, and some of them may
be more suggestive in one way or another than analogues noted by
Marvell's editors. Even if so, these are potshots, more or less, and thus
by definition haphazard: With luck, they may land on target. In what
seems to me a clear-cut contrast, the material given earlier is relatively circumscribed and is possessed, moreover, of much greater internal coherence. In looking at it—and this point in my view is also of
considerable significance—one is not dealing with anything at all like
the grand biblical archetypes which inform so much of earlier literature. It is true that Northrop Frye recently mentioned (in order to
take mildly to task) "Immanuel Velikovski, a writer with still a considerable vogue," who "has written books to show that this event"—the
solar miracle performed for Joshua—"along with an equally improbable story about Hezekiah in 2 Kings 20, did take place in much he way
described, the cause being, he tells us, the settling of the new planet
Venus into its orbit."[24] But for Frye himself, Joshua and Hezekiah,

---

24. *The Great Code: The Bible and Literature* (New York and London, 1982,
1981), 44; a footnote (238) refers to "Immanuel Velikovsky, *Worlds in Collision*
(1950)." For some of my earlier material, cf. Frye's remark on Eccl. 3.11 ("He
has made everything beautiful in its time; also he has put eternity into man's
mind, yet so that he cannot find out what God has done from beginning to
end"): "In Koheleth's inexhaustible treasury of common sense one of the
shrewdest is that God has put *'olam* into man's mind (3.11). The word usually
means something like 'eternity,' but in this context has rather the sense of
mystery or obscurity. Eternity is a mental category that, in Keats's phrase,
teases us out of thought" (124). [Frye's form, *'olam*, perhaps should be explained: the ' indicates rough breathing—cf. note 13 above—and "holam" is
sometimes used in transliteration.]

not to mention glue, are scarcely even minor cyphers, and understandably so, in the Bible's great code. Even Babylon herself, while a prominent figure indeed in the myth of exile and return, is a recognizably different lady in the patterns I have been tracing. The chariot of Ezekiel, at least at one time, was of profoundest import in Jewish tradition since the "Merkabah" ("quadrigus," four-wheeled, in the commentaries) and "Bereshith" ("beginning," "Genesis") were the polar symbols of Yahweh's mysterious, transcendent essence on the one hand and of his reality as manifested in the visible handiworks of creation on the other. J. H. Adamson evoked a part of this tradition for Milton's "Chariot of Paternal Deity" (*PL*, 6.750), but for my purposes the relevance at very most is tangential.[25] If these contrasts are representative, then it seems improbable that mere fortuity can account for the simultaneous presence of so many parallel elements in the set of materials I have described and also in one short poem.

Biography might be used to replace chance as a connection, though I personally discount its value in this particular case. Both Poole and Marvell enjoyed the patronage of Lord Fairfax. As all students of Marvell know, he tutored the general's daughter in the 1650s. One of the bequests in Fairfax's will was this: "I give to Mr Matthew Poole the sume of Tenn pounds towards the carryinge on of his Synopsis."[26] When the work was published, Fairfax was among the benefactors named by Poole in the "Praefatio." Fairfax himself maintained a library stocked with biblical and theological books—the biographers mention polyglo Bibles as well as the works of Saint Jerome—and, in addition to trying his own hand at verse paraphrases from Psalms, Fairfax adorned his portal with an inscription:

> Think not, O Man! that dwells herein,
> This House's a stay, but as an inn
> Which for convenience fitly stands
> In way to one not made with hands.
> But if a time, here thou take rest,
> Yet think eternity the best.

25. "The War in Heaven: The Merkabah," in W. B. Hunter, C. A. Patrides, and J. H. Adamson, *Bright Essence: Studies in Milton's Theology* (Salt Lake City, 1971), 103–14; rpt. from *JEGP*, 57 (1958): 690–703.

26. Quoted by Clements R. Markham, *The Great Lord Fairfax* (London, 1890), 444. The inscription next quoted is taken from M. A. Gibb, *The Lord General: A Life of Thomas Fairfax* (London, 1938), 233.

In 1666, while representing Hull in Parliament, Marvell wrote, "We have adjourned till Saturday next. I thank you for your kind present of our Hull liquor" (Margoliouth, 2.48). Two years later, he reported to Mayor Duncalfe, "as we sat there drinking a cup of sack with the General Coll: Legg chancing to be present there were twenty good things said on all hands tending to the good fame reputation & advantage of the Town" (2.80). The *DNB* records of Poole that

> The evening he spent at some friend's house, very frequently that of Henry Ashurst where 'he would be exceedingly but innocently merry,' although he always ended the day in 'grave and serious discourse,' which he ushered in with the words, 'Now let us call for a reckoning.'

The *DNB* also reports that Ashurst himself (1614?–80) "acted as treasurer for the Society for the Propagation of the Gospel" and "had the intimate acquaintance of . . . Matthew and Philip Henry." Philip (1631–96) was the father of Matthew, and Matthew was the author of the commentary I have often cited. Although Matthew, born in 1662, would have been young at the time of Marvell's death in 1678 and Poole's in 1679, some of these men may have been busily peering over one another's shoulders to see what had been or was being written. Conceivably their evenings were enlivened with sack and billiards and table talk of Babylon and Cynthia and thus of eternity and time. This fancy has considerable charm, but it is not the picture I am trying to see, at least not at this moment.

The point instead is the visibility of patterns of usage with overlapping configurations in authors who had occasion to consider a number of the topics also included by Marvell. Since the patterns can be seen in terms of both positive correlation and negative comparison, the probability seems strong that Marvell was working from within a tradition, using concepts and words with connotative values and associations at one time recognized though now largely unfamiliar. Marvell's own gleaming language, while astonishing enough in isolation, virtually leaps forth from the dun backdrop of some of the material given here. Despite its obviousness, that may be the most important point to be made. Disparity of purpose in this case, however, is of no consequence. Had Poole been called upon for a reckoning, the balance sheets of Marvell's poem presumably would have been suspect. Also presumed, however, is that Poole would have understood the terms used by Marvell and that both writers might have been rather puzzled by some of the later commentary.

Astonishment might be a better word for their reaction to the commentary given here, with its laborious scratching away at the surface of biblical and classical texts. Marvell surely could not have written as he did without having absorbed, rather than merely accumulated information about, the values of the words he chose to use. And so, one may fairly ask, what words *did* he use? And what lies beneath the surface of his own text? The best textual evidence we have indicates that Marvell did indeed include glue, and one of the things that seems clear to me is that any attempt to discard the word will have to be based on firmer ground than a presupposition about its impropriety. Efforts to defend it as deliberately grotesque or to rewrite it so it means "glow" also appear anachronistically misguided. "Hue" and "dew," moreover, were not words of greater inherent luster and thus are not preferred on the basis of aesthetic sensibility. In terms of theoretical pecking order, glue was the most useful of the three; dew, second; and hue, a distant third. Since there seems little question about that order, my supposition is that Marvell found hue of initially absorbing interest as he made his very close examination of this lady's flesh, specifically her skin; the "color" of her (unpejorative) "hide," after all, is a superficial but undeniably attractive place to start. When one moves on (or down) to the level of "every pore" (36), however, then dew and glue are words of much greater exactitude. If Marvell had been a poet whose manuscripts were widely circulated (as Donne's were), one could speculate not only that at least two versions are equally authentic but that they were designed for slightly different audiences. As it is, at least so far as is now known, only two of the three words can be retained in a conventional text. Hue almost certainly is the one to omit, but the reading which really ought to be given would look something like this:

> Now therefore, while the youthful hew: glew
> Sits on thy skin like morning glew: dew.

The suggestion is probably impractical, but not, I think, theoretically extreme. There would be a considerable advantage, as I see it, if a comparable crux in *Hamlet* were similarly handled:

> O that this too too solid: sullied: sallied flesh would melt,
> Thaw, and resolve itself into a dew!

One at least would be confronted by the problems instead of unearthing them from a textual note, often buried at the back of the play or even the book.

Hugh Richmond observed, several years ago, that the "Lesbia" to whom Catullus sometimes addressed himself "was recognizably a real person, Clodia, wife of Quintus Metellus Celer," but "no scholar has felt that the identity of Marvell's coy mistress was a matter worth research or controversy." Rosalie Colie's remark about "The Gallery" is perhaps applicable here as well: "It doesn't matter who the lady is, or whether she is real or not."[27] If one supposes that Marvell's mistress had poetic existence rather than the autobiographical kind and that her flesh, to borrow a phrase from Colie, was "an artefact of the imagination," then even so the situation imagined by Marvell is not thereby reduced to unreality, nor is it a mere poetic fiction totally remote from actual human experience. The situation is separable, however, from *urgent* matters as determined by the speed of everyday clocks, and it can be contrasted to variant circumstances on either side. Donne thought he was dying (erroneously, as it turned out) when he wrote *Devotions upon Emergent Occasions* or, as we would say, "emergencies." According to Rosalind, "Men have died from time to time, and worms have eaten them, but not for love" (*AYLI*, 4.1.101–2). In Marvell's poem, urgency is of neither of these kinds.

With or without a nameable lady in mind (or in tangible flesh before him), Marvell thus could and did delay time's winged chariot long enough to examine this particular situation both specifically and broadly. Glue signifies physical and metaphorical perfection but not necessarily at the same time, and within the traditional usage resides an implicit tension of the kind which informs the entire poem. To seize the day amorously is to use and enjoy the physical perfection while it exists and with full cognition that the perfection of the "willing soul" (35) must be a secondary consideration or possibly no consideration at all. The glue which bonds one to God and to humans created as divine images differs markedly from the sexual kind. Gates, whether of death or life, are ambivalent, as is the grave itself. The world and the time which measures it are expandable constrictions, and the dry and thirsty land of existence can be remedied by more than one kind of dew. Colie (125) proposes that the poem, "for all its marvellously understanding presentation of sexual desire, . . . does not suggest that its speaker has a fuller awareness of love than of the kind he is talking about in the poem." My notion, however, is that her comment on "The Garden" in most ways would have been more appropriate: "The mind is an envelope of possibilities, enclosing within itself all conceivable to any mind" (120). Marvell weighs carefully—or rather, asks the lady to consider with meticulous care—the disparate

27. Richmond, *The School of Love* (Princeton, 1964), 59; Colie, "*My Ecchoing Song*: *Andrew Marvell's Poetry of Criticism* (Princeton, 1970), 109.

choices of the present instant in the continuum of nearly infinite past and future, and it is the "now" (as in "Now, therefore") which results in and requires Marvell's immediacy and precision. The context (as in "world enough and time") results, however, in a breadth which also is extraordinarily deep. Herrick cut through some of this complexity by means of marriage, a bond which sanctions sexuality: "Then be not coy, but use your time; And while ye may go marry."[28] Marvell chose instead to incorporate allusive references which finally have the effect of expanding the poem within our minds so that one irrationally believes, at least momentarily, that the lines actually embody a vast tradition of which they can in fact be merely a part and on which they depend. Whatever Marvell's coy mistress decides, and even if she should decide not to decide, at least not yet, her choice will be informed by an awareness of not quite innumerable implications at the narrowest and broadest limits of human experience.

This poem and its companions among Marvell's lyrics often are veiled oxymorons in that they are contemplative or exploratory and yet address themselves to actions and reactions. Poems which deal with ongoing current events, especially those of a political nature, have less room for contemplation for the simple but sometimes terrifying reason that profoundly significant action either is or ought to be happening even as one writes the poem. Emergent occasions certainly ought to be handled with great caution lest a fatal mistake be made, but they leave no time in which to decide to postpone decision. Habits of mind and long-cherished methods are not easily changed, however, and this fact is evident in Marvell and Waller as well. Waller evidently believed that his customary occasional verse did not meet the needs of the times when King Charles was rebuilding England in St. James's Park and when a war with Holland was being waged. He temporarily shifted mental gears—not to abandon his style and methods but to reapply them—and he later shifted them again for the religious verse of his extremely old age. When Marvell became Hull's representative in Parliament, coy and uncoy mistresses became relatively less important, even if the ones in question were Charles's own. Absolutes did not and could not change, but Marvell's relationship to them as a writer did. He abandoned his usual methodology no more than Waller did, but he had to alter his style, and since he died unexpectedly, there was literally no opportunity—either to take or to decline—for a final modulation back from satire into lyric.

28. "To the Virgins, to make much of Time," in *The Complete Poetry*, ed. J. Max Patrick (New York, 1963), 118.

3

Waller and King Charles in St. James's Park

In 1687, when Waller died, every short list of famous English poets almost certainly would have included his name, though not Marvell's, and he continued to be greatly praised for about fifty years. Both Dryden and Pope admired Waller's manner and style; Elijah Fenton (d. 1730), Pope's protégé and the translator of several books of "Pope's" *Odyssey*, usually thought the substance was faultless as well. By 1744, however, Pope himself was dead, the reissue in the same year of Fenton's edition of Waller's *Works* probably was not greeted with the enormous enthusiasm its editor had himself expressed, and admiration has been in singularly short supply ever since. The nadir occurred in 1984, if not for all of Waller's verse, then at least for "On St. James's Park As Lately Improved by His Majesty," for in that year the poem more or less ceased to exist. Nicolas Jose quoted the final couplet—"Reform these Nations, and improve them more / Than this fair Park from what it was before"—as a preface for his own final, devastating attack.

But such rhetoric seems cheap, coming alongside the senselessly self-indulgent scene we were shown initially:

> The gallants dancing by the river's side
> They bathe in summer, and in winter slide.

> Waller's attempt to graft rhetoric of the order of Virgil's fourth eclogue on to his urbane pastoral is sadly self-defeating. The highly ornate centrelessness of the poem attenuates the relationship between the eternal king and the fleeting modernity of the park, until it is beyond the reader's grasp. The huge classical claim collapses into a much more precarious idyll and Waller's world-weary sense of the ephemeral leaves his idea of the restoration in the background.[1]

In effect, obviously, Jose has argued the so-called "poem" out of existence since its stature has diminished to the vanishing point. His charges, moreover, are themselves so numerous and seemingly scattered that simultaneous defense on all fronts looks to be impossible. Perhaps, however, Jose supposes that senseless self-indulgence, self-defeating engraftments, and world-weary ephemerality are surface manifestations of two deeply fundamental flaws, "ornate centrelessness" on the one hand and "cheap" rhetoric on the other. If so, then what is required is close attention to the context of the poem (for valuation of rhetorical strategy) and to the text itself (for awareness of central focus). Luckily, the title and opening lines of the poem enable one to address both of these issues in fairly close proximity.

Had the Park not been "lately improved by his Majesty" in a quite literal way, then the poem could only have been greatly different both in detail and structure. Pepys was much taken with the "great and very noble alterations" (16 August 1661), "the brave alterations" (3 September), "the new works" (27 July 1662), and the scene so offensive to Jose was not so to him: ". . . it being a great frost still, and after a turn in the Park seeing them slide . . ." (2 February 1663); "I and Captn. Ferrers to the Park, and there walked finely, seeing people slide" (8 February).[2] Waller watches Charles playing the game of Pall

---

1. *Ideas of the Restoration in English Literature 1660–71* (Cambridge, MA, 1984), 52. It is not easy to see how that which is mindless can be intelligent, but see Jack W. Gilbert, *Edmund Waller*, TEAS 266 (Boston, 1979), 94: "Mindless compliment may cloak, however, the cunning of a poet who ventures intelligent admonition." The latter part of the statement, in my opinion, is accurate and will be developed here, but my much greater debt is to Earl Miner, *The Cavalier Mode from Jonson to Cotton* (Princeton, 1971), 24–37.

2. Pepys is quoted from *The Diary*, ed. Henry B. Wheatley (London, 1893–99; rpt. 1946). "On St. James's Park" is quoted from Miner's appendix (see also my own References). The most accessible text is the one in *Ben Jonson and the Cavalier Poets* (Norton Critical Edition), ed. Hugh Maclean (New York, 1974).

Mall on a "well-polisht" surface (57); Pepys explains that "all over there is a cockle-shells powdered, and spread to keep it fast; which, however, in dry weather, turns to dust and deads the ball" (14 May 1663). A game preserve was added for birds; in the diary, "the King and Duke came to see their fowl play" (16 March 1661/2), and in the poem, "a flock of new sprung fowl / Hangs in the ayr" (27–28). A newly cut canal linked the Park to the Thames. Pepys evidently found this particular improvement less interesting than others, though he refers to "the several engines to draw up water" (11 October 1660), but Waller thought it very fine work indeed, for " 'tis of more renown / To make a River than to build a Town" (11–12).

The first point, therefore, is that Waller could not have made his poem what it is apart from Charles making the Park what it was in the process of becoming. Even so, Waller imposes on or creates out of the topographical details a distinct order of his own. The introductory four lines balance the lasting fame—despite the loss—of the first paradise and the potential fame of its modern counterpart.

> Of the first Paradise there's nothing found,
> Plants set by heav'n are vanisht, and the ground;
> Yet the description lasts; who knows the fate
> Of lines that shall this Paradise relate?

Passing over the unforeseen irony of the rhetorical question, one may notice that for Waller to be more assertive would be presumptuous and rash, for much depends not only on what Waller and Charles can accomplish by their makings inside the Park but also on what Charles alone can perform in realms outside it. At the end of the poem, the world lies all before the king, as it does in 1667 for Milton's Adam and Eve. But Milton already knew what choices would be made, whereas Waller can be no more than hortatory and prophetic. Visions are thus glimpsed of a paradigmatic past and of a possible future, but finality cannot be asserted, for the poem is predicated not only on those improvements already made but on continuing reform as well. Inside the Park, often in the present tense, Waller and Charles are viewers who survey two distinguishable prospects. Waller (5–66) sees peaceful activities of various kinds, one of them being angling and thus specifically that which Walton calls the contemplative man's recreation. Charles (67–134) contemplates decisively forceful action arising from and consonant with the principles of deeply meditated thought. This double bifurcation of viewers and scenes in the poem as a whole is reflected locally by the antitheses of its couplets, and these binary unities depend on or spring from initial interaction between "that" paradise and "this" Park.

> Instead of Rivers rowling by the side
> Of *Edens* garden, here flowes in the tyde;
> The Sea which always serv'd his Empire, now
> Pays tribute to our Prince's pleasure too:
> Of famous Cities we the founders know;
> But Rivers old, as Seas, to which they go,
> Are nature's bounty; 'tis of more renown
> To make a River than to build a Town.
>
> (5–12)

Genesis 2.10 records that "a river went out of Eden to water the garden; and from thence it was parted, and became into four heads"; hence, for example, Milton's "four main Streams" (*PL*, 4.233) as well as these "Rivers rowling by the side."[3] Thanks to the new canal, however, in this case the "tyde" of one river "flowes in." A commonplace but nonetheless remarkable fact about the Thames is that it actually is tidal and thus permits reciprocal motion. It goes down to the sea, as rivers customarily do, but the sea in this case also flows up and through "the new stream" (14) into the Park. Sea-nymphs, emissaries of Thetis, later enter with "the swelling tyde" (38) and next re-exit "to make report, / And tell the wonders" they have seen (39–40). The canal admits the "Sea," the servant of "Empire," but empire itself depends on maritime expansion, not contraction, on movement down and outside the Thames as well as a return by means of it. Antithetical direction of flow is an inescapable fact, in short, but not yet a prominent one in the poem. Due process is important for this poem as a reflection of historical process itself, and embedded in Waller's lines are implications only later unfolded. Waller certainly is mindful of outward expansion, including the kind achieved by commercial interchange, and he makes obvious that fact when Charles contemplates methods of "restoring trade" (118) and next considers how "our bounds" may be "inlarg'd" (120). At this earlier stage, however, the lines stress the bringing *in* of due "tribute" and the concomitant supplying of "nature's bounty" to Charles as its rightful recipient. Charles has no need to exact homage, but he has made possible its payment by affording tidal ingress, and since this is a work of "renown," he

---

3. Milton is quoted from *The Complete Poems and Major Prose*, ed. Merritt Y. Hughes (New York, 1957).

confers honor upon himself as well as receiving it from others. Unruffled on the surface, these lines thus possess considerable depth, and there is an appropriate retrogression to them despite or rather because of the precise form of their sequential linearity:

$$\text{sea} \left\{ \begin{array}{c} \text{rivers . . . tide} \\ \\ \text{rivers . . . river} \end{array} \right\} \text{(sea)}$$

Even as the verse paragraph ends, however, forward movement is continued by means of a nice distinction between the relative worth of two claims for fame: not that building a town is *inglorious* work, absolutely considered, merely that making a river is of *more* renown. Famous cities and their founders, as Waller says, are known, and he supplies an example almost immediately (in line 15) by mentioning not the town itself but rather its maker, the semi-divine "Amphion," who played upon the lyre to raise the walls of Thebes. "The voice of *Orpheus*" in the same line indicates that the ordering power of harmony is the primary point being made. Waller, however, does not always particularize names in this poem. A possibly surprising proof is that the king is personally and pervasively present, but "Charles" occurs only in line 77, and in another passage (discussed below), where one expects to hear the syllables "Cromwell," there is loud silence instead. Despite the silence here, "Of famous Cities we the founders know" is a line which invites exemplification, and Rome is not a bad choice to make, especially since Waller later alludes to "*Romes* Capitol" (88) and to its unnamed but identifiable "proud founders" (90). The eponymous figure in this case, of course, is Romulus, who

> is universally supposed to have laid the foundations of that celebrated city, on the 20th of April, according to Varro, in the year 3961 of the Julian period, 3251 years after the creation of the world, 753 years before the birth of Christ, 431 years after the Trojan war, and in the fourth year of the sixth Olympiad.[4]

4. *Lempriere's Classical Dictionary* (London, 1984; 1st ed., 1788), s.v. "Roma." Cf. also the prefatory "Chronological Table from the Creation of the World," v.

These dates, despite the momentous events which establish them, probably are not specifically included in Waller's own long view, but if history of this sort is to the point in even a general way, then the line about famous cities and founders begins to look like understatement, and the reference to "Rivers *old*" suggests a rather precise antiquity. Waller's title, the poem's occasion, and a comparison often made in connection with the name of Charles all indicate that an additional founder of renown may be specified with considerable confidence, the more so since Waller does mention him in line 123, referring to "great *Augustus*" and his "fame." Kenneth Scott gathered from numerous Roman sources the evidence (to quote his title) for "The Identification of Augustus with Romulus-Quirinus,"[5] but the example of the *Aeneid* alone may be sufficient to establish familiarity with the idea in later times. In Virgil's eyes, Augustus founds ("condet," 6.792) not the city itself, of course, but a second golden age for it and its empire. "See," as Dryden translates, "*Romulus* the great" (*Aeneis*, 6.1055) and behold Augustus, "Born to restore a better Age of Gold" (1080).[6]

Hindsight thus indicates the relevance of Rome and its double founders, but foresight is required by the poem's initial frame of reference, for the comparison to paradise cannot help but raise expectations about what kind of place the Park itself must be. Merely to mention this point is to risk belaboring it, but the comparison is too important to be taken for granted. Waller does place Eden first, and he was under no obligation to place it anywhere at all. Jonson managed quite nicely without it in "To Penshurst," a work more or less directly behind Waller's own, and he did so despite other religious references of various kinds. My reason for displacing this basic point from its initial prominence and deferring it until now is that the use of hindsight to restrict foresight is not merely helpful in this case but essential. Eden was so comprehensive a symbol compounded of such numerous values that a principle of selectivity must be found in order to deal with it at all. This procedure is not entirely arbitrary, however, for whatever the widest limits of expectation may have been in Waller's audience, including Charles, some narrowing presumably occurs because of the ongoing delimiting process in the poem itself. It can be seen, in fact, that of the myriad meanings of "Eden," all of them potentially important, a specific one very quickly becomes

5. *TAPA*, 66 (1925): 82–105.
6. Dryden is quoted from *The Poems*, ed. James Kinsley, 4 vols. (Oxford, 1958). (I later refer, however, to the California Dryden for editorial comment.)

quite clearly relevant. This is the concept of "pleasure," the Hebraic denotation of the word itself.

The idea first emerges as Waller apparently emphasizes a difference, not a similarity, between the two landscapes, but the notable new feature of the Park which he chooses to stress actually makes it more Edenic, not less. The sea had always served the king's empire, but now, thanks to the canal, it "Pays tribute to our Prince's pleasure too" (8). Pleasure is exaggerated by—and may be responsible for—Waller's initial de-emphasis of commerce, not to mention war. Both pursuits later on are brought into the foreground: "What Nation shall have Peace, where War be made" (79); "mending Laws" and "restoring trade" (118). That kind of thing, however, Waller himself defers in order to stress first that the Park is a veritable garden of earthly delights.

Seasonal pleasures are among those available, including those of "Summer" and "Winter" (24), and this too can be admirable despite a marked difference from the perpetual Spring enjoyed in paradise. Since Adam and Eve surely were vegetarians, the pleasing recreation of angling also represents change within continuity, especially in this case, in fact, since much of the fishing is mildly and pleasantly amorous: The feminine anglers "make the fishes and the men their prize" (36). The strife of Venus with Mars, of course, had long been a prime example of concordant discord because their offspring was Harmonia. In "Cooper's Hill," to cite a closely proximate work, Denham refers (39) to Windsor Castle, "where Mars with Venus dwells."[7] Waller, however, prefers innocent sportiveness: "A thousand Cupids on the billows ride" (37) in company with those sea-nymphs previously mentioned. "Harmonia," even so, by no means is excluded from this scene but instead assumes varying forms, including the most literal one. Music was among the traditional charms of the "locus amoenus"—from this point of view, Eden necessarily is the "locus amoenissimus"—and according to some authorities, work in paradise was very like a dance.[8] Here, the "Gallants" are "dancing" (23), "Musick" resounds from the "boats" (25), and "the loud Echo . . . returns the notes" (26). This also is the proper context for those mythic figures

7. Quoted from Maclean (see note 2).

8. For Edenic work as dance, see Dubartas, *The Devine Weekes and Workes*, 3.1.1, trans. Josuah Sylvester, 2d ed. (London, 1608), 234. Cf. Plato's concept of dance as a reflection or imitation of song and discourse (e.g., *Laws*, 7 [816A]). For the "locus amoenus," see Ernst R. Curtius, *European Literature and the Latin Middle Ages*, trans. Willard Trask (New York, 1953), 194–95.

earlier referred to: "young Trees" are so well placed that "The voice of *Orpheus*, or *Amphions* hand / In better order could not make them stand" (15–16). (The preceding italics are Waller's or his printer's, but those which immediately follow are mine.) "*Silver* fishes" (31) in "the *Crystal* lake" (33) play about "*gilded* Barges" (32). The fish, moreover, are "beneath" (31), while "over head" is that "flock of new sprung fowl" from the game preserve, and the birds themselves are among the sources of shade, another requirement of the "locus amoenus": The flock "Hangs in the ayr" and "does the Sun controle" (28). The benefit of shade is not a likely result of specifically "young Trees" (13), but this new growth anticipates "rich *fruit*-trees" which are fully grown so that "loaded branches hide the lofty mound" (45–46), and this mature stand is later balanced in turn by "A living Gallery of *aged* Trees" (68).

These harmonies of fish and fowl, sport and love, youth and age, and echoing music itself are not individually of great importance, but they have a way of adding up. They thus prepare for the fact that the verse paragraph concludes with reconciliations on the grandest of scales between the two traditional books of God, the Bible and Nature, with each of these vast tomes being presented in terms of dichotomous unities to which those of the Park may be compared. Waller evidently supposed the equal familiarity of both biblical parts of what is—in effect, but not in appearance—an extended simile:

> here you may descry,
> The choicest things that furnisht *Noahs* Ark,
> Or *Peters* sheet, inhabiting this Park.
>   (42–44)

The Ark, no doubt, identifies itself as clearly now as in former times, but the "sheet" may be something else again. As the Ark is from the Old Testament, so its chiastically placed counterpart is from the New, and the story of it is given in Acts 10. Peter

> 10 . . . became very hungry, and would have eaten: but . . . he fell into a trance,
> 11 And saw heaven opened, and a certain vessel descending unto him, as it had been a great sheet knit at the four corners, and let down to the earth:
> 12 Wherein were all manner of four-footed beasts of the earth, and wild beasts, and creeping things, and fowls of the air.
> 13 And there came a voice to him, Rise, Peter; kill, and eat.

With this narrative in hand, one sees that plenitude is an obvious point of comparison here but also that Waller's allusive strategy suggests progressively increased selectivity: from the Ark (totally comprehensive of every zoological creature that survived the Flood) to the Sheet (copiously full but not quite so commodious) and thence to the Park (where the "choicest things" of either or both of the preceding may be descried). Narrowing once again indicates improvement, however, not deterioration, since conditions are approaching the zoological—perhaps also the botanical—purity of prelapsarian existence prior to the Flood and the consequent destruction of Eden. A parallel progression marks the succession of symbols since Eden, the theoretical beginning, is the fullest of them. The Ark and the Sheet were taken to be images of one another in biblical commentaries (details follow momentarily), and each—depending on point of view—may be thought of as either more and/or less inclusive than the other. Thence one moves again to the symbolic Park as a restricted image of Eden restored.

To see how this pattern actually emerges, one ought to notice first that the commentators, in explaining Peter's sheet, felt obligated to consider its Old Testament prefiguration.[9] They thought of the Ark as the Ship of the Church Universal, of its passengers as voyaging—in Milton's words—"Betwixt the world destroy'd and world restor'd" (*PL*, 12.3), and of Noah—to quote Milton again—as the "one Man found so perfect and so just" (11.385) and thus as one of the "shadowy Types" (12.303) of Christ. From one point of view, therefore, nothing could be more comprehensively perfect—until, that is, one observes the implications of a world not yet replaced and of a shadowy type not yet fulfilled. The Sheet also represents the Church Universal, one which specifically embraces, moreover, Gentiles as well as Jews. Gentile commentators were much gratified to find this so, and they discovered several proofs of confirmation. Peter at first declined to eat, despite supernatural injunction to do so, lest he violate Hebraic dietary law by feeding on "common"—the word, in this particular case, means "unclean"—flesh, but "the voice *spake* unto him again the second time, What God hath cleansed, *that* call not thou common" (v. 15). This entire vision, moreover, was to prepare Peter in advance lest he reject a deputation from "a certain man in Caesaria called Cornelius,

9. The References below give information about the biblical commentaries cited and the system used in citing them. Pepys (9 February 1664/65) reports that a number of wild animals actually were among the Park's denizens.

a centurion of the band called the *Italian* band" (1). As Poole points out, the man was "a Gentile by title" and "a Roman by his name; which name was ordinarily to be found amongst the families of the Scipios and Syllas." He "was at present quartered in . . . a strong city," to quote Matthew Henry, one "called Caesarea in honour of Augustus." The place "was not so far from Jerusalem," Henry says, but geographical proximity was of no moment in this case since it did nothing to diminish the alienation between Gentile and Jew. The reconciliation of a Gentile was therefore "a better work wrought upon them than they had expected" and was, in fact, "so great a surprise to the believing as well as the unbelieving Jews" that some reactions were hostile. "But thus often," Henry comments, "are the prejudices of pride and bigotry held fast against the clearest discoveries of divine truth." To those of more open mind, happily, the case is otherwise. Henry introduces Acts 10 with this observation: "It is a turn very new and remarkable which the story of this chapter gives," a turn of events which is "good news indeed to us sinners of the Gentiles."

Divine reconciliation and restoration are the morals of this tale, but only the concord of Peter and Cornelius was complete, not that between Jerusalem and Rome. Part of the structure of the book of Acts depends on spiritual geography as the good news of the gospel spreads outward from Jerusalem to both Jews and Gentiles in areas farther and farther afield. One can trace this expansion through the book and on a historical atlas until Paul finally arrives at Rome in the last chapter, and even then more work remains to be done: "Be it known therefore unto you, that the salvation of God is sent unto the Gentiles, and *that* they will hear it" (28.28). Diodati prefaces Acts as a whole with the comment that the book charts "the new form of conduct and government . . . a new shape, as being risen again from death and darkness." For further information about what the shape finally is to be, one naturally reads, first of all, the next biblical book, Paul's Epistle to the Romans.

A point-by-point allegory for England's Restoration probably could be constructed from this biblical material since it concerns preservation and regeneration as well as a proclamation of fullest reconciliation when time shall be. Waller, however, is not writing allegory, nor does he force a total harmony from biblical elements which merely lead in that direction. Rather, he continues his extended comparison by turning to Nature and its divided realms. The terms now change, but here too reconciliation is stressed and yet the unity of dichotomous entities, while genuine as far as it goes, once again remains partial rather than total. The shift from written Book to Nature's text occurs when Waller's "Muse" becomes "doubtfull" about "what path to tread" (48) amidst such plentitude. Apparently by accident, but of course by careful design, a pause is made to take notice of "the lofty mound" (46):

> Yonder the harvest of cold months laid up,
> Gives a fresh coolness to the Royal Cup,
> There Ice like Crystal, firm and never lost,
> Tempers hot *July* with *Decembers* frost,
> Winters dark prison, whence he cannot flie,
> Though the warm Spring, his enemy draws nigh;
> Strange! that extremes should thus preserve the snow,
> High on the Alps, or in deep Caves below.
>
> (49–56)

Natural antitheses of cold and hot, December and July, Winter and Spring, the Alps and caves, heights and depths—all these are yoked together because of a lofty mound which preserves ice within its lateral depth. Like the canal, the mound pays liquid tribute, here frozen in form, to the monarch's pleasure. The act is proleptic, at least in part, since the usefulness of it is not fully apparent until one encounters the vigorous sport described in the next verse paragraph: the flying balls of the game of Pall Mall, played with fury and smoke. The coolness of the cup mentioned here thus anticipates royal need for it. Cups, moreover, are artifacts which therefore mediate natural materials and human use, and in this particular case, the mediation occurs at an exalted level, for this is, quite explicitly, the *royal* cup. This object, even if capacious (a magnum, say), is thus a microcosm of the Park, which is itself an artifact dependent on a natural landscape subject to human improvement. By the end of the poem, this narrowing process will have been reversed so that the Park represents what the macrocosm of the kingdom is or ought to be, with England in turn a microcosm of the world at large. Here, however, inwardness has now arrived at its most specific point, a (relatively) small cup in the hand of the king inside the (relatively) small Park, a place where opposites not merely balance but momentarily coincide in an oxymoron: "harvest of cold."

That oxymoron has inherent significance in this context, but also worth noticing is that the location of the phrase is nearly central to the line, but not to the passage, in which it occurs. The cup itself, moreover, is a pivot for the concepts, but not for the versification, of the lines in which it is placed. The versification, in fact, calls attention to its own imperfection by proclaiming the tempering of extremes in lines which inexactly articulate the concept. There may be more than one way of approaching this fact. From one point of view, the oppositions of July and December apparently meet in an English equivalent of the second line of a Latin elegiac couplet:

Témpĕrs / hót Jŭ / lý // wíth Dĕ / cémbĕrs / fróst.[10]

This scansion places two and a half feet on either side of a medial caesura with a nice balance of half-lines to present, with seeming propriety, bifurcated oneness. Prosody of this kind was standard, of course, in Roman elegy, a verse form with which Waller was demonstrably familiar since he himself was using it at the age of seventy-three for "Ad Comitem Monumetensem" (To the Duke of Monmouth). And since poets have been known to be their own arbiters on metrics, a Latinate scansion is not impossible, but there are several objections to it. It assumes the presence of a split spondee ("ly"–"frost"), normal enough in Latin with quantitative principles but not in English, and in this case resulting in six weighted syllables, not five. Even if both sides of this point are minimized, the line is highly unusual for *this* poem. The further difficulty is that "July" was stressed on the first syllable "as late as Dr. Johnson's time," according to the *OED*, which adds, "the modern Eng. pronunciation is abnormal and unexplained." Suckling rhymes the word with "newly," and R. G. Howarth, his editor, remarks that "other words often take the stress required by the line," but "*Júly*" is "invariable."[11] Evidently the number of accents in Waller's line must be reduced from six to five by scanning

Témpĕrs / hŏt Jú / lў̆ wíth / Dĕcém / bĕrs fróst,

but balanced precision and polish are not to be gained in this way.
   Whether this entire matter is worth worrying about may well de-

10. My argument needs only blunt scansions, but the sophistication of Richard Flantz's scansions of Jonson may be appropriate for Waller as well: "The Authoritie of Truth: Jonson's Mastery of Measure," in *Classic and Cavalier*, ed. Claude J. Summers and Ted-Larry Pebworth (Pittsburgh, 1982), 59–75. See also Alexander W. Allison, *Toward an Augustan Poetic: Edmund Waller's "Reform" of English Poetry* (Lexington, KY, 1962).
   11. Suckling, "A Ballad Upon a Wedding," in *Minor Poets of the Seventeenth Century*, ed. R. Howarth (London and New York, 1931; rev. 1953); see Howarth's "Note on Pronunciation," xviii.

pend on what one concludes from the versification of the line which specifically illustrates "extremes":

> Strange! that extremes should thus preserve the snow
> Hígh oň / thĕ Alṕs / ŏr ín / dēep Cāves / bĕlów.

The line is not a bad one, but *in* is overstressed at the expense of *deep* despite the absence of any metrical or syntactical need. Greater balance, with no loss of clarity, would be achieved by continuing the inverted word order with which the line begins:

> Hígh ŏn / thĕ Alṕs / ŏr déep / ĭn Cáves / bĕlów.

Whatever one thinks of Latinate scansions and syllabic stress in the line about "tempers," the one about "extremes" lacks the precision it might easily have had. Control has not lapsed, however, through want of skill. Waller was fully capable of pointing his couplets when he so chose, a fact I hope to demonstrate in connection with the closing lines of the poem. But he does not make that choice here. Instead, partial dislocation and asymmetry occur so that concordant discord, even as it is alluded to, remains incomplete despite the royal cup and the loftily deep mound.

Nor is the mound the topographical climax of this section of the poem, for a second path leads to the "well-polisht Mall" (57). If one is to remember the cockle shells mentioned by Pepys, then the smooth surface represents a minor tribute of the sea to further the cause of pleasure, specifically the sport enjoyed by Charles. In any case, his athletic prowess also affords pleasure to others, in part because it augurs well for a continuation into future times of present order. "Manly posture," "gracefull" appearance, "Vigor and youth"—all "Confirm our hopes we shall obey him long" (59–62). Important also is that the activity of the game is far more forceful, strenuous in fact, than anything earlier described. Charles employs "matchless force" (58); the ball is "No sooner . . . toucht" but is "already more than half the mall" (63–64);

> And such a fury from his aim has got
> As from a smoking Culverin 'twere shot.
> (65–66)[12]

---

12. R. Chambers, *The Book of Days* (London, 1869), 1.464–65, relies in part on Pepys (16 May 1663) in giving an account of the game as played in the Park.

The game, while undeniably peaceful, metaphorically approaches the conditions of war and thus prefigures, as this section of the poem now does conclude, important alternatives to be examined in the second half.

Waller himself is ending one part by looking ahead to the next, but it may be useful at this point to look back at what has been happening thus far. Figure 1 charts Waller's principal disjunctions but necessarily depends on schematic oversimplification and is further distorted by the major displacement of the "Royal Cup" from its true inward location.

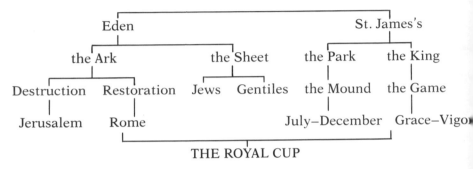

Fig. 1.   Dichotomous unities

Despite the vast scope, both geographical and temporal, all of this material is only part of the picture. Many extremes, it is true, have been tempered into concord of a peaceful, recreative kind. The martial imagery of the game, however, forcefully represents the implications also discoverable in references to empire, trade, amorous angling, and so on, none of which can possibly call attention to the life of the mind in any explicit way. On the contrary, harmony has been evidenced in physical rather than mental terms in the topographical improvements made to the Park as a fit place for, among other things, the athletic activity and corporeal demeanor of the king. And yet, of course, the microcosmic Park also ought to be like Milton's macrocosmic world in "Answering" the "great Idea" of its maker (PL, 7.556–57). At this stage, therefore, the manly figure of Charles gives way to "his nobler thoughts" (76), and Waller gives way to Charles as the one who contemplates and interprets the scene. Waller, moreover, has been viewing topographical features inside the Park, but Charles meditates on that which is visible immediately outside its bounds. As a result, this also is the place where outward expansion begins to reverse the earlier narrowing process.

To initiate these changes, Waller levies upon an ode in which Horace balances himself and Augustus. Waller greatly compresses the Latin poem (most of Horace's poetic "autobiography," for example, is omitted as inapplicable here) but retains material important in establishing a framework. Both poets, moreover, include the initially surprising irruption into the peaceful scene of a terrifying war. The Loeb translation of Horace—much shortened, partly for the reason just given—is this:

> O Queen Calliope . . . sing with thy clear voice . . . Methinks I hear her and am straying through hallowed groves, where pleasant waters steal and breezes stir. . . . 'Tis ye who in Pierian grotto refresh our noble Caesar, when he seeks to soothe his cares . . . Ye give gentle counsel, and delight in giving it . . . Full well we know how the impious Titans and their frightful horde were struck down . . . who strove to set Pelion on Shadowy Olympus . . . and Enceladus, bold hurler of uprooted trees . . . Brute force bereft of wisdom falls to ruin by its own weight. Power with wisdom tempered, even the gods make greater. . . .
> (*Odes*, 3.4)

In no sense does Waller *translate* Horace. He manages, in fact, to adapt so as to include specifically English details in his own lines. The hybrid product is this:

> Near this my muse, what most delights her, sees,
> A living Gallery of aged Trees,
> Bold sons of earth that thrust their arms so high
> As if once more they would invade the sky;
> In such green Palaces the first Kings reign'd,
> Slept in their shades, and Angels entertain'd:
> With such old Counsellors they did advise
> And by frequenting sacred Groves grew wise;
> Free from th' impediments of light and noise
> Man thus retir'd his nobler thoughts imploys:
> Here CHARLS contrives the ordering of his States,
> Here he resolves his neighb'ring Princes' Fates.
> (67–78)

Major parallels between Waller and Horace are the presence of the Muse (though not identified by Waller as Calliope since this is a name in no way needed), the sacred haunts of hallowed groves as places of recreation ("recreatis," v. 40) and counsel ("concilium," 41) in which the Muse herself delights ("gaudetis," 42), and most notably, perhaps, the "pleasant" ("amoenae," 7) circumstancing of a poet and his monarch. Remembering some of Waller's slightly earlier emphases, one probably ought to notice the "*tempered* force" ("vim temperatam," 66) attributed by Horace to Augustus, especially since the idyllic landscapes of both poets are disrupted by an attempted invasion of heaven by bold sons of earth. T. E. Page explained the Latin by arguing that Horace "with singular abruptness but singular force introduces a dramatic account of the defeat of the giants, which at once suggests the thought how Jove's great vicegerent on earth shall in like manner be victorious over his foes."[13] In Waller the "aged Trees" appear to be a much less dangerous threat, but within their "Gallery" Waller allusively places some portraits of recent English uprisings.

To see this fact, one needs to know that trees were still abundant in St. James's when Charles began his improvements, but some of them had been uprooted (cf. Horace's "evulvis," 55) by a violent storm on the night of Cromwell's death. In September 1658, that fact appeared to be Nature's testimony to the magnitude of England's loss, as in Waller's own poem, "Upon the Late Storm, and of the Death of His Highness Ensuing the Same":

> We must resign! Heav'n his great soul does claim
> In storms, as loud as his immortal fame:
> His dy ng groans, his last breath, shakes our isle,
> And trees uncut fal for his fun'ral pile
>
> . . . .
>
> Nature herself took notice of his death.

Sir W. G.'s "Answer to Mr. Waller's Poem" seems an unnecessarily savage retort:

> The Pines and Oaks fell prostrate at his Urn,
> That with his Soul his Body too might burn:
>
> . . . .
>
> Nature her self rejoiced at his Death.[14]

13. *Carminum libri IV* [*et*] *Epodon liber*, ed. Page (London, 1883–84; rpt. 1953).

14. "An Answer . . . ," in *State Poems; continued From the time of O. Cromwel, To The Abdication of K. James [and] . . . to the Year 1697*, 2 vols. (London, 1703), 1.246–47.

But the Restoration did require reinterpretation of this incident, as of so many others. Cowley, in "Upon His Majesties Restoration and Return," claims that "a *Tempest* carried" Cromwell "away" (stanza 4).[15] "God came not till the storm was past" (7), and Cromwell was like "The proud gigantick son of earth, / Who strives t'usurp the gods forbidden seat" (16). Proud usurpation, moreover, was now seen as having been widespread. In *Astraea Redux*, Dryden alleged that "Madness the Pulpit, Faction seiz'd the Throne" (22); the California editors cite Brome's "Congratulatory Poem": "This did invade the Pulpit, and the Throne."[16] "Invade" is also Waller's word ("As if once more they would invade the sky"), but this particular similarity may be coincidental, and trying to pin down particular English sources may be fruitless since "one might almost conclude," along with Dryden's editors (214), "that all drew from a common pool of ideas." For my purposes, of course, the primary point in any case is that another conjunction of disparities is allusively made in Waller's lines since English details support the Horatian structure.

One further point about that structure ought to be noticed. In the ode's concluding lines, not quoted above, Horace presumes to instruct Augustus by presenting a series of negative examples, patterns the emperor should eschew, not follow. Most of these illustrations are derived from well-known myths so that Horace's practice, in this respect unlike Waller's, is to mention the names and thus dispense with retelling the tales. The example emphasized by terminal position, however, is historic rather than mythic, and the personage is left nameless. Page, referring to "similar eloquent omissions" elsewhere in Horace, confidently rectifies this one: "Considering to whom the Ode is addressed . . . there can be little doubt who the fallen foe hinted at is—the Roman Antony." This is the place where loud silence, mentioned much earlier as one to listen for, is heard in Waller too, for there can also be little doubt in this case who the principal bold son of earth had been even though the word "Cromwell" itself is suppressed.

Waller tactfully avoids boldness himself, however. He offers no direct instruction to his ruler but rather allows Charles to be his own best mentor by viewing various nearby buildings: "His Fancy objects from his view receives, / The prospect thought and Contemplation

15. Cowley is quoted from *Poems*, ed. A. R. Waller (Cambridge, 1905).
16. See the California *Works*, 1, ed. Edward N. Hooker and H. T. Swedenberg, Jr. (Berkeley and Los Angeles, 1956), 221.

gives" (83–84). With one major exception (specified in the next paragraph), a silent roll call of names in this case probably is *not* being made, for these buildings were and for that matter still are evocative of so many personages that no short list could be representative. General import emerges by means of language which evaluates rather than describes. The House of Commons is "where all our ills were shapt" (99); at coronation time, Westminster Abbey is "Where Royal heads receive the sacred gold" (92). These structures are so massive, of course, that one could hardly fail to perceive them, both inside the Park and out, but their history probably has less immediacy now than formerly, and Waller occasionally alludes to that history in a way which by some standards is densely compact. Especially is this true of what Charles first sees:

> The structure by a Prelate rais'd, *White-Hall*,
> Built with the fortune of *Romes* Capitol;
> Both disproportion'd to the present State
> Of their proud founders, were approv'd by Fate.
> (97–90)

These lines, while not at all opaque, take for granted a fairly large number of historical details. Whitehall, originally constructed in the thirteenth century, later became the London residence of the archbishops of York. It was substantially rebuilt by Wolsey ("by a Prelate rais'd"), who became Archbishop in 1514, both a Cardinal of the Church and Lord Chancellor of England in 1515, and papal legate in 1518. This prince of the Church remained much in the public eye until his death in 1530 while journeying from York to London to answer charges of treason after his failure to obtain papal permission for Henry VIII's divorce from Catherine of Aragon. Whitehall itself, while scarcely a hermitage from the public's gaze, nonetheless was not a public building but a private residence until appropriated from Wolsey ("disproportion'd") by Henry for state use. As Fenton points out, the relevant history behind the reference to "*Romes* Capitol" is that the Capitoleum—planned by Tarquinius Priscus and completed by Tarquinius "Superbus" ("proud")—at first was a private arsenal and then became a temple to Jupiter when appropriated by the state. These lines of cross-reference between Whitehall and the Capitol thus emerge: both "founders" were "proud" (though only one of them was called "Superbus"), and both were Romans (though one was so by faith, not birth); their two buildings became public, but the residence of the religious authority became secular while the arsenal of the secular ruler became sacred.

These disproportionments, while proportional to one another, do not occur at the same time nor in the same place and are perceivable only by the eye of the mind. This fact lends additional force to Waller's next point, that the Abbey simultaneously unites within itself both affairs of state and functions of the Church: *royal* heads and *sacred* gold. The geographical oneness of the place itself also serves as a unifying circle of chronologically separate beginnings and endings, and those temporal limits are examined from a point of view which is both political and religious. The Abbey

> gives them Crowns, and does their ashes keep;
> There made like gods, like mortals there they sleep
> Making the circle of their reign compleat,
> Those suns of Empire, where they rise they set.
> (93–96)

Also "compleat" is the perfection of the Abbey itself, but only in its own terms and only for so long as one refuses to look at buildings close to it. Standing in opposition is the House of Commons, and against the Abbey's unification of antitheses is an uneasy conjunction of opposites found, by means of a simile, on Mount Aetna.

> Hard by that House where all our ills were shapt
> Th' Auspicious Temple stood, and yet escap'd.
> So snow on *AEtna* does unmelted lie,
> Whence rowling flames and scatter'd cinders flie;
> The distant Countrey in the ruine shares,
> What falls from heav'n the burning mountain spares.
> (99–104)

Auspicious preservation despite volcanic eruption and destruction is the explicit point, possibly with implicit recollection that the Prayer Book had been banned, the head of the Church executed, the monarchy and House of Lords—including bishops—abolished, and so on. Yet the Abbey itself escaped, and that for which it continued to stand, literally and metaphorically, was to be restored. Lucretius (6.639ff.) explained scientifically why Aetna erupts, but Waller clearly has in mind the mythic reason: Enceladus, incarcerated after the rebellion against Jove, there spouts forth flames from his mouth and causes tremors with restless turnings of himself. Horace's allusion to this myth has already been quoted. Virgil gives a comparable reference in the *Aeneid* (2.570ff.), but the passage to cite here is the one in the *Georgics* (1.472–73), where the active volcano is linked with the murder of Julius Caesar. "When *Rome* in *Caesar* fell," as Dryden translates (1.629), "What Rocks did *AEtna's* bellowing Mouth expire / From her torn Entrails! and what Floods of Fire!" (636–37). Cowley contrived to invert this symbolism in his Restoration poem by seeing all England as an Aetna erupting with joy for the return of Charles: "He's come, he's safe at shore; . . . All *England* but one *Bonefire* seems to be, / One *AEtna* shooting *flames* into the *Sea*" (stanza 16). Cowley's ode to Hobbes is even more to the point because Waller's snow and flame surely derive either from that ode or from those classical sources (Claudian, Tacitus, Silius Italicus, and Seneca) whom Cowley scrupulously footnotes. As Cowley puts it,

> So *Contraries* on *AEtna's* top conspire,
> Here hoary *Frosts*, and by them breaks out *Fire*.
> A secure *peace* the *faithful Neighbours* keep,
> Th'emboldened *Snow* next to the *Flame* does *sleep*.
> (86–89)

The resemblances between Waller's Aetna and Cowley's are close, but there are differences as well. When Cowley says that "contraries . . . conspire" on the mountain's top, he must be thinking, etymologically, of "conspiro": "breathe with" and hence "join together." It may be doubted, however, whether he can succeed in blocking the unfavorable English sense of "conspiracy" despite the seeming impropriety. The developed sense, however, is not remote from Waller's allusions since in the latter case there is destruction as well as escape therefrom, and further tension is introduced by the explicitly heavenly origin of the snow: "What falls from heav'n the burning mountain spares." Waller's point, clearly, is not "secure *peace*," as Cowley has it, but rather the reverse. The devastation of churches, including stained glass, organs, and altars, at one time had been rampant, but the mere fact of the Abbey's continuing existence "did presage / The Crown should triumph over popular rage" (97–98). From this perspective, it is at the Restoration, not earlier, that what Cowley calls "faithful neighbours," including the buildings themselves, may peacefully coexist.[17]

17. For some of the remarks in the preceding paragraph, cf. Paul J. Korshin, *From Concord to Dissent: Major Themes in English Poetic Theory 1640–1700* (The Scolar Press, 1973): Waller "must also have been acquainted with [Cow-

A developing theme, therefore, but only for Waller and not Cowley, is unity and/or disunity of church and state. Waller continues it by taking advantage of the medal struck for the coronation of Charles and the scene stamped thereon. Maclean describes it as "representing the king as a shepherd tending his flock," and this may be all that is needed for Waller's lines: "Here like the peoples Pastor" Charles "do's go, / His flock subjected to his view below" (109–10). In Fenton's reproduction, however, the medal's shepherd looks to be a Roman wearing a toga, and the sheep crook, heavily stylized, may be a bishop's crozier. Whatever the iconography, in Waller's scene there is no place for "private passion" (112) or youthful "pleasures" (113). In view of the previous emphasis on varied pleasure, this change is itself emphatic, but "publick care" (114) now takes explicit precedence. Strictly speaking, *care* probably ought also to be a curate's *cure*, a sacred office in a secular world. That double role is later suggested, but for purposes of illustrative detail Waller first brings forward each half of it in turn.

Antithetical elements once again are greatly in evidence: The "peacefull Olive" (117), paralleled by "mending Laws" and "restoring trade" (118), is balanced by the "Laurel" (119) of triumph with its attendant associations of "Nations conquer'd and our bounds inlarg'd" (120). With "ancient Prudence" Charles "ruminates, / Of rising Kingdoms and of falling States" (121–22). Since names can be appropriately mentioned in this particular context, Charles specifically considers

> What Ruling Arts gave great *Augustus* fame,
> And how *Alcides* purchas'd such a name.
> (123–24)

Waller's model for himself in these lines is another poem by Horace (soon to be quoted), and the precedents for Charles may be those commentators who speculated on the ruling arts of Augustus as perceived by Virgil. Segrais, as translated by Dryden in his "Dedication" of *The Aeneis* (Kinsley, 1020), comments,

> Virgil had consider'd that the greatest Virtues of *Augustus* consisted in the perfect Art of Governing his People; which caus'd him to Reign for more than Forty Years in great Felicity. He

---

ley's] classical source, Claudian's *De Raptu Proserpinae*" (60); "the classical reference, given deeper meaning, provides both description of, and analogy to, contemporary affairs" (61).

> consider'd that his Emperour was Valiant, Civil, Popular, Elo-
> quent, Politick, and Religious.

When the *Aeneis* itself was published, this comment may have had ironic over- or undertones vis-à-vis the current English monarch, but Waller could deploy ideas of this kind with straightforward serious-ness. Such ruling arts, so worthy of fame, certainly would well repay Charles's study. The second line of Waller's couplet suggests, however, not that the king already has mastered them but rather that he may learn how to do so. To see this point one needs to go behind the reference to Alcides, one of the names of Hercules, in order to notice a similar allusion in Horace's celebration (*Odes*, 3.14.1–4) of the return home of Augustus from Spain.

> *Herculis* ritu modo dictus, o plebs
> *morte* venalem petiissee laura
> *Caesar* Hispana repetit penatis
> *victor* ab ora.

> *Caesar*, O citizens, who but now was said, like *Hercules*, to be in quest of the laurel purchased at the price of *death*, rejoins again his household gods, *victoriously* returning from the Spanish shore. (Loeb; italics added in both quotations)

Augustus, it is true, had been putting down rebels while abroad rather than seeking temporary refuge from them, but the parallel of the triumphant return is close enough for Waller's needs. The change of name, moreover, is probably not casual. "Hercules"—the fact is more clear from the Greek spelling, *Hera* + *cles*—means "glory of Hera," a sardonic theophoric in view of Hera's implacable enmity toward her husband's son. "Alcides" means "valiant," a prominent quality in the twelve famous labors and their various perils. Horace used the first name, possibly because "valor" would be redundant when speaking of the laurel purchased by death. Waller uses the second but does not go so far as the author of "On the Return of King Charles II": "Twelve Labours" the "banisht" demi-god "sustain'd, / Twelve tedious yeares great *Charles* in Exile reign'd."[18] Indeed, Waller's praise is for antici-pated achievement rather than past action since Charles's thoughts

18. In *State Poems* (see note 14), 2.243. The poem is "signed" by R. South; a Latin version also is given (242): "Dicitur Alcides bis subiisse labore / Exul: totque annos *Carolus* exul agit."

are of "how his Brows may be with Laurel charg'd" (119), not of how they already have been.

Waller also redistributes Horace's material to some extent, and this too is significant. The italics added above were to underline the fact that Horace alternately parallels the two names even as he contrasts death and victory. Waller, however, establishes similar linkage not with parallel but with chiastic placement supported by assonance:

> . . . *Augustus*
>
> *Alcides* . . .

And yet the parallelism of structure emphasized by the "fame . . . name" rhyme balances chiasm. Since effects of Waller's versification become more intense as the poem insistently drives toward its conclusion, Waller again looks ahead to prepare for what is to occur in the final vision granted to Charles. This anticipatory signal is entirely appropriate, among other reasons, because the vision itself is of future expectancy. It begins in the present, however, and also harks back to the past.

> His eyes upon his native Palace bent
> Close by, suggest a greater argument,
> His thoughts rise higher when he does reflect
> On what the world may from that Star expect
> Which at his birth appear'd to let us see
> Day for his sake could with the Night agree;
> A Prince on whom such different lights did smile,
> Born the divided world to reconcile:
> What ever Heaven or high extracted blood
> Could promise or foretell, he will make good.
> (125–34)

A curious phenomenon on the day of Charles's birth was the sighting of a star about noon. Perhaps it was only Venus, as claimed by those who refused to be impressed by a fact which they did not, however, deny. For others, the significance was profound even at the time, and the scene was depicted on a medal, also reproduced in Fenton, that celebrated the birth. Reference to this incident in *Astraea Redux* prompts Dryden's editors (232) to remark that it "was an open invitation, both in 1630 and in 1660, and royalist poets in droves responded to it, accepting the phenomenon as a miraculous event

presaging the exaltation of Charles to honor and greatness." They also
note (233) that Dryden was but one of many in choosing "to parallel
the King's return and the birth of Christ" when the star of Bethlehem
was seen. This is the religious aspect, obviously, of the secular-sacred
curacy which I mentioned earlier, and the basic material for it was
commonplace. Full appreciation of how carefully Waller shapes the
material may, in fact, require venturing into wastelands outside St.
James's such as the effusions offered in 1660 by Oxford and Cambridge.[19] Waller does not suffer, however, from a comparison of his
version to those of Cowley and Dryden.

Cowley's semi-Pindaric expansiveness demands or at least permits
treatment of the star at considerable length, but an abridgement of
the closing lines of the first stanza and those which begin the second
can illustrate the methods as a whole. The star which appeared
"thirty years ago" served to "foreshow" "future *Glories*." "In despight /
Of the proud *Sun*'s Meridian Light," it "could out-face the *Sun*, and
overcome the *Day*."

> Auspicious *Star* again arise,
> And take thy *Noon-tide Station* in the skies,
> Again all *Heaven* prodigiously adorn;
> For loe! thy *Charles* again is *Born*.

Dryden economizes as follows:

> That Star that at your Birth shone out so bright
> It stain'd the duller Suns Meridian light,
> Did once again its potent Fires renew
> Guiding our eyes to find and worship you.
>
> (288–91)

The oft-noted contrast between Cowley's "old-fashioned" style and
the newer one of Dryden is easily seen in these passages since the
factual basis for them is the same. Less immediately apparent but for
my purposes more important is a difference between Dryden and
Waller. Direct comparison would be misleading, however, unless one
first takes into account the fact that the two passages occupy different

19. *Britannia Rediviva* (Oxford, 1660) was one of the sources used by H. T.
Swedenberg, Jr., in "England's Joy: *Astraea Redux* in Its Setting," *SP*, 50
(1953): 30–44; evidently he overlooked the similar outpourings of *Academiae
Cantabrigensis* (1660), but the fact does not alter his conclusions.

positions in their respective poems, Waller's nearly at the end but Dryden's significantly earlier.

The importance of location arises from the fact that the couplets of *Astraea* become increasingly more pointed as Dryden gradually approaches and finally arrives at his own forceful close. There is no practical way to substantiate this point conclusively since it rests upon nothing less than the versification of the entire poem, but the following examples may serve as signposts to a developing pattern which Dryden allows to emerge with increasing clarity.

> The winds that never Moderation knew
> Afraid to blow too much, too faintly blew.
> (242–43)

> It is no longer Motion cheats your view,
> As you meet it, the Land approaches you.
> (252–53)

"Rapprochement" continues in the couplets quoted earlier about the star, and the last lines of the poem are these:

> Oh happy Prince whom Heav'n hath taught the way
> By paying Vowes, to have more Vowes to pay!
> O Happy Age! Oh times like these alone
> By Fate reserv'd for great *Augustus* Throne!
> When the joint growth of Armes and Arts foreshew
> The World a Monarch, and that Monarch *You*.
> (318–23)

The anaphora of "Oh happy," reinforced by "Oh times," neatly points to the idea that the "Age" is singularly blessed because of its "Prince"; mutuality of shared gratification is balanced by a specifically "*joint* growth" of antithetical "Armes" and "Arts"; climax occurs as the general finds its focus in the particular, the "World . . . and *You*," with a double appearance of "Monarch" in between.

Waller's versification in almost terminal position certainly is not less remarkable and may even be more skillful in the technical precision with which the couplets reconcile their own internal elements as they advance the reconciliation of temporal and spatial disparities. "Day" and "Night" "agree" so that a "Star" above alerts the "world" below to be on watch for Charles. "A Prince" initiates the next couplet, and at the end of it what he does is "reconcile," although "divided world," the object of reconciliation" itself divides the agent from the action performed even as it balances the "different lights" of the preceding line. The divine and human resources of "Heaven" and "high extracted blood" next cooperate so as to "promise or foretell" that which "he will make good." And each of those four monosyllables probably ought to be enunciated with increasingly emphatic stress to thrust forward in prophetic affirmation. Without discounting Dryden's expertise in the slightest, I suggest that it might be difficult to find lines where versification is more a function of meaning than here. Preparation for them, moreover, has been seriatim throughout the poem, including occasional irregularity as well as anticipatory harmonies. In a sense, these lines thus unfold brilliantly the initial implications, as they now can be seen to have existed, of the two makers present in the Park at the outset, one of the landscape and the other of the poem: Charles mediates the concepts in these lines, and Waller measures the versification of them.

Also important is the difference within similarity of the prognostications offered by these three poets. Cowley and Dryden interpret the star as serving to foreshow that which the Restoration triumphantly shows forth. Among readers of other Restoration poems, Waller may arouse comparable expectations that his celebration will also assert finality. If so, then "to reconcile" at first may appear to be a telic purpose partially fulfilled by the earlier birth and totally vindicated by the later Restoration so that the optation implicit in "promise" and the vaticination explicit in "foretell" achieve spatial reification with temporal simultaneity. Bombast, however, is what Waller himself avoids. His own making is nearly done, but not so with Charles since the Park is improved but not yet perfected. Charles had further plans for the Park in mind, and at least some of these were later realized, as Pepys records. Much remained to be done outside the Park as well, and Waller exhorts Charles to the undertaking of it. Resuming control from the king, from whose perspective the scenes in the latter part of the poem were described, Waller insists on being the poet of this landscape by having the final word. Despite the complaints of Nicholas Jose, the note sounded, to my ears, is exactly on pitch.

> Reform these Nations, and improve them more,
> Than this fair Park from what it was before.

Panegyric traditionally offers hyperbolic praise to those who genuinely merit applause and extends unmerited flattery to those who do not in the fervent hope that with encouragement they may: "exhorting to virtue," as Erasmus put it, "under pretext of praise."[20] Or so the theory goes. In practice, no doubt, pious justifications have often been no more than self-serving excuses for sycophantic work. Waller's praise is unquestionably hyperbolic, though it scarcely could be more so than that of other poets and poetasters of the time, but he does much to align his poem with the ideal posited by the theoretical purposes of the form. Dr. Johnson long ago observed in his life of Pope that "the design of *Windsor Forest* is evidently deriv'd from *Cooper's Hill*, with some attention to Waller's poem on *The Park*."[21] St. James's certainly ought to be on the list of places to visit when on one's way from Denham to Pope. Its attractions, as I see them, make even a special trip worthwhile.

What would have happened had Charles busied himself with the precepts as well as the pleasures available from St. James's Park is anybody's guess. Waller certainly would have continued to write poetry, but very possibly something quite different from his "Instructions to a Painter." There might have been no need at all for a satiric "Second Advice to a Painter" or a "Third," a "Fourth," a "Fifth," and a "Last Instructions." Not, of course, simply because Waller's poem would not have existed to be responded to; satire can always find fuel to feed its flames, after all. The political conditions themselves, however, might have elicited very different reactions, conceivably even praise. Speculation necessarily is vain, of course, since Charles increasingly pursued his own pleasures until he became, as Farley-Hills puts it, "a living satire":

> At the centre of the nation's life in his reign there was a man whose symbolic life as supreme monarch was ludicrously discrepant with his personal life as roué and debauchee. To his hierarchically minded subjects he appeared a living satire; and with the centre awry all else seemed discordant.[22]

Waller made one further effort to persuade Charles that this geometry needed to be corrected, and he chose, characteristically, an occasion

20. Quoted by James D. Garrison, *Dryden and the Tradition of Panegyric* (Berkeley, 1975), 21. See also Ruth Nevo, *The Dial of Virtue: A Study of Poems on Affairs of State in the Seventeenth Century* (Princeton, 1963).

21. *Lives of the English Poets*, 2 vols. (London, 1906; rpt. 1967), 2.310 (The World's Classics edition).

22. David Farley-Hills, *The Benevolence of Laughter: Comic Poetry of the Commonwealth and Restoration* (London, 1974), 18.

which seemed to be a glorious moment which held the promise of a monarchy and an England as they might yet exist. It is possible that 1667 may already have been too late for that dream, if indeed 1660 itself had not previously set a pattern not reversible until after Charles's death. The answers to Waller's "Instructions" proceed, however, from the very different assumption that where praise and exhortation have failed, satire just possibly may succeed.

4

Waller and the Painter

On 3 June 1665, English forces commanded by James, Duke of York, defeated a Dutch navy under the admiralty of Jacob Wassenaer, Baron von Opdam, in a battle fought in the North Sea off the coast of Lowestoft, the easternmost extreme of England. That much is clear enough, and since almost everything thereafter was evidently mishandled, it probably is true that "the English victory off Lowestoft" was "the high point of this Second Dutch War."[1] The first one (1652–54) had been ended by the Treaty of Westminster, some of the terms of which included Dutch reparations for actions dating from as far back as 1623, but this second one was to be concluded indecisively, and part of it was to be humiliating. As of July 1664, the Dutch were sufficiently wary to avoid the English Channel, preferring—when feasible—to send cargos north around Scotland

---

1. George deF. Lord, ed., *Poems on Affairs of State*, 1:1660–78 (New Haven and London, 1963), 20. Lord does not say so, yet his remark is surely designed to indicate not the historical reality but the English reactions (in large measure ill-founded) to reports from Lowestoft. Pepys, for example, records (8 June 1665), "and the sum of the newes is:—VICTORY OVER THE DUTCH, JUNE 3RD, 1665" (quoted from *The Diary*, ed. Henry B. Wheatley [London, 1893–99; rpt. 1946]). Painter poems, including Waller's, those of "Marvell," and "The Last Instructions," are quoted from Lord's edition. The References at the end of this book give information about other works often cited and the system used in citing them.

despite the longer distance. One month later, an English fleet was so ill-prepared to counter the Dutch presence at Guinea that it got as far as Portsmouth but not out of that port. On 20 November, however, some Dutch ships en route from Bordeaux were seized, and the taking of two more off Smyrna on 29 December was followed, two weeks later, by an official declaration of war by Holland on 14 January 1665. Presumably this was the action that England, which had not yet declared war itself, had been trying to provoke. In early May, a divided Dutch fleet declined to leave the harbors of Texel and Vlie to encounter English ships on patrol between those ports, but by the middle of the month the English themselves withdrew to Harwich to replenish provisions. The Duchess of York turned the occasion into a fête of sorts with a visit which began on 16 May, and the Dutch improved on the occasion by taking unprotected English merchant ships sailing from Hamburg.

The battle of Lowestoft is foregrounded against this unstable backdrop, and in view of subsequent English disasters, it is as important as it may be difficult to remember that this engagement was the first direct confrontation between official instruments of war and that it seemed, at first or possibly even second glance, to put England in a commanding position. Not long afterwards, true enough, it was abundantly clear that a splendid chance for decisive victory had somehow been squandered rather than made the most of. Parliamentary questions were asked, acrimonious charges laid, scapegoats sought, and sardonic instructions written for imaginary painters of bungled battles. Waller, however, had no reason to anticipate the deeply troubled waters which actually lay ahead. In writing a poem about Lowestoft, he supposed, in fact, that he had an entirely different set of problems on his hands, one of them being that the Duchess of York had unaccountably neglected to bring with her a shield when visiting the Duke and the fleet at Harwich in May.

A difficulty of that kind may seem trivial, but my phrasing is not meant facetiously, or not entirely so, for the implications are by no means minimalistic from an artistic point of view. It can be shown that Virgil and Homer are specifically relevant for Waller's poem, but a brief way to introduce evidence for the point just suggested is to recall, first of all, the title of a work by Hesiod. When the Greek poet invited his hearers to attend to "The Shield of Heracles," the initial impact must have been notably different from whatever impression is made by the title Waller had to settle for:

INSTRUCTIONS TO A PAINTER
For the Drawing of the Posture and Progress of His

Majesty's Forces at Sea, under the Command of His
Highness-Royal; together with the Battle and Victory
Obtained over the Dutch,
June 3, 1665.

The abyss which seems here to yawn between the two titles admittedly was less deep in Waller's day than now, partly because of topical
excitement generated by the event and partly because ponderous titles were not only less unfashionable but may even have had some
sales value. Waller, however, was aware of considerable difference
between his subject and Hesiod's, a fact clearly evident from two
strategies which initially appear to be self-contradictory: He calls
attention to the gap on the one hand and yet tries to bridge over it on
the other. The bridging techniques must be postponed until I am in a
better position to offer an explanatory account of them, but an illustrative example of more or less explicit discrepancy is easily given now.

In visiting Harwich, "Th' illustrious Duchess and her glorious
train" had made their appearance "Like Thetis with her nymphs"
(81–82);

> The gazing sea-gods, since the Paphian queen
> Sprung from among them, no such sight had seen.
> (83–84)

Thetis, however, had brought a shield to Achilles; Venus—"the Paphian
Queen"—had done the same for Aeneas. In doing so they had not only
armed those heroes but also supplied them with art works measurably
superior to and even more famous than Hesiod's. In appearance, or so
Waller can hyperbolically claim, the Duchess out-rivals her divine and
classical counterparts, but the heroes visited differ in at least one noteworthy respect.

> The great Achilles march'd not to the field
> Till Vulcan that impenetrable shield
> And arms had wrought.
> (127–29)

"Our bolder hero," however, "on the deck does stand / Exposed" (131–
32). Another difference is that Waller, with no impenetrable shield to
describe, must resort to giving instructions to a painter instead. Or
rather, as "bolder hero" partly indicates, Waller is determined to
make poetic capital from deficiency in two ways.

He describes not only what the painter is to paint but also what he is not. Indeed, until nearly the end of the poem, absence will be fully as important as presence is. The finished canvas could be impressive, no doubt, if the instructions were literally real and well executed, but the picture fictionally envisaged is in process and not yet finished, and Waller cannot guarantee results since he himself can only instruct, not paint. The same is true of another work, the impressive kingdom for which the canvas is intended to be the artistic and expressive symbol. If that larger work which Waller has in mind is ever to exist, then Charles will certainly have to oversee its production and probably will need to be the painter of much of it. Mythic and poetic pasts can be incorporated into present-tense directions to one of these artists in order to offer suggestions to the other of them, but the perfected works themselves are future possibilities, not certainties, because the only work that Waller himself can control is his own poem. A fundamentally important point here is the metaphoric principle which informs Waller's ingenious device of advising others both explicitly and implicitly, along with producing polished art himself as a specific illustration of what might be accomplished, in a picture or a kingdom, by following his example.

The only thing that has seemed important, however, is the chain reaction to the device which Waller so shrewdly chose to adopt. Fictional instructions about imaginary pictures began to appear almost immediately, including but by no means limited to Marvell's "Last Instructions to a Painter," and these painter poems, as they came to be called, were still going if not going strong when Steele, forty years later, expressed the belief or perhaps the fervent hope that the form could not survive what Blackmore had done to it.[2] Osborne published a finding list of painter poems in 1949, and they have attracted considerable attention since then, notably by those who necessarily have had to take them into account in assessing Marvell's later work and career.[3] The fictional necessity for the fictional instructions, however,

2. Robert Anderson, ed., "The Life of Blackmore," in *The Works of the British Poets* (London, 1795), 7.583: "In 1706, he published his *Advice to the Poets* . . . and [in 1709] *Instructions to Vanderbank*, a sequel to the *Advice to the Poets*, which Steele ridiculed . . . with such success that he put an end to the species of writers who give *advice to painters*." *The Tatler*, 3 (16 April 1709): "Waller and Denham had worn out the expedience of 'Advice to a Painter': this author has transferred the work, and . . . that thought is worn out also."

3. Mary Tom Osborne, *Advice-To-A-Painter Poems 1633–1856* ([Austin?] The University of Texas, 1949).

originally had been the space left vacant by the missing shields of classical antiquity, and that fact apparently has been lost sight of. This is a development which almost certainly would have taken both Waller and Marvell by surprise.

To regain the earlier perspective, one ought to look at Waller's starting point in some detail so as to be able to see where he left off and thus where subsequent painter poems began. A useful critic to cite for these purposes—this statement will look anachronistic only for a moment—is Pope. His translation of the *Iliad*, both luckily and unluckily, was intended for the carriage trade, underwritten by advance subscription, and first published in imposing folio form. The expensive format is especially important toward the end of the eighteenth book because the engraving supplied for the Shield of Achilles otherwise could not have been included at all and/or the details depicted thereon would have been microscopic to an unaided eye. This is a fact which the Twickenham editors discovered to our sorrow, and they chose to leave out the plates rather than supply a magnifying glass with each set sold. They do include a bonus, however, which eighteenth-century buyers did not receive since they reproduce Pope's own rough drawing for the finished design. Both formats also, of course, include Pope's elaborate and at times highly schematic verbal descriptions of what an actualized version of the shield would be like.[4]

Pope assures us that he was "very careful to consult both the best Performers and Judges in Painting . . . the most distinguish'd Masters of that Art. Sir *Godfrey Kneller* in particular . . . entirely agrees with my sentiments on this Subject" (370). This self-protective coloration appears at the end of an account in which he ventures "to consider this Piece" (Homer's of course, and not his own, or at least not explicitly) "as a complete *Idea* of *Painting*, and a Sketch for what one may call an *universal Picture*" (363). He also offers what he refers to as "an Attempt . . . to shew with what exact Order all that [Homer] describes may enter into the Composition, according to the Rules of Painting" (366), an attempt which is needed, in part, because a fundamental "rule"—indeed, one of the inherent limitations of the art form—appears to be violated. Or so, at any rate, say those who complain that in painted work it is manifestly "impossible to represent the Movement of the Figures" (358) or to "*hear*" (359).

A comparable argument was used not too long ago to discredit the

4. Pope is quoted from *The Poems*, 8 [*Iliad*, 10–24], ed. Maynard Mack *et al.* (London and New Haven, 1967).

idea that Marvell could have written two of the painter poems sometimes attributed to him since they incompetently allow painted figures to speak.[5] Waller must have had more than a little sympathy for
this realistic position since at one point he finds it incumbent to
justify his own departure from it.

> Painter, excuse me, if I have a while
> Forgot thy art and us'd another style,
> For, though you draw arm'd heroes as they sit,
> The task in battle does the Muses fit.
> They, in the dark confusion of a fight,
> Discover all, instruct us how to write,
> And light and honor to brave actions yield,
> Hid in the smoke and tumult of the field.
>
> (287–94)

Even here, however, Waller aligns himself with classical practice
rather than modern commentary. On the shield of Aeneas, as Dryden
puts it, "Th' approaching *Gauls*, / Obscure in Night, ascend, and seize
the Walls" (*Aeneis*, 8.873–74).[6] And Virgil next chooses to give some
particulars despite the fact that in doing so he "oversteps the limits of
possibility," as Page (658 n) points out, since "if the night was dark the
many details . . . would not be visible." Waller prefers to allow the
muse to reveal more than a painting could actually show, and his own
perspective, therefore, is rather like Pope's view concerning movement and speech on the shield.

"There is," Pope observes, "a great deal of difference between the
Work itself, and the Description of it" (359). On the shield, the scene is
certainly silent and almost as certainly static as well. Eustathius,
Homer's twelfth-century commentator, had speculated "That 'tis possible all those Figures did not stick close to the Shield, but that they
were detach'd from it, and mov'd by Springs, in such a manner that
they appear'd to have Motion," but all this is "without any Necessity"

5. See E. G. Fogel's attack on Lord's claim for Marvell as the author of "The
Second Advice to a Painter" and "The Third Advice": "Salmons in Both, or
Some Caveats for Canonical Scholars," *Bulletin of the New York Public Library*,
63 (1959), 223–36; rpt. in *Evidence for Authorship: Essays in Problems of
Attribution*, ed. D. V. Erdman and E. G. Fogel (Ithaca, 1966).

6. Dryden is quoted from *The Poems*, ed. James Kinsley, 4 vols. (Oxford,
1958). Virgil is cited from *The Aeneid* [7–12], ed. T. E. Page (London, 1900;
rpt. 1956).

and, in any case, explains only movement, not sound. Eustathius—
and others, one might add—overlooked the fact that a description
quite properly may describe what the scene itself can only mutely,
motionlessly, or even darkly suggest. "In explaining a Painting of
Raphael or *Poussin*," Pope wants to know, "can we prevent animating
the Figures, in making them speak conformably to the Design of the
Painter?" By way of indirect answer, "*Pliny* says of *Apelles*, that he
painted *Clytus* on Horseback going to Battel, and demanding his Hel-
met of his Squire" (360). Indeed, "the same Author has said much
more of *Apelles*," that "he painted those things which could not be
painted, as Thunder." (Apelles and thunder and especially Zeus the
Thunderer, I should parenthetically say, will need further attention
later on.) "And of *Timanthus*," Pliny goes so far as to claim "that in all
his Works there was something more understood than was seen."
(This too is a pregnant observation.) "No one sure will condemn those
ways of Expression," or at least not rightly so, and especially not in
this case because the vast immensity of the scene demands them. For
the truth of the matter is that the scope of the shield, as forged out by
Hephaistos and described by Homer, is nothing less than "the whole
World . . . and all the Diversions of Mankind" (358).

One needs to remember, however, that the divine artificer was "the
God of Fire," not of Water. In consequence, Homer writes (or rather
Pope does),

> Thus the broad Shield complete the Artist crown'd
> With his last Hand, and pour'd the Ocean round,

but "he passes over this part of the description negligently" (357 n).
Oceanic matters are, however, the only omission of any consequence,
and even that one has long since been remedied by Mulciber and
Virgil for the comparable shield of Aeneas. Virgil "makes half his
description of *Aeneas*'s buckler consist in a sea fight" precisely "because *Homer* had describ'd nothing of this kind" (ibid.). "The *Latin*
Poet," moreover, when he "imitated the *Greek* one, always took care to
accommodate those things which Time had chang'd, so as to render
them agreeable to the Palate of his Readers" (360).

In the shield of Aeneas, therefore, though not in Achilles',

> We see the famous Battel of *Actium*, where we may distinguish
> the Captains: *Agrippa* with the Gods, and the Winds favorable;
> and *Anthony* leading on all the Forces of the *East*, *Egypt*, and
> the *Bactrians*: The Fight begins, The Sea is red with Blood,

> *Cleopatra* gives the Signal for a Retreat, and calls her Troops
> with a *Systrum. Patrio vocat agmina Systro* <696 [this insert
> and the one below are the Twickenham's]>. The Gods, or
> rather the Monsters of *Egypt*, fight against *Neptune, Venus, Mi-*
> *nerva, Mars* and *Apollo*: We see *Anthony's* Fleet beaten, and the
> *Nile* sorrowfully opening his Bosom to receive the Conquer'd:
> *Cleopatra* looks pale and almost dead at the Thought of that
> Death she had already determined; nay we see the very Wind
> *Iapis* <actually *Iapyx*>, which hastens her Flight: We see the
> three Triumphs of *Augustus*; that Prince consecrates three hun-
> dred Temples, the Altars are fill'd with Ladies offering up Sacri-
> fices, *Augustus* sitting at the Entrance of *Apollo's* Temple, re-
> ceives Presents, and hangs them on the Pillars of the Temple;
> while all the conquer'd Nations pass by . . . (360–61)

In Pope's view, "Nothing can better justify *Homer*, or shew the Wisdom and Judgment of *Virgil*." Virgil, quite rightly, "was charm'd with
Achilles's Shield, and therefore would give the same Ornament to his
Poem." "But as *Homer* had painted the Universe, he was sensible that
nothing remain'd for him to do"—except, that is, an amplifying of the
seascape and a "Prophecy" to "shew what the Descendant of his Hero
should perform." Pope does not bother to say so, but from Virgil's
standpoint, of course, though not that of Aeneas, the prophecy had
already been fulfilled so that the future history displayed on the
shield had become a living and present reality. This was not to prove
true for Waller, or not without significant restrictions.

Pope also makes no comment, though he could have, on that profu-
sion of painter poems which Waller inadvertently called into existence
when he looked about, or rather behind, him to see whether Virgil had
exhausted the only possible extension of Homer or whether there remained something that a poet might yet do with a sea battle in which
the ducal brother of the reigning "Augustus" had played a major role.
Here, in a sense, we return to well-charted territory, since Waller's
precedents for describing the painter's task have themselves been often described.[7] Regularly mentioned in this connection are Anacreon,
Horace, and the tradition of *ut pictura poesis* which regards poems as
speaking pictures and pictures as silent poems. Waller's prime source,
however, has been identified as a poem by Giovanni Busenello in which

7. The best account of this background is given by Annabel M. Patterson,
"The 'Painter' Poems," in *Marvell and the Civic Crown* (Princeton, 1978), 113–
67 (especially 127ff. on "pictorial theory").

the painter Liberi is told how to depict (or possibly how he was already in the process of depicting) a climactic event of a twenty-five-year war, the defeat inflicted in 1655 by Venice on the Turks at Crete. The painting, as of 1949, "still occupies its appointed place in the *Sala dello Scrutinio* of the Palace of the Doges" (Osborne, 9) and thus has long overshadowed Busenello's poem and, one supposes, Waller's as well.

I have not seen the fact mentioned in connection with the painter poems, but Busenello, in this respect also like Waller, was better known formerly than now. A respected writer of poems to be read in their own right, he also was a librettist for Monteverdi, who wrote his last two operas, *Il ritorno d'Ulysse* (The Return of Odysseus, 1641) and *L'incoronazione di Poppea* (The Crowning of Poppea, 1642) for Venice, at that time the operatic capital of Italy.[8] Sir Thomas Higgons, sometime ambassador to Venice, may have seen some analogues in such works for happenings in England when he published his translation of Busenello's victory poem as *A Prospective of the Naval Triumph of the Venetians over the Turk* (1658). I also have seen no mention of the fact that this is the same Higgons who, as MP from New Windsor, was to be one of Marvell's satiric butts in "The Last Instructions" (197–98), but Waller's debt to Busenello, directly and/or through Higgons is well established. Indeed, it is so much taken for granted that Waller's commendatory poem "To his Worthy Friend Sir THOMAS HIGGONS, upon his Translation of the VENETIAN TRIUMPH" (Fenton, 95–96) evidently is no longer read any more than Higgons and Busenello are. The assumption appears to be that the mere fact of its existence is all that usefully needs to be known, but that is not, I think, the case.

Waller begins by carefully distinguishing among several levels of artistic merit in different artistic mediums. The heraldic Lion of Venice, as displayed on that city's coat of arms and by the famous sculptures before San Marco, is "not so fierce in fight, / As LIBERI's hand presents him to our sight." Yet the painter's brush ("his pencil") does not show him "half so fierce, / Or roar so loud, as BUSINELLO's verse." And yet Higgons's English translation "does all three excel, / The fight, the piece, and lofty BUSINEL." If, moreover, words are sufficiently lofty, then even loftier deeds may be inspired by them. It thus is not beyond all hope that

> If, list'ning to your charms, we could our jars
> Compose, and on the TURK discharge these wars;

8. Donald Jay Grout, *A History of Western Music*, 3d ed. (New York and London, 1980), 312.

> Our BRITISH arms the sacred tomb might wrest
> From Pagan hands, and triumph o'er the east:
> And then you might our own high deeds recite.
> And with great TASSO celebrate the fight.

Waller in extreme old age abandoned such ideas, a point made at the outset of this study, but Tasso had earlier been such a great favorite of Waller's that Fenton (xxx) gives a brief biography. Jerusalem delivered was Tasso's theme, of course, but there was no point in worrying about taking that city back from the Turks when dissonant jarring was not composed at home. Shakespeare's Henry IV made that discovery years earlier when, receiving battle news from Wales, he observed, "It seems then that the tidings of this broil / Brake off our business for the Holy Land" (1.1.47–48). And that conclusion could hardly have been less compelling in 1658. The return of Charles in 1660 temporarily papered over only some of the deep divisions and only in some quarters. In "On St. James's Park," Waller had already urged the king to press forward with the further reforms still so very much needed. By 1665–66, moreover, factional strife at home, while not evident in verse and restricted almost exclusively to "radical prose pamphlets" (as Lord [xxxiv] calls them), was dangerously accompanied by Dutch threats abroad.

Seen in this light, it is quite clear, I think, that Waller proposed to celebrate an external victory in terms that would also invite the further composing of internal "jars" and thus enable British arms, whether literal or verbal, to be discharged on someone other than the British themselves. His failure on the second of these proposals was to be conspicuous, among other reasons because he did not anticipate the ignominy of a Dutch fleet sailing more or less unopposed up the Thames and the jeering painter poems which "celebrated" that shaming "triumph." What Waller could and did do was take a relatively long view of the past as it might be brought to bear upon the present and upon a future which (unrealistically as it turned out) he hoped would come to pass. He therefore certainly looked at the more or less current work of Busenello and Higgons, but in doing so also looked long past them to the example of Homer and Virgil and the heroic leadership of antiquity. Discrepancies between the now and the then were obvious, sometimes blatantly so, and thus had to be taken into account, but they also had to be bridged over wherever and insofar as possible lest the future distance between present and past become greater, not less. Waller evidently saw that quite clearly. What he could not have foreseen was that from the satiric perspective of subsequent painter poems, the distance was already grotesquely absurd.

Strictly speaking, simultaneous affirmation of presence-absence is as impossible in a poem as on a canvas where audible figures are seen to move; some suspension of disbelief is required of those who attend to either kind of work. Waller also suffers the further disadvantage inherent in his own verbal medium: He can set forth the pictorial framework of the whole only by tracing out its sequentially linear parts. On the other hand, by the time Waller's reader is actually asked to visualize the Paphian and Thetis-like Duchess and the unshielded and therefore bolder Duke, an ongoing system of referential allusion has already been gradually but firmly established. I earlier lifted those movable figures from their true position in Waller's scene because of the immediate usefulness of the allusive language whereby they are described. Waller, however, is more circumspect both in his approach to and recessional from them. In theory, as Pope indicates, the example of Homer, or at least of Homer and Virgil combined, would justify the inclusion of anything and everything in the surrounding canvas area since the classical scope is universal. This open-door policy of indefinite expansion proved very handy, in fact, for satirists eager to scatter broadside shot at diverse targets of not quite miscellaneous kinds, but it was also an invitation to disordered lack of structure and seemingly endless prolixity which was not always declined. Waller is circumspect on these matters too, but his instructions do run to 336 lines—Marvell's "Last Instructions" run to 990, in this case not a pejorative fact—and several locales at separable time periods are on view. To manage a firm control requires blocking out the painting's compositional scene with considerable care.

Waller begins, therefore, not with the Duchess and Duke at Harwich nor the other events leading up to 3 June 1665, but rather, as it were, *in medias res*. "First draw the sea," he says, or more accurately, "that portion which between / The greater world and this of ours is seen" (1–2). The initial effect, surely, is diminution since a greater world can only contrast with a smaller one presumably less significant. Virgil, however, effects a transition from earlier events on land to those at sea in a verbally similar way. "Haec inter," between these, he says (8.671); or as Dryden translates, "Betwixt the Quarters, flows a Golden Sea" (8.891). "The groups hitherto described," to quote Page's explanation,

> are on the border of the shield and have been mentioned beginning with those 'at the top' ([v.] 652) and ending with those

representing the under-world, which would naturally be at the bottom. Then 'between these' groups and the central groups (675 *in medio*), which all deal with the exploits of Augustus, is a band of gold, representing (cf. *imago*) the circumambient Ocean.

For those able to see this background, either now or after it has been more clearly limned, Waller's opening lines probably expand as well as contract. The circumambient English channel, North Sea, Atlantic Ocean, and so on implicitly establish England as nearer to, not farther from, the controlling center of everything, namely the exploits— or more probably the figure—of an Augustus. From this point of view, the greater world is so in size but not in significance. "Vast floating armies," watched closely by "the whole world" (4–5), further reveal where the truly important focus is, and the painter is to confirm that fact with watchful heavens: "Make Heav'n concern'd and an unusual star / Declare th' importance of th' approaching war" (7–8).

Lord's note suggests that this is "perhaps the comet reported by Pepys on 6 April 1665: 'great talk of a new comet.'" The note could have cited Dryden's allusions in *Annus Mirabilis* (64–72, 1161–64) or Waller's own later reference to the Duke's "dreadful streamer, like a comet's hair" (269). But if the comet of 1665 specifically is meant, then Waller's "unusual" is itself an unusual adjective since comets regularly are "baneful," "dread," or—as Dryden (1162) has it—"dire." This "unusual star," while possibly modern, is in any case the counterpart to Virgil's "patrium . . . sidus" (8.681): The "beamy Temples" of "Young *Caesar*" "shoot their Flames afar, / And o'er his Head is hung the *Julian* star" (Dryden, 899–902); "*i.e.*, the star of . . . Julius Caesar, which appeared shortly after his death and was supposed to mark his reception into heaven" (Page, 680 n). That we are to glance back at the regicide of January 1649 seems doubtful to me since I doubt that Waller would here have wanted to refan those flames, but I shall later question Waller's artistic control in two passages, and an inflammatory allusion here is not impossible. More certain is that, having set this scene, Waller next asks that we look back at the "early deeds" of the "valiant Duke" (11) and to those events of the immediate past which prefaced or rather provoked the confrontation about to begin. A summary was given at the outset of this discussion and needs no repeating, but some of the details given earlier were chosen precisely because Waller alludes to them. The editorial notes repeatedly (and necessarily) say (to quote one example from many), "these lines . . . refer to" (48–50 n). The notes also point out with some regularity that

"Waller tactfully omits all reference to . . ." (55–64 n) or that "Waller's account is especially fanciful here" (65–76 n).

Since these notes are factual rather than interpretive, it would be totally unfair to complain that they miss the point, but it can be said without prejudice that they may be misleading in an unintentional way. By line 65 it ought to be obvious that Waller is busily translating history into myth and that one of his methods of doing so is to re-design some of the strategies often employed by Homer and Virgil.

> So hungry wolves, though greedy of their prey,
> Stop when they find a lion in their way.
>
> (23–24)
>
> While his tall ships in the barr'd channel stand,
> He grasps the Indies in his armed hand.
>
> (27–28)
>
> Like falcons these, those like a num'rous flock
> Of fowl which scatter to avoid the shock.
>
> (57–58)
>
> Europe and Africa, from either shore,
> Spectators are and hear our cannon roar,
> While the divided world in this agree,
> Men that so fight deserve to rule the sea.
>
> (61–64)

The last lines quoted include line 64; line 65 itself ("But nearer home, thy pencil use once more"), to which is appended the note about Waller being "especially fanciful," merely initiates a new variation on a process which began much earlier.

When Waller wrote this poem, he probably was right in thinking that he could take liberties with this kind of historical material and that, to requote Pope, "No one sure will condemn those ways of Expression." Shakespeare, admittedly dealing with a past more remote but even so a very famous one, had worked comparable transformations with the reign of Henry IV, partly in the business about the holy land and notably in making Hotspur roughly the same age as Prince Hal despite the historical reality that Percy was twenty-three years older and thus older than the king himself. But once the hard facts of 1665–66 became not merely known but publically satirized, then it was Waller, of course, who appeared to mislead, and not unintentionally. When, moreover, Waller introduces the Duchess of York as a goddess, he must have been sailing very near the wind even in 1666. It has to have been well known in court circles, if not well publicized elsewhere, that Anne Hyde was pregnant at the time of her marriage and that she gave birth two months afterward. In "The Last Instructions," Marvell exclaims upon her ingenuity in finding a method whereby "royal heirs might be matured / In fewer months than mothers once endur'd" (55–56). "The Second Advice to a Painter" drives home the point with sexual vulgarities. Venus, now "the Cytherean girl" had made do with "One thrifty ferry-boat of mother-pearl" (63–64), but the Duchess must have "navies" as stage "properties" for a "small sea-masque" (65–66). She is addressed as "dear" (66), a cheapening title for a duke's wife but also expressive of the idea that she was uncheap or dear at any price despite being a cheap piece of goods. Waller claims that Harwich is "where such beauties spring" (88) and that

> The soldier here his wasted store supplies
> And takes new valor from the ladies' eyes.
>   (89–90)

But in "The Second Advice," the soldier is leaving it behind in a different place.

> See where the Duchess, with triumphant tail
> Of num'rous coaches, Harwich does assail!
> So the land crabs, at Nature's kindly call,
> Down to engender at the sea do crawl.
>   (55–58)

Waller's allusions to Venus and Thetis surely cannot have been prudent, not even before the satiric adaptations were made, but Waller needed his picture of the Duchess, or one very like it, to continue tracing out the border for the shield that is not quite there. The two further extensions which almost immediately follow were, however, much safer to draw in every way, and both are about as explicit as possible.

> For a less prize, with less concern and rage,
> The Roman fleets at Actium did engage;
> They, for the empire of the world they knew,
> These for the old contend and for the new.
>   (113–16)

This is Virgil's scene, of course. Homer's appears quite shortly, in lines earlier quoted but abridged.

> The great Achilles march'd not to the field
> Till Vulcan that impenetrable shield
> And arms had wrought, yet there no bullets flew,
> But shafts and darts which the weak Phrygians threw.
> Our bolder hero on the deck does stand
> Expos'd, the bulwark of his native land:
> Defensive arms laid by as useless here
> Where massy balls the neighboring rocks do tear.
> Some power unseen those princes does protect,
> Who for their country thus themselves neglect.
>
> (127–36)

This résumé conveniently overlooks, of course, the presence of Hector, not to mention Paris and the arrow that found its way to Achilles' vulnerable heel. That very fact, however, underscores the point that the diminution with which the poem apparently began has been openly inverted; by this stage, it is the world of Achilles, inhabited by weak Phrygians, that now seems small. Not only that, the absence of the shield has now become a disadvantage which is turned into an asset; taking it away reveals the presence of a courage all the more to be admired. It might be thought that if Waller supposes he can get away with hyperbole of this kind for the Duke, then the illusion of the Duchess vis-à-vis the realities of the former Anne Hyde would not have troubled him at all. York himself, however, was never seriously discredited for his personal conduct in this engagement, though others were, whereas the Duchess had small credit, by some standards, well before it began.

The question of artistic control does not arise, however, in considering the fact that the lines on Augustus at Actium, anachronistically in terms of literary (and world) history, precede those on Achilles at Troy. Foregrounding Virgil at the expense of Homer is not accidental and not bad strategy. Waller is more than willing to have the Dutch compared to "trembling *Indians* and *Egyptians*" or to "soft *Sabaeans*" (Dryden, 8.937–38). Indeed, he refers to "the trembling Dutch" (273) as "sheep" (274) and jests at proverbially "Dutch" courage: "The Dutch their wine and all their brandy lose, / Disarm'd of that from which their courage grows" (43–44). Some of them, presumably the still softer sort, "At home, preserv'd from rocks and tempests, lie, / Compell'd, like others, in their beds to die" (71–72).

But Waller has no intention whatsoever of elevating "greedy mariners" (69) to the status of Hector and Paris or of raising The Hague and Amsterdam (which "tremble" [266]) to the heights of towered Ilium. He cannot discredit the enemy entirely, of course, since to downplay the foe too much is also to minimize the victory. The Dutch admiral is justifiably "Proud of his late success against the Swedes" (139). They were *merely* Swedes, of course, not English, but nonetheless he is "Made by that action and his high command / Worthy to perish by a prince's hand" (139–40). Since not all of the hyperbole can be reserved for the English side,

> we reach our foes,
> Who now appear so numerous and bold,
> The action worthy of our arms we hold.
> A greater force than that which here we find
> Ne'er press'd the ocean nor employ'd the wind.
> (98–102)

And yet in referring to the Dutch admiral, Waller is derisive in the way in which he uses the man's name. Abridgement of "Jacob Wassenaer, Baron von Opdam" to "Opdam" is itself insignificant since Charles Sackville, to pick an example *not* at random, is usually referred to as (the Earl of) "Dorset," and Dorset himself shortened the Dutchman's name to "Opdam" in his "Song: Written at Sea, in the first Dutch War, 665, the Night Before the Engagement." The point is that Dorset stressed the first syllable: "Should foggy Opdam chance to know."[9] In "The Second Advice," a comparable metrical pattern is visible in lines 45, 178, and 198:

> Then in kind visit unto Opdam's gout

> And still fights Opdam through the lakes below

> And promises to do what Opdam failed

Either metrical inversion occurs in "Opdam sails in, plac'd in his naval throne" (163), as seems likely, or in this instance Waller's practice, deliberately or not, has been echoed. In any case, Waller uses the name twice (in lines 137 and 170), with the second syllable stressed, not the first.

9. Sackville is quoted from *The Works of Dorset*, in *The Works of the British Poets*, ed. Robert Anderson (London, 1795), 6.511.

> Against him first Opdam his squadron leads.

> For such a loss Opdam his life must pay!

Juxtaposition of these lines indicates that leading in this case leads to loss; up-Dam quite definitely is not up and may be worse than down. His name in effect proclaims him.

Waller also wants his painter to depict the Dutch fleet, both men and ships, as now drunk on Dutch courage and tipsily reeling.

> Brandy and wine (their wonted friends) at length
> Render them useless and betray their strength.
> (243–44)

> Their reeling ships on one another fall,
> Without a foe, enough to ruin all.
> (249–50)

The scene at times becomes Conradesque in its grimly comic absurdity, as in "The flame invades the powder-rooms, and then, / Their guns shoot bullets, and their vessels [shoot] men" (255–56). Grim also is the irony that

> Ingenious to their ruin, every age
> Improves the arts and instruments of rage.
> Death-hast'ning ills Nature enough has sent,
> And yet men still a thousand more invent.
> (237–40)

Waller's references to the brother of Charles are worth noticing too. Opdam, despite his name, was "worthy to perish by a prince's hand" (140) but not specifically by the hand of "James" or "York." Elsewhere, it is "His Highness-Royal" (subtitle) or "the Duke" (146, 199, 268) or "our royal Admiral" (259) who customarily leads the way. But "York appears" (123) at one point, and at another, the name is emphasized by terminal position and by rhyme: "English valor" may "wonders . . . work" when "Led by th' example of victorious York" (277–78). "Jacob" is mentioned once, but far from being an opponent surnamed Wassenaer, the reference is to the biblical patriarch even though the occasion for introducing the name is a particularly horrible incident.

A rumor soon reached Paris that York himself had perished, and it could easily have been the truth. As Pepys (8 June 1665) reports, three men standing nearby did die, "their blood and brains flying in the Duke's face; and the head of Mr. Boyle striking down the Duke, as some say."[10] Lord's note to line 147 omits Pepys but does identify all three men:

Charles Berkeley, Earl of Falmouth, better known as Lord Fitzharding; Charles MacCarthy, Lord Muskerry (in the Irish peerage); and Richard Boyle, second son of the Earl of Burlington, "a youth of great hope, who . . . took the first opportunity to lose his life in the King's service." (Clarendon, *Life*, section 643).

Waller introduces dark comedy when he writes that these persons not only died but "dyed his [the Duke's] garment with their scatter'd gore" (148). What he does not do is mention their names. They are merely "three worthy persons," and suppression of their honorifics and claims to fame has the effect of underlining "Jacob" when it does appear. A further interesting fact is that the name is transferred to otherwise nameless bystanders or witnesses to the triple death. Momentarily "struck with horror" (155), they erroneously suppose the gore to be the Duke's own, and their reaction is comparable to Jacob's when shown the parti-colored, blood-stained coat of Joseph (Genesis 37.31–34):

> And they took Joseph's coat, and killed a kid of the goats, and dipped the coat in the blood. And they sent the coat of many colours, and they brought it to their father; . . . And Jacob rent his clothes.

"So trembl'd Jacob," Waller says, "when he thought the stains / Of his son's coat had issu'd from his veins" (157–58).

Both reactions, strictly speaking, were equally ill-founded, but in the modern instance three men, not the kid of a goat, had lost their lives, and it is precisely for this "loss" that "Opdam his" own "life must pay!" The prince "Before for honor . . . fought," but "now" for "revenge" (160–61), and he boards the Dutch ship resolved to exact vengeance "while yet their blood is warm" (174). These horrors are maximized, if anything, by the ironies of die and dye, by the horrible humor of reeling ships, and by the fiendish ingenuity of death-

10. The rumor mentioned above is documented by Wheatley (see note 1), annotating Pepys's entry.

hastening ills. In no sense, therefore, does Waller minimize the magnitude of the "sacrifice" (153) made. These young men

> their youth,
> Their worth, their love, their valor, and their truth;
> The joys of court, their mothers, and their wives,
> To follow him, abandon'd—and their lives!
>
> (163–66)

The focus of Waller's attention, even so, must in no sense be distracted from the Duke himself. The witnesses are Jacob-like in their reaction, in part at least, because they can express the stunned reaction which their leader must himself repress in favor of immediate and vigorous response. At this point, if not earlier, one presumably is to realize that not only have "Berkeley," "Fitzharding," and "Boyle" been suppressed, but so has "James," the Duke's own name. Or rather, one is to recall that "James" and "Jacob" are variant appellations of one another. The private horror of James is expressed through others so that the public personage of York can appropriately react. One also realizes that the Dutchman named "Jacob" has been a mere pretender, though a valiant one, now in the process of being unmasked, displaced, and destroyed. Pepys further mentions, "Admirall Opdam blown up," and Waller comments, "Their . . . commander from his charge is toss'd" (187).

Waller's treatment of names needs to be watched closely, partly because of what was and was not done with them by Waller himself in "On St. James's Park" and partly because of the nominal strategies adopted in subsequent painter poems, especially "The Last Instructions." More immediate, however, is that this careful device of naming and not naming prepares for Waller's instructions after the battle is won. However important the three worthies were, they were less important than York, and however much James-Jacob of York transcends Jacob Wassenaer of Opdam, he himself is transcended by the king. The point is glanced at in such lines as "His bright sword now a dearer int'rest draws, / His brother's glory and his country's cause" (13–14); and—later and more briefly—"he pleads his brother's cause so well" (215). It ought to be noticed, however, that while Charles is being represented in these lines, he does not present himself personally. The focus of much of the poem quite appropriately has seemed to be, perhaps actually is, the lesser of the two brothers. And indeed, Waller's prophetic hope for James, for his poem, and for future time is that "Ages to come shall know that leader's toil / And his great name on whom the Muses smile" (295–96). Nevertheless, at this point the painter is to depict a "great Monarch" whose own great name needs no mentioning at all. The modern substitute for the shield of Aeneas which Waller has and has not been describing is now to blazon forth in full glory the royal presence which hitherto—as one belatedly realizes—has been conspicuous by its absence.

> Then draw the Parliament, the nobles met,
> And our great Monarch high above them set.
> Like young Augustus let his image be,
> Triumphing for that victory at sea,
> Where Egypt's queen and eastern kings o'erthrown
> Made the possession of the world his own.
> (299–304)

One of the splendors of this passage is that it completes and embellishes the conceptual border of the picture with highly refined brushwork from Virgil and manages to unveil a portrait of the central, dominant figure of both pictures, Virgil's and Waller's, at one and the same time.

Lacquered surface and polished sheen notwithstanding, Waller must have been feeling especially venturesome or especially driven by urgent need when he wrote this poem. Otherwise it is difficult to account for the fact that he risked going beyond the magniloquent luster of the "image" which the lines just quoted reveal. But risk it he did, and some of the final touches—but unfortunately not all—actually succeed in adding to the gloss. Two of them take the painting device about as far, evidently, as it could go; subsequent satiric versions were able to find numerous twists whereby to subvert Waller's form but not many genuinely new ones whereby to extend it. Having finished the formal portrait, Waller ends with a formal address "To the King." I earlier mentioned the tentative theory of Eustathius, as reported but also rejected by Pope, that Homer's figures were detached from the surface of the shield so as to be capable of motion external to the work of which they were a part. With an ingenious inversion of his own, Waller now invites the king to step inside the picture and be his own living portrait:

> Great Sir, disdain not in this piece to stand,
> Supreme commander both of sea and land!
> (311–12)

Waller has been giving all the instructions up to this point, but if Charles were to fuse art and life within his royal figure, then further directions from Waller himself would become superfluous. With another inversion of control—from the perspective of life rather than art, it is instead a reversion—Charles himself should now become that overseer who is to "Instruct the artists" (328).

In "The Third Advice to a Painter," the painter is told to stop after painting the "the monkey Duchess" of Albemarle "all undress'd"; the reason is that she herself is better suited, as it were, to "paint the rest" (171–72). The satire follows Waller at a distance and possibly indicates that both poems, though at even greater distance, are following the Pygmalion myth of the art object becoming a living reality. The satire does not improve upon Waller in either sense of that word, but one reason why it could be written is that Charles failed to issue the instructions that Waller urges upon him. The "artists" whom the king is said proleptically and prophetically to instruct are not painters, after all, but those who need to know "How to build ships and dreadful ordnance cast" (327). The model for Charles, flatteringly enough, is to be "Jove himself" (329), but in times of strife that deity did not think it beneath himself to descend from an Olympian throne to ensure the safety of his realm, and neither should Charles.

> You as the soul, as the first mover, you,
> Vigor and life on ev'ry part bestow:
> How to build ships and dreadful ordnance cast,
> Instruct the artists and reward their haste.
> So Jove himself, when Typhon Heav'n does brave,
> Descends to visit Vulcan's smoky cave,
> Teaching the brawny Cyclops how to frame
> His thunder mix'd with terror, wrath, and flame.
>   (325–32)

Teaching by example is sometimes sooty work, but Waller thought it had to be done and done with "haste" lest Typhon actually prevail at the next encounter at Actium or Lowestoft, wherever and whenever that battle actually would be waged. Waller was in no position to give this kind of instruction; Charles was. For much of the poem Waller has reshaped, in seriatim fashion, the history and artwork described by Homer and, more especially, Virgil. In ending his own work, however, he evidently recalls not only the more recent poetry of Busenello and the nearly contemporary history of 1655, when the Venetians defeated the Turks at Crete, but also the far more ancient report that

Crete had been the birthplace of Zeus. In the last four lines of the poem, the small island becomes Great Britain (though not, one recalls from the poem's second line, "the greater world"), and the Thunderer is displaced by Charles. History is or could be rewritten in the present or, less unrealistically, if not today then tomorrow; the implication is confident hope and future expectancy. But the verb tense is a conditional past, and the syntax pivots on an unwritten "if" which, by its very absence, signals the presence of a condition not yet fulfilled.

> Had the old Greeks discover'd your abode,
> Crete had not been the cradle of their god:
> On that small island they had look'd with scorn
> And in Great Britain thought the Thunderer born.

Marvell used similar syntax to posit a situation contrary to actual fact: "Had we but world enough and time." The potential contrariness in Waller's language was also to be actualized. The old Greeks never could have made the discovery to which Waller refers, but that is scarcely a problem. Many Englishmen, including Marvell, were becoming convinced that in the present political climate that discovery would not be made by modern Greeks, by the Dutch, or by any one else, including the English themselves.

Waller succeeded admirably in bridging the gap between the Shield of Heracles and the Portrait of York, but his success certainly cannot have been hindered and may have been helped by the fact that in this case art really did imitate life. The editorial notes, as earlier quoted, refer to Waller's "fanciful" manipulation of reality, but they also indicate that in lines 213–20,

> Waller did not exaggerate York's violent encounters with the Dutch. One of the best accounts of the end of the action is in Harris' *Life of Sandwich*, pp. 304–05 [I abridge the quote which follows]: ". . . The vessels were grappled and locked together; the fighting at close quarters was furious; man after man was cut down, or his brains were blown out by pistols held only a few feet away. . . . After an hour's desperate struggle the *Oranje* was compeled [*sic*] to yield, her men were taken prisoners, and she was set on fire."

The notes further document the fact that after the battle was won, both houses of Parliament "expressed to the King their resolution to assist him with their lives and fortunes against the Dutch, or any others that would assist them. . . . The large sum of £1,250,000 was voted for the next year" (299 n). Given this reality, the following picture also does not "exaggerate" the facts of the matter, but Waller may later have rued the drawing of it:

> Last draw the Commons at his royal feet,
> Pouring out treasure to supply his fleet;
> They vow with lives and fortunes to maintain
> Their King's eternal title to the main.
>
> (305–8)

The trouble with these lines is neither fancifulness nor accuracy as such but rather that this abasement of Parliament at the royal feet follows hard upon—the lines are literally contiguous—the humiliation of "Egypt's queen and eastern kings" beneath the triumphant Augustus. Bridging the gap between Charles and Augustus couldn't really be done, as it turned out, but this cannot have been a tactful or appropriate strategy to try out even when Waller wrote the poem. In these lines, he appears, recklessly, to have let himself be carried much too far away by hyperbolic exaltation. Even this might not have mattered had Charles listened hard and painted well, but he did not. It is hindsight, of course, which influences this view of Waller's conclusion, but the subsequent painter poems have long since established hindsight as a nearly inescapable perspective, and they did so on the basis that foresight had been outrageously and shamefully nonexistent except on the part of those with eyes fast fixed on their own main chance. By 1666–67, if not earlier, those with a corrupt personal vision of this kind were alleged to include the Duchess of York, the man who was both her father and the principal minister of state, and even—though some experienced vertigo at this point—the monarch named Charles who was her brother-in-law. By 1688, of course, James was no longer the name of a hero but an exiled king, and instead of the *Oranje* being set afire, a Dutchman named William of Orange became the English Thunderer. Fourteen years old at the time of Lowestoft, William has no more than a walk-on role in Waller's poem; he is merely "that young Prince" (187).

5

Waller Repainted by "Marvell"

"Every one knows that *Nero*, for the first Five Years of his Reign, either really was, or pretended to be, Endow'd with all the amiable Qualities that became an Emperor." The comment is James Welwood's, prefacing Nicholas Rowe's translation (1718–19) of Lucan.[1] If the evidence from verse is at all reliable, then a similar statement is true about Charles II. "From 1660 to 1666," to quote Lord, "both Charles and his ministers seem to have received nothing but panegyrics from the poets."[2] The primary reasons for change were, of course, Nero and Charles themselves and momentous events—including two very famous fires—over which they both had less than total control. From a purely poetic point of view, however, the Roman figures prominent at the turning point from praise to criticism were thought at one time to be Lucan and Persius, and two of the English ones are Waller and Marvell. All sorts of problems arise, however, some of them apparently not solvable, as soon as one descends from this generality to particulars. The panegyric to Nero in Lucan's first book may rise to heights of hyperbole that not even Waller ever dreamed of, but in the seventeenth century

1. *Lucan's Pharsalia* (London, 1718), iii. Since Welwood's "Preface" is dated 26 February 1719, the printer's date presumably is old style.
2. George deF. Lord, ed., *Poems on Affairs of State*, 1:1660–78, (New Haven and London, 1963), xxxiv. Painter poems, including those of Waller, "Marvell," and "The Last Instructions," are quoted from this edition.

Lucan's "praise" was thought by some to be heavily ironic and to exemplify the standard satiric strategy of inflating in order to deflate. Since Lucan and Persius were said to be close friends, the case for irony appeared to be supported by an idea which classicists now reject, that Persius specifically satirized Nero's bombastic verse by quoting and deriding some of it in his own first satire. To see how tangled an affair this was in times past one might notice that Welwood takes it for granted that Persius satirized Nero and was good friends with Lucan but supposes that Lucan's panegyric was written before 1666, as it were, and therefore was appropriately adulatory.

The English side of this coin is also hard to make out. It was "Waller's eulogistic *Instructions to a Painter*," Lord adds, that "brought the honeymoon to an end" (between Charles and English poets) "by providing the model for Marvell's parodic *Second Advice to a Painter*." It is curious that one particular panegyric from among so many should have caused the proliferation of hostile responses that Waller's did, but perhaps one may suppose that Waller's poem was seen as having gone so outrageously far that it could not itself be allowed to go unchallenged. This issue, however, is relatively minor when considered in context. The assertion just quoted from Lord does not indicate the fact in any way, but it is far from certain that Marvell actually did write the "Second Advice" or "The Third" which followed it. Marvell's authorship of "Last Instructions to a Painter" is not disputed, but that poem and its two predecessors confront one with what seems to me to be the most serious problem of them all, the difficulty of reconciling satiric advice about the kingdom with the praise apparently offered in the addresses "To the King" with which all three of the "Marvell" poems end. My notion is that Lucan and Persius, despite the difficulties those authors pose, are helpful in addressing problems raised by the English poems; the one I most want to get to is "Last Instructions to a Painter," an anti-epic of considerable satiric expertise and enormously energetic force, but I shall have to sneak up and back to these points from various indirections.

The response to Waller's celebration of Lowestoft was not only unmistakably hostile but also appears to have been remarkably quick. A broadside publication of Waller's first version of the poem was entered in the Stationers' Record for 10 March 1664–65, and presumably appeared prior to the Lowestoft engagement, fought the following month.[3] I have not seen a copy of the publication, but Osborne's

3. Mary Tom Osborne, *Advice-To-A-Painter Poems 1633–1856* ([Austin?] The University of Texas, 1949), 26.

description indicates that it corresponds to lines 1–50 and 55–64 of the later text. These lines make sense in that grammar and syntax are not problematic, but they can compliment the "valiant Duke" only for "early deeds" (21), sketch in some earlier deeds by others, and merely position the "spectators" (62) for a conflict in which the Duke is "Resolv'd to conquer or resolv'd to die" (18). Perhaps Waller was prudently laying down the groundwork on which to paint, as the case required, either a glorious victory or a glorious death. Except for the festival visit of the Duchess to Harwich, also in March, there was not yet even a notable absence to write up or play down. Osborne refers to "the greatly expanded version" entered on 1 March 1665–66, and since Waller must have been busily at work sometime in the preceding months, it is possible that manuscript circulation preceded actual publication of the finished work. An advantage of this supposition is that it allows more time for the writing of "The Second Advice," a work already in existence in April, the following month.

For the "Third Advice," not to mention the "Fourth" or "Fifth" or "The Last Instructions to a Painter," speedy response is not an issue, but the question of authorship certainly has been. Marvell's name is firmly attached to "The Last Instructions," and his name and John Denham's are prominent in some seventeenth-century publications of the others as well, but perhaps for the sake of publicity regardless of truth. "Marvell," and to a lesser degree, "Denham" have been attached and detached with some frequency since then, and dispute over attribution at times has been conducted, as Patterson put it in 1978, "acrimoniously."[1]

Patterson wanted Marvell to be the author of the "Second" and "Third Advice," a possible reason being (though never stated quite this way) that the importance of "The Last Instructions" seems even greater when viewed as Marvell's climactic effort. Chernaik proved to his own satisfaction that Lord's textual evidence for Marvell as the author of the "Second" and "Third" does not hold up; perhaps coincidentally, he not only omits them from his discussion but also finds "The Last Instructions" less interesting than Patterson does.

Controversy over attribution is one of those problems alluded to

4. Annabel M. Patterson, *Marvell and the Civic Crown* (Princeton, 1978), 115 (part of a review of the debate, with bibliographical references.) See also Warren L. Chernaik, "Appendix[:] Manuscript evidence for the canon of Marvell's poems," in *The Poet's Time: Politics and Religion in the Work of Andrew Marvell* (Cambridge, 1983), 206–14 (a vigorous dissent from previous assumptions and conclusions, notably Lord's).

earlier which probably cannot be resolved on the basis of the evidence now available, but for my purposes it need not be. Whoever the author(s) of the "Second" and "Third Advice" may have been, it cannot be reasonable to approach the "Last Instructions" except by means of the prior poems since Marvell could not or at any rate did not leave them out of his own account. And his first readers would surely have been surprised had he tried. "Last" has little meaning, after all, without positing the existence of something(s) between it and whatever was "first." One could look at the "Second," of course, having looked only at Waller's poem (not called the "First" by Waller himself but retrospectively an accurate title), and for a short time the two works would have been companion poems to be read in approximately the same way that one reads Crashaw's "For Hope" and Cowley's "Against Hope." There is, in fact, an advantage even now in approaching the initial response to Waller's poem in isolation from those which came later. To approach this particular point, it may be helpful to remember, first of all, that the most famous sequel of all time surely has to be Deuteronomy (deutero-"second" + nomos-"law"). Matthew Henry prefaces his commentary on the book by observing that the name "signifies the *second law,* or a *second edition of the law,* not with amendments . . . but with additions."[5] "The former laws" he says, "are repeated and commented on," and that is precisely the method adopted in "The Second Advice": What Waller had said is resaid and commented on, but since the viewpoint is satiric, in this case amendments are also made in effect. Waller's poem does not disappear at this point, but "The Second" becomes the immediate new impetus for "The Third," which in turn generates "The Last." The so-called "Last" did not stop the chain, but neither, for that matter, was Deuteronomy the only "second." "The gospel is a kind of Deuteronomy," Henry adds, "a second law, a remedial law, and it is a law that *makes the comers thereunto perfect.*" This remedial process, no doubt, is what the painter-poems are predicated on, but perfection remained elusive so that not even the "Last" could fulfill its own title in any literal way.

Three poems, however, are quite enough to try to juggle at one time. This is especially true when the three assume the presence or absence of a fourth one, Waller's own, and when, moreover, the "Last" poem, regardless of its position in an ongoing sequence, is unquestionably the response to Waller most worth one's attention. Also important is

5. The References give information about works often cited (including Henry's) and about the system used in citing them.

the fact that the "Marvell" poems, whether or not Marvell actually wrote all three, do have a cumulative effect quite clearly visible if all three are taken together but necessarily imperceptible otherwise. That statement, largely speaking, does not hold true, however, for the "Fourth Advice" and the "Fifth," both of which acknowledge the existence of preceding work in their titles and in occasional allusions but otherwise depend less on prior poems and more on the device itself on which all painter poems necessarily rely. Comparable in this respect are other "continuations," including "Further Advice to a Painter," a poem which Lord claimed for Marvell in 1963 but rejected as spurious in 1968.[6] No one questions the canonicity of "Clarendon's House Warming" or "The Loyal Scot," to mention two poems with very close connections to material in "The Last Instructions," but in these cases the titles themselves signal different points of departure.

My own ax, at any rate, has a different edge, and in order to grind it, I need to narrow things down gradually. Cutting Waller down to size was a continuing aim of the three "Marvell" poems which followed, but the more important purpose, of course, was to lay bare and belittle the personages and events which Waller, from the opposing point of view, had wrongly admired. Virgil, and to a lesser degree Homer, had been helpful and appropriate, even when not actually present, for the kind of heroism that Waller wanted to encourage, and those classical authors continue to be relevant, often in inverted or subverted form, for subsequent response. But even to speak of "response" is to indicate that Waller himself, as distinct from his background materials, now becomes a prominent new source. The "Marvell" poems almost necessarily answer one another if for no other reason than that they all answer Waller and thus share similar, though not identical, frameworks and bodies of material. In these "Marvell" poems, moreover, it is helpful to reintroduce Persius and Lucan, partly because the example of Nero rather than Augustus begins to seem, frighteningly so, the model which Charles, whether consciously and willingly or not, was dangerously close to adopting. "The Last Instructions" stands on the brink to peer into a Neronic chaos and looks far beyond the mere reconsideration of whether the battle of Lowestoft had been won by heroes or bungled by fools and rogues. The narrowest issue— but also, of course, the broadest—now concerns exemplary merit and

6. Cf. *State Poems*, 1.163: "*Further Advice* . . . marks a change in Marvell's attitude . . ."; *Complete Poems* (New York, 1968), xxxii: the poem is one of those "formerly attributed to Marvell . . . which may now also be excluded as spurious."

demerit: how the concept is to be defined, for whom, of what kind, and on what basis. Waller and Marvell were not so far apart on fundamentals as they usually seem to be, but the only method that Marvell evidently could find to dismantle the superstructure raised aloft by Waller was to undermine the foundations. Or, to return to the metaphor used by the poems themselves, Marvell found it necessary to repaint Waller's picture. I have hopes of supporting these statements and thus showing that Waller's "Instructions" and Marvell's "Last Instructions" are complementary mirrors of one another, but I ought to say in advance that it might be misleading to refer to the subsections below as five "easy" stages whereby to proceed from one poem to the other.

I
Parodic Subversion of Waller

When "The Second Advice" parodies Waller's account of the Duchess at Harwich, it includes more than that crawl, cited in the preceding chapter, of land crabs to the sea. With a sudden reversal which is itself satiric, the pomp and circumstance of her visit is compared to the absence of ceremony at her wedding to the Duke. Lord (annotating line 69), quotes from Lodge's *Political History of England, 1660–1702*, to explain,

> "The Duke of York had courted Anne Hyde, the Chancellor's daughter, when she was a Maid of Honor in attendance on the Princess of Orange. Her pregnancy compelled the Duke to admit a binding promise of marriage, and the ceremony was secretly performed in her father's house on September 3, 1660" . . . Hence the meanness of her "nuptial pomp."

Either her father was not present or almost immediately regretted that presence or he lied both belatedly and blatantly (and risked having the lie exposed by other witnesses) when he went on record as having urged Charles to commit Anne to the Tower, next have her tried, and then have her beheaded. Hyde's version of the story, though quoted by Lord (see "The Second Advice," 153–54 n), may not have been widely known, but enough information was available for Waller's flattering compliment to seem fanciful in one direction and the satirist's deflation of pomp by means of deliberately misinterpreted circumstance to seem fanciful in the other.

> O Duchess! if thy nuptial pomp were mean,
> 'Tis paid with in'trest in this naval scene.
> Never did Roman Mark within the Nile
> So feast the fair Egyptian Crocodile,
> Nor the Venetian Duke, with such a state,
> The Adriatic marry at that rate.
>
> (69–74)

"Nor would I love at lower rate," from "To his Coy Mistress," while surely not a genuine echo here, is a line conveniently cited to underline the provocative coarseness of tone and attitude. Lord cites Cleveland's *Mark Antony* (1647): "Never Mark Antony / Dalli'd more wantonly / With the fair Egyptian Queen." One might want to pause to note also that the treacherous implications of the crocodile's toothsome smile and, more notoriously, its tears are suggested by the poet's request,

> Now, Painter, spare thy weaker art, forbear
> To draw her parting passions and each tear;
> For love, alas! has but a short delight.
>
> (75–77)

Lord also refers to "the wedding of Venice to the sea, a magnificent ceremony which still commemorates on Ascension Day that city's maritime importance." All of this information is quite useful, especially the part about Ascension Thursday for a passage so clearly concerned with demeaning movements in the other direction. The complaint, therefore, if one may be made, is not about what is put in but what is left out. Perhaps, however, Lord thought that reminders of Waller's evocations of the *Aeneid* and the Venetian victory in 1655 at Crete were by this point superfluous. A later allusion to Waller's own name, in strategic opposition to Denham's, nonetheless appears: "Now may historians argue con and pro: / Denham saith thus, though Waller always so" (335–36). And Waller's next theme, we are told, "must be" not the already lowered Duchess of York but Denham's wife, otherwise known as York's mistress and here named (with a "bawdy pun," as Lord chastely calls it) "Madam l'Édificatresse" (339–40). "To the King" ends this satire as it did Waller's panegyric. Crete reappears, and the Chancellor now is placed there, too.

Thou, like Jove's Minos, rul'st a greater Crete
And for its hundred cities count'st thy fleet.
Why wilt thou that state-Daedalus allow,
Who builds thee but a lab'rinth and a cow?
If thou art Minos, be a judge severe
And in's own maze confine the engineer;
Or if our sun, since he so near presumes,
Melt the soft wax with which he imps his plumes
And let him, falling, leave his hated name
Unto those seas his war hath set on flame.

(351–60)

Hyde's name, appropriately enough, is suppressed; it is hated and should be hidden, first of all, in the convoluted maze of his own devious construction. His stately corpulence is evident in Lely's portrait (for a reproduction, see Lord, 158) and the swelling of his hide was attributed by his enemies to living on the fat of the land ("Second Advice," 118–19: "Hyde, whose transcendent paunch so swells of late / That he the rupture seems of law and state"). Here his soft underbelly becomes synonymous, as it were, with soft wax to be melted by flame too high above for him to control and by flame below for which he himself is responsible. Once the outer Hyde is rendered down so that the inner man is not hidden, his own self-destruction ought to follow inescapably.

This is a fine comeuppance for the Lord Chancellor, to be sure, and all sorts of other put-downs have preceded it, some of which gesture in the general direction of Waller's background materials. One might cite Edward Montagu for being reduced or, in a sense, elevated from the queen's Master of the Horse to hold the reins of Homer's Trojan horse as "the wooden horse's master" ("Second Advice," 276). Or there is the recommendation given in the "Third": " 'Leave then,' said he, 'th'invulnerable keel; / We'll find their foible, like Achilles' heel' " (79–80). Additional allusions more or less like these will be put on view later in connection with the several conclusions of these poems, but a different point to be seen here is that Waller himself and not his sources is now providing, to some extent, the framework or the border of the new pictures. "Nay, Painter," the "Second Advice" begins, "if thou dar'st design that fight / Which Waller only courage had to write" (1–2). In "The Last Instructions," "Old Waller, trumpet-gen'ral, swore he'd write / This combat truer than the naval fight" (263–64). "The Last Instructions," moreover, presents one remarkable scene which should not be passed over before moving on. Waller had made reference to "the brawny Cyclops" visited by Jove, and the satiric response paints a vivid picture of furious inactivity of an un-Cyclopean kind, which indicates why Virgilian heroism, while seemingly relevant for Waller, seems irrelevant later. Waller's own model was *Aeneid* 8.439–45, just prior to the forging of Aeneas's shield, a fact that I earlier omitted as unnecessary in discussing Waller's poem but worth noticing now.

> My sons, said *Vulcan*, set your Tasks aside,
> Your Strength and Master Skill must now be try'd.
> Arms for a Heroe forge: Arms that require
> Your Force, your Speed, and all your forming Fire.
> He said: They set their former Work aside:
> And their new Toils with eager haste divide.
>   (Dryden, 8.579–84)[7]

In "The Last Instructions," only the first part of these instructions is given or heard.

> Meantime through all the yards their orders run
> To lay the ships up, cease the keels begun.
> The timber rots, and useless axe doth rust,
> Th' unpractic'd saw lies buri'd in its dust,
> The busy hammer sleeps, the ropes untwine,
> The stores and wages all are mine and thine.
> Along the coast and harbors they take care
> That moncy lack, nor forts bc in rcpair.
>   (317–24)

This technique depends on pointing to that which ought to be visible but which in fact is not. Waller, as I tried earlier to show, was extraordinarily adroit at making references to absent items of very considerable importance. But the past master of the technique, in both senses of past, probably was Lucan, and a notable example is his description of a wedding ceremony as fully unfilled with pomp and circumstance as any wedding, even Anne Hyde's, could be. Duff, the Loeb translator, quotes Heitland's comment: "The marriage takes 22 lines, 17 of which describe the usages dispensed with by the pair, 3 those complied with; 2 are introductory."[8]

7. Dryden, unless otherwise indicated, is quoted from *The Poems*, ed. James Kinsley, 4 vols. (Oxford, 1958).
8. Duff, 82 (annotating Lucan, 2.354ff.). For Heitland, see *Pharsalia*, ed. C. E. Haskins, "with an introduction by W. E. Heitland" (London, 1897), lxxii;

The statistical count is accurate but scarcely conveys the magnitude of the effect:

> No Garlands gay the chearful Portal crown'd,
> Nor wooly Fillets wove the Posts around;
> No Genial Bed, with rich Embroidery grac'd,
> On Iv'ry Steps in lofty State was plac'd;
> No Hymeneal Torch preceding shone,
> No Matron put the tow'ry Frontlet on,
> Nor bad[e] her Feet the sacred Threshold shun.
> No yellow Veil was loosely thrown, to hide
> The rising Blushes of the trembling Bride;
> No glitt'ring Zone her flowing Garments bound,
> Nor sparkling Gems her Neck encompassed round;
> No silken Scarf, nor decent winding Lawn,
> Was o'er her naked Arms and Shoulders drawn.
>   (2.551–63)

"All these were absent." The terse summary is Duff's, and he translates the next verse with, "No members of the family and no kinsmen assembled." Edward Hyde and the Doge of Venice were not there either, possibly a mixed nonblessing. Eris, she of Discord and the delusory Golden Apple, also held aloof, and the Trojan War which stemmed from the wedding of Thetis, mother of Achilles, the wedding to which Eris was conspicuously not invited, was a conflict that therefore did not occur. What took place instead was the Roman civil war, but even though it definitely happened, the vacuity of its negative achievements was inevitable. As Lucan saw it, no victors could possibly emerge when Rome itself had been its own self-destructive enemy, and the ashen fruits of defeat were later symbolized by Nero, the reigning

---

Haskins, annotating 2.354, remarks that "throughout this passage the negative is carried on in Lucan's favorite manner." I usually quote Rowe's translation (see note 1 above) even though Marvell evidently adapted part of Thomas May's earlier translation for the Horatian ode on Cromwell. May's style is of an older kind than the one which Marvell was helping to create; the verse form at times mixes alternate quatrains with couplets. I later cite *Lucan's Pharsalia*, tr. Thomas May (London, 1631) in making a couple of points, but Rowe is usually the better choice as a less distant approximation of Marvell's language. "Tom May's Death," accepted as genuine by Donno but placed among "Poems of Doubtful Authorship" by Lord, satirizes the translator and possibly Lucan as well.

monarch of Lucan's day. Juvenal (1.30) later said it was hard *not* to scribble satire ("Difficile est Satyram non scribere"), and Lucan suggests that negative syntax can be the right language for nefarious times, even when a wedding ceremony is, or rather is not, taking place.

II
Accentuate the Negative

According to one rumor, perhaps still proverbial, Nero fiddled while Rome burned. The older version reported that he recited his own inept poetry to the accompaniment of the harp, and it was sometimes added that he himself had ordered the fire set to clear the way for a new Rome to be built in his own image. Lucan evidently was among the first to turn this belief to literary use; the work is now lost but mentioned by Statius in his poem for Lucan's birthday (*Silvae*, 2.7.60–61) as concerning how "the impious fires of the guilty monarch ranged the heights of Remus" (Loeb). According to a later rumor, reported in Burnet's *History of My Own Time*, Charles was "at supper with his mistress" on a similar fateful night. I borrow the quotation from Lord, who gives it in annotating "The Fourth Advice to a Painter":

> As Nero once, with harp in hand, survey'd
> His flaming Rome and, as that burn'd, he play'd,
> So our great Prince, when the Dutch fleet arriv'd,
> Saw his ships burn'd and, as they burn'd, he swiv'd.
> So kind he was in our extremest need,
> He would those flames extinguish with his seed.
> But against Fate all human aid is vain:
> His pr—— then prov'd as useless as his chain.
> (129–36)

Marvell bared a similar shaft in connection with Henry Jermyn, Earl of St. Albans. "Widely-rumored," to quote Lord yet again, to have had an "affair with Henrietta Maria . . . the Queen Mother," Jermyn also was an ineffective ambassador to France. "His breaches," according to the "Last Instructions," "were the instrument of peace";

> Who, if the French dispute his pow'r, from thence
> Can straight produce them a plenipotence.
> (42–44)

In addition to Jermyn's name, at least eighty others, some of them now so obscure as to defy confident annotation, are given in this poem, but infamous "Nero" is not one of them. This omission will or will not seem surprising depending in part on what one has been reading earlier, and since "The Fourth Advice" comes later than "The Last Instructions," some backtracking is in order.

"The Second Advice" opens with a scene in which Sir Thomas Allin, earlier praised toward the outset of Waller's poem (55–64), is "tilting at the coast of Spain" (8). In the scene which immediately follows, the Great Fire is fought with equal ineffectiveness, and two Londons, the ship and the city, become symbolic equivalents.

> Next, let the flaming *London* come in view,
> Like Nero's Rome, burnt to rebuild it new:
> What lesser sacrifice than this was meet
> To offer for the safety of the fleet?
>
> (13–16)

One of the measures actually taken to fight the fire was the setting of counterfires, apparently in much the way that forest fires sometimes are fought today. This passage nevertheless incensed the author (possibly Christopher Wase) of the "Divination," a work which, in Lord's words (54), "is one of the very few political satires which support the government in this period." Since the style of the poem often is elliptic or even cryptic, Lord's note should precede quotation of the lines themselves: "A man who could joke about the loss of the *London* by fire (cf. *Second Advice*, 13–18) would not, perhaps, go so far as to set fire to the City—fear would prevent him—yet he would be content to have the 'town in ashes sit' as a subject for his satires."

> Words prove the man: Caesar could not have wrote
> So well unless as well he could have fought.
> He that dares with a flaming *London* sport,
> If fear to act what fearless to report,
> Would not perhaps the city wrap in flames,
> Cover with flying boats the busy Thames,
> Yet be content a town in ashes sit
> To guide the pencil of his wanton wit.
>
> (193–200)

I cannot tell whether "Wase" was or was not remembering Lucan's contempt for a "Wretch" (Rowe, 2.135) who beheld "Proud *Carthage* in her Ruins" (143): "Amidst her Ashes pleas'd he sate him down, / And joy'd in the Destruction of the Town" (144–45). In any case, these ashes recur in variant forms. The latter part of "The Third Advice" is spoken by the coarse—but often admirably outspoken—seamstress whom General (now Admiral) Monck had married. Toward the end, however, she rises to the heights of a madly prescient Cassandra so that Troy and London burn almost simultaneously. Sackcloth is not mentioned, but ashes and mourning are among the details, and one of the things she wants to know is, "Who rais'd the fire?" (One of the rumored answers, I should say, though no annotation to that effect is given here, was "Roman Catholics.")

> Woe's me! what see I next? Alas, the fate
> I see of England and its utmost date!
> · · · · · · · · · · · · · · · · · ·
> War, fire, and plague against us all conspire;
> We the war, God the plague, who rais'd the fire?
> See how men all like ghosts, while London burns,
> Wander and each over his ashes mourns!
> · · · · · · · · · · · · · · · · · ·
> Curs'd be the man that first begot this war,
> In an ill hour, under a blazing star.
> · · · · · · · · · · · · · · · · · ·
> So of first Troy the angry gods unpaid
> Raz'd the foundations which themselves had laid.
>
> (413–28)

St. Paul's Cathedral was largely lost in the Great Fire, and Hyde bought up its stones for the finishing of Clarendon House. "Clarendon's House Warming" (the title itself is incendiary) points out that he thus had no need to bother about demolishing as well as selling "Dunkirk" or sending to "Tangier" when "he had nearer the stones of St. Paul's" (41–44). A satire of 1666, outside the painter series, was "J'ai vendu Dunkerque" (*State Poems*, 419). One of the boasts by the "Hyde" of this poem concerns foisting off his "putaine" of a daughter on York, a second is the sale to which the title (actually the first line) refers, and a third is pillaging "l'Église." The "House Warming," however, adds lament to satiric comment:

> Fond city, its rubbish and ruins that builds,
>   Like vain chemists, a flow'r from its ashes returning,

Your metropolis house is in St. James's fields,
And till there you remove, you shall never leave burning.
(93–96)

Satiric lines about the Fire certainly were circulated in London itself, and some of them may have penetrated to Wiltshire, where Dryden was writing *Annus Mirabilis*, the latter part of which addresses the disaster from a royalist point of view.[9] Dryden alleges that "a *Belgian* wind" fanned the flames (917); "The Ghosts of" past "Traitors" join "bold Fanatick Spectres" of religious dissenters "to rejoyce" (889–90). Dryden refers to Waller, but it is the poet's celebration of the rebuilding of St. Paul's by Charles I that is recalled. "Nor could thy Fabrick, *Paul*'s, defend thee long, . . . Though made immortal by a Poet's Song" (1097–99). The burning destruction of Troy, specifically its river, is also remembered. "Old Father *Thames* rais'd up his reverend head, / But fear'd the fate of *Simoeis* would return" (925–26). Dryden's editors note that Homer has Hephaistos burn "the Scamander or Xanthus, not the Sinois," but Dryden is preparing, well in advance, for the Thames to imitate the winding of the Sinois around Troy. "The silver *Thames*, her own domestick Floud, / Shall . . . often wind" (1189–91). That, however, is to occur after the fire is out, when the ashes, even more abundantly present in Dryden's poem than the others, may be swept and washed away. Dryden, evidently with very considerable basis in fact, stresses the vigorous personal activity of Charles and York in combating the fire and also indulges his fancy by letting us eavesdrop on the king as he prays for even diviner aid. Antiroyalist sentiment, in short, is deflected, returned with good measure, or turned topsy-turvy, but one idea was too insidious to include even if stood on its head. To say that Charles is not Nero nor was ever meant to be is a negation that simply must be avoided.

The received view of Marvell is that on this point he and Dryden, in a sense, agreed. Lord (163), proceeding on the premise that all three "Marvell" poems actually are by Marvell, comments that "in the second and third *Advices* and *Last Instructions* he had treated the King with respect, while laying the blame for administrative malfeasance

9. *Annus Mirabilis* is quoted from *The Works*, 1: *Poems 1649–1680*, ed. Edward Niles Hooker and H. T. Swedenberg (Berkeley and Los Angeles, 1956). The commentary appears to have been overlooked by those who discuss the painter poems but contains much useful information about the battle of Lowestoft, the Fire, theories of poems based on history as distinct from myth, the relationship between painting and poetry, and other relevant matters.

and misfeasance on his ministers and other officials." Two of these attributions, as noted earlier, are questionable, but attribution is not the issue here. Lord also says (xxxiv) that "it is only in the disenchantments of the 1670s that attacks on monarchy begin. Before that time nearly all the verse satirists seem to have accepted, or to have made a pretense of accepting, the institution of monarchy." This statement is unexceptionally worded, but Lord's next sentence, previously quoted for a different reason, is that "Charles . . . received nothing but panegyrics" at this time. This implicit equation of monarchy with the monarch himself looks questionable to me. Here is the place, therefore, to reintroduce Persius, Lucan's panegyric to Nero, and the question of Lucan's own pretense. I do not need to propose that Lucan must be a direct "source" for Marvell in the sense that Plutarch is a source for Shakespeare's Roman plays. The two situations are, if anything, upside-down versions of one another. Shakespeare borrowed large quantities of reworkable details without having to adopt Plutarch's biographical standards. Marvell, however, had plenty of details to work with already, perhaps too many for ready assimilation. Lucan was not needed for that kind of thing at all, but he was a famous precedent in some circles for a less-than-optimistic attitude toward timely events and their causes. Despite apparent anachronism, Pope's report on the shield was a very handy way to sketch that particular background, and Welwood's report is convenient for similar reasons here.

III
Lucan and Persius

Welwood's basic assumption is that the panegyric in Lucan's first book could not possibly have been written after Nero's true colors became visible.

> For it is not to be imagin'd, that a Man of *Lucan*'s Temper would flatter *Nero* in so gross a manner, . . . No! *Lucan*'s Soul seems to have been cast in another Mold: And he that durst, throughout the whole *Pharsalia*, espouse the Party of *Pompey*, and the Cause of *Rome* against *Caesar*, could never have stoop'd so vilely low, as to celebrate a Tyrant and a Monster, in such an open manner. (Preface, iii)

The point Welwood stresses, therefore, is that the adulation appears very early in the poem in lines which doubtless had already been written before "the Mask of Virtue" had been "thrown off." In the early years of Nero's reign, after all, the *"Poetical Incense"* could be "offer'd up" with exaggeration but without impropriety. This chronological solution presumes that Lucan's suicide, ordered by Nero himself, prevented authorial revision which Lucan certainly would have made had he lived to do it. Indeed, the principal reason why Welwood discounts even as he reports the fact that "some Commentators have judg'd that Compliment to *Nero* . . . to be meant Ironically" is that "if *Nero* had been as Wicked at that time, as he became afterwards, *Lucan's* Life had pay'd for his Irony." Otherwise, the argument on the other side is as fully consistent with Lucan's life, character, and poem as the "Commentators" have argued it to be.[10]

Lucan, biographically speaking, was early attracted both to rhetoric and the Stoics and "contracted an intimate Friendship with *Aulus Persius* the Satyrist" (ii), a poet of similar leanings. The two friends probably "diverted themselves often alone, at the Emperor's Expense," and Persius himself "went so far, that he dar'd to Attack openly some of *Nero's* Verses in his first Satyr" (iv). Whichever way the influence went, "if we consider *Lucan* critically, we shall find in him a strong Bent towards Satyr" (ii):

> His Manner, it's true, is more declamatory and diffuse then *Persius*: But Satyr is still in his View, and the whole *Pharsalia* appears to me a continued Invective against Ambition and unbounded Power.

The remark is accurate enough for Marvell's poem as well as Lucan's, unmistakably so in those parts of it which inveigh against Hyde

10. Hugo Grotius—or Huig van Groot (1583–1645), to use the Dutch form—is now the seventeenth-century commentator usually mentioned (cited by Duff in the Loeb, by C. E. Haskins, A. E. Housman, and other editors). Thomas Farnaby's edition (London, 1618) was for school use (it includes a marginal note, "per ironiam," for the passage on Nero). See also *Lucan's Pharsalia*, tr. Sir Arthur Gorges (London, 1614), 4: "This is meere Ironicall flattery"; "he teacheth Nero how he should governe, by an Imagination." George Granville (1667–1735), a determined royalist, said that "Lucan was a determined republican; no wonder he was a free thinker"; see his note to the "Essay" in verse, "Upon Unnatural Flights in Poetry," *The Poetical Works*, in *The Works of the British Poets*, ed. Robert Anderson (London, 1795), 7.714.

and his minions. At least one further fact, however, ought to reckoned with. Lucan and his uncle Seneca are linked by more than family ties, their involvement in The Conspiracy of Piso to topple Nero from the throne, and their subsequent suicides. Indeed, the important point of similarity, stylistically speaking, is the extraordinarily ornate rhetoric which both authors employ. The characters of Seneca's tragedies, however, are those of myth whereas Lucan's are historical personages of the recent past. "The *Pharsalia*," as Welwood points out (vii–viii), "is properly an Historical Heroick Poem, because the Subject is a known true Story." (This too is at least partly true of Marvell, of course.) As a result, the rhetoric often seems overblown though acceptable in the uncle but often needs to translated down, mentally if not verbally, in the nephew. This may be the case even for the passage of extraordinarily negative negation of marriage ceremonies quoted earlier, but it definitely is necessary elsewhere. Many lines, especially if taken without a surrounding context, seem so impossibly hyperbolic that temptation to invert apparent meaning is frequently strong even when one has every reason to think that the writing, by Lucan's own uncommon standards, was essentially straightforward. The apotheosis of Pompey at the beginning of the ninth book, presumably in structural counterbalance to the deification of Nero, is an obvious case in point. Lucan often has to be read, in fact, rather as Waller must be, even though their styles are for the most part quite different. After one has made every possible allowance for these facts, the passage offering "poetic incense" to Nero nonetheless shows how strong the case for irony can be. Despite the length, fairly extensive quotation (for the most part from Rowe) is necessary since length itself is significant to the effect.

Italy (1.67ff.) is a scene of "universal Desolation" because "Her impious Sons have her worst Foes surpass'd, / And *Roman* Hands have laid *Hesperia* waste. . . . But if our Fates severely have decreed / No way but this for *Nero* to succeed," then " 'Tis just . . . nor ought we to complain." Therefore (with a chain of concessives almost as strong as the negatives earlier quoted),

> Opprest with Death tho' dire *Pharsalia* groan,
> Tho' *Latian* Blood the *Punick* Ghosts attone;
> Tho' *Pompey*'s hapless Sons renew the War,
> And *Munda* view the slaughter'd Heaps from far;
> Tho' meagre Famine in *Perusia* reign,
> Tho *Mutina* with Battles fill the Plain;

> Tho *Leuca*'s Isle, and wide *Ambracia*'s Bay,
> Record the Rage of *Actium*'s fatal Day;
> Tho servile Hands are arm'd to Man the Fleet,
> And on *Sicilian* Seas the Navies meet;

In short, or rather at length, though all these things are true,

> All Crimes, all Horrours, we with Joy regard,
> Since thou, O *Caesar*, art the great Reward.

Anticipating Nero's death and the deification which then must surely occur, Lucan next supposes that "Heaven" will "resound with Joy" in the future fully as much as Rome will. Nero, it is possible to think, was not so interested in that future as Lucan appears to be. In May's translation, "Earth will not feare" this particular "change." Perhaps, therefore, one also may think that the alteration might be welcomed below as enthusiastically as it is to be on high. Heaven, at any rate, will acquiesce to whatever role Nero chooses to play. Rowe puts it this way:

> Whether great *Jove* resign supreme Command,
> And trust his Scepter to thy abler Hand;
> Or if thou chuse the Empire of the Day,
> And make the Sun's unwilling Steeds obey;
>
> . . . .
> Wher-e'er thou reign, with one consenting Voice,
> The Gods and Nature shall approve thy Choice.

Lucan requests that, wherever that "where" be, let it not be a place whence "thy blest Rays obliquely visit Rome." Oblique glances, like the dark clouds which momentarily follow, perhaps had already been too numerous. "Serene for ever be that azure Space"—there will be a good deal of it, of course, in between Nero and Rome—"No black'ning Clouds the purer Heav'n disgrace."

Whatever one makes of the preceding, the hope next expressed cannot be ironic in any way—except, quite obviously, that the hope also cannot become a reality, if ever, until after Nero's departure.

> Then shall Mankind consent in sweet Accord,
> And warring Nations sheath the wrathful Sword;
> Peace shall the World in friendly Leagues compose,
> And *Janus*' dreadful Gates for ever close.

And the conclusion, whether or not read through the eyes of a Persius, may seem to go more than a bit too far even for Lucan's frequently exaggerative technique. May's version makes this point more clearly than Rowe's, though paraphrasable content is the same in both.

> Oh be my god: If thou this breast inspire,
> *Phoebus* from *Cirrhaes* shades I'll not desire,
> Nor Nysa's *Bacchus, Caesar* can infuse
> Verse enough into a Roman muse.

"But to me you are divine already," as Duff more prosaically has it; "you alone are sufficient to give strength to a Roman bard."

This is, for lack of a better word, Lucan's invocation. It is placed early but not quite so early as the invocations of Homer and Virgil. One reason is that Lucan has already subverted Virgil's "Arms and the man I sing," the *Aeneid*'s first line, with his own beginning, "Of war I sing, war worse than civil" (Duff), and instead of inquiring, as Virgil does, whether divine minds might harbor so much wrath as to trouble Aeneas so greatly, Lucan has previously asked, "what madness was this, my countrymen, what fierce orgy of slaughter?" "To Nero," if one may invent a separate title for Lucan's lines, thus appears about as early as was practicable. One of the items being held back is a sea fight; reserved for the latter part of the third book, Lucan's account was clearly intended to outgo all previous ones, among other ways by depicting two losers and no winners. The picture given is truly ghastly to behold, and it was of no use to Waller, who sensibly bypassed it completely. What Lucan placed at the very end is a scene in which Caesar is granted—more accurately, threatened by—a terrifying vision of Pompey's decapitated head as a fearful portent of future events which lie beyond the scope of the poem; Lucan breaks off so abruptly that Caesar's reaction is not even indicated. Terminal position in Waller's poem is taken, of course, by "To the King," and subsequent imitations, even though they subvert Waller as Lucan subverts Virgil, perforce must do likewise.

Comparison of these various starting and stopping points can be instructive, I think, since it can point up reversal strategies of varying kinds, some of them extreme both in technique and implication. The envoy to the king at the ends of the satires is self-evidently the place to get to; it also will be the point at which to return to Lucan's not quite initial invocation of the monarch. The way to approach those passages, also self-evidently, is to look at what these poems start with. "Waller," it might be supposed, answers that question even before it can be asked, and that is quite true but yet only partly so. "Advice to a Painter" (whether "Second" or even "Fifth") is a title which certainly invokes Waller's own, but not necessarily for purposes of satiric inversion. Deuteronomy is not, after all, a satire. "The Second Advice," however, interposes between its title and its first line an epigraph from Lucan's friend Persius, and as soon as one sees *that*, the only question probably concerns what kind of satire is to follow. It is the second beginning which starts up a line of thought running underneath and counter to Waller's own.

IV
Displaced Beginnings and Replaced Painters

Taken from the fifth satire of Persius, the epigraph is given, first of all, to suggest the futility of depending on high-shoed landlubbers, especially when fighting the high-shoed Dutch. "The High-shoo'd Plowman," in Dryden's translation,

> shou'd he quit the Land,
> To take the Pilot's Rudder in his hand,
> Artless of Stars, and of the moving Sand,
> The Gods wou'd leave him to the Waves and Wind:
> And think all Shame was lost in Human-Kind.
> (5.147–51)

Casaubon's outline for this satire's structure reveals, however, that the entire second part develops "the Stoic paradox that without wisdom all are slaves and no one is free," or—as Dryden paraphrases in his headnote—"that the Wise or Virtuous Man is only Free; and that all Vicious Men, are Naturally Slaves."[11]

Exposition of this idea explicitly began at verse 73 (Dryden's line 100), and to the dialogue adopted for the satire as a whole there is now added occasional internal dialogue as well. The form enables the counterbalancing of contrasting viewpoints and hence is parallel to

11. Dryden, *The Works*, 4: *Poems 1693–1696*, ed. A. B. Chambers, William Frost, and Vinton A. Dearing (Berkeley and Los Angeles, 1974), 682 (for Casaubon), 323 (for Dryden). The introduction to Dryden's translations includes information about early editions of Persius and Casaubon's commentary.

the poising of two or more sets of instructions about how and what a painter is to paint. "Freedom" may indeed be the "first Delight of Humane Kind" (100), but definitions can be contradictory, and the disputants question one another's premises. Persius's opinion, in fact, is evidently that "Fond Notions of false Liberty" (131) are more prevalent than true ones. These issues need to be settled, in part because raising them after the boat has sailed (assuming, to break the chronology, that the Dutch have left any still afloat) may well be too late. "Resolved for Sea, the Slaves thy baggage pack" (206); but "What do'st thou make a-Shipboord? to what end?" (211). Persius ends with a ruffian's contempt for Greek philosophy, and Dryden's adaptation was written in the 1690s, but the lines, even so, are coincidentally appropriate. "The dull fat Captain," if told about True Liberty,

> Wou'd bellow out a Laugh, in a Base Note:
> And prize a hundred *Zeno*'s, just as much
> As a clipt Sixpence, or a Schilling *Dutch*.

Dispensing with epigraphs from a satire about true liberty and false, the "Third Advice" and "Last Instructions" charge into the related question of true and false pictures. In the "Advice," a "new painter" (2) is required, but it must not be Sir Peter Lely: "Lely's a Dutchman, danger in his art; / His pencils may intelligence impart" (3–4). Richard Gibson is called upon instead, presumably less dangerous, if for no other reason than because he was "three feet and ten inches" tall. The information is given by Fenton (xcii) in connection, of course, with one of Waller's poems. We are back to Waller once again, therefore, but not to the "Instructions." Instead, the poem is "Of the Marriage of the DWARFS." Fenton adds that "Mr. *Gibson*'s genius led him to painting," and that "His paintings in water-colors were well esteem'd: but, the copies he made of *Lely*'s portraits gain'd him the greatest reputation." Waller had found Gibson's marriage (to a lady "of an equal stature," according to Fenton) an occasion for ponderous puns—"Thrice happy is that humble pair / Beneath the level of all care"—but also one in which short appearance was accompanied by an enviable internal reality: "Secured in as high extreme, / As if the world held none but them." "The Third Advice" offers less to admire:

> Thou, Gibson, that among thy navy small
> Of marshall'd shells commandest admiral
> . . . .

> Come, mix thy water-colors and express,
> Drawing in little, how we do yet less.
>
> (5–10)

One of the realities in this case, however, is that Lely is to be displaced by a dwarf whose "greatest reputation" arose not from original work but from copying the work of the painter he is to replace. This procedure is singularly apt for a poem explicitly copying two prior productions–both Waller's original and its inverted duplication by "The Second"–but it may or may not have the advantage of trying to reduce problems of state to manageable proportions. As Gulliver learned, disputes between high heels and low heels are no less real for being small. We may also be moving deeper into Plato's cave and farther away from Truth by looking at a miniature copy of a bigger copy of that which is real. Lely's "pencils" are dangerous, after all, precisely because they "may intelligence impart" (4).

In "The Last Instructions," Marvell evidently dismisses the two preceding "Advice" poems as insufficient rough sketches for the finished picture. "After two sittings, now, our Lady State, / To end her picture, does the third time wait" (1–2). And now, instead of a dwarf copier, what is needed is a painter who can "paint without colors" (5). If the one being addressed can do that,

> Then 'tis right:
> For so we too without a fleet can fight.
> Or canst thou daub a sign-post, and that ill?
> 'Twill suit our great debauch and little skill.
>
> (5–8)

An unskilled dauber may have to be taken on as the best practical substitute, but the "ideal," presumably, is an inept artist using no colors to produce a blank canvas of uncreated nothingness. Nonpainting, however, has occasionally been successful in the past. Protogenes, in a tale told by Pliny, exemplified that fact long ago. Frustrated in trying to paint the froth on a dog's mouth, he hurled his sponge in anger at the canvas and was unexpectedly gratified by the result. Farley-Hills regards the story as "an early example of action painting," and Patterson sees in it "an anticipation of twentieth-century 'action' paintings," "a crazy celebration of the unintentional."[12]

---

12. David Farley-Hills, *"Last Instructions to a Painter,"* in *The Benevolence of Laughter* (London, 1974), 79; Patterson, 161.

The comparison at first seems apt, but the allusion to Pliny's story in "The Last Instructions" in fact supports the sometime fortuity not of action painting nor of any other kind but rather of no painting at all: "His anger reach'd that rage which pass'd his art," but "Chance finish'd that which art could but begin" (24–25). In this poem, moreover, the result of chance is a slaphappy grin on the painter which is matched by one on the canvas which shows the one on the dog being painted: As models (including "our Lady State") are said to "sit," so also Protogenes "sat smiling how his dog" (presumably both painted and real) "did grin" (26). Martial's poem (1.109) on a painter and his pet dog concludes with the idea that the living dog is not as like itself as the image of it is and that a viewer would suppose both to be real or both to be painted. Art and life thus become so confused as to be interchangeable and not recognizably distinct. If Marvell's version is action painting prefigured, it is also a prototypical shaggy-dog story which reduces both painter and model to the status of that which ought not be real even though they are.

Apelles, a painter mentioned much earlier because mentioned by Pope in discussing shields, appears here too.

> Ah, Painter, now could Alexander live,
> And this Campaspe thee, Apelles, give!
> (103–04)

One of the points here turns on the existence of Lely's painting, "Alexander and Campaspe"; Gibson, the dwarf, is still copying Lely who has been copying Apelles who had been copying life. Another point arises from Pliny's report that Apelles became enamored of his model, a Theban slave taken but also freed by Alexander; the painter marred his own work lest the sittings (theoretically three, as we learned at the outset of this poem) be ended. This tale also had a fortuitously happy end, at least for Apelles, when Alexander handed over (the theoretically free) Campaspe to the painter. Perhaps the lady was past caring at that point; Pliny doesn't say, and neither does Marvell. But at this stage, when theoretically good painters are producing spoiled pictures for devious motives, the reality mirrored by art and by artists is an ugly one, whatever the beauty of the model. In Marvell's case, moreover, the model itself is ugly since one of the paired lovers in the verse paragraph which Campaspe concludes is Lady Castlemaine, whose love affairs, including one with the king, were notorious. At this time of her life, what she needs is not so much to be painted as to paint herself up: "Paint Castlemaine in colors that will hold / (Her, not her picture, for she now grows old)" (79–80). The other of the pair is neither Alexander nor Apelles but a "footman" with "brawny thighs" (84–85) whom the painted-up Lady strips down.

In a world where appearance contradicts reality, when false or deliberately disfigured or no art at all is the very best kind for a perverse subject matter, where moral and mental topsy-turviness is rampant—in this kind of world, only an idiot would follow ancient custom in placing invocations at the beginning. Waller's placement, while in no sense irrelevant, in another sense is as fortuitously at hand as the painter's sponge turned out to be. Invocations simply have to be placed at the end for their own indecorous impropriety to make any (non)sense at all. These diverse preparations dependent on varying kinds of materials ought to arouse expectations of seeing something closer to photographic negatives of pictures instead of fine color prints at the end. Straight praise, after all, would be surprising and perhaps artistically corrupt in these circumstances. Since these poems are not nihilistic but merely negative, the possibility of color prints is not dismissed as a merely delusive mirage or a visionary pipe dream, but the suggestion made is that very meticulous darkroom work will be required to bring them to the light of day. "Pretense" is here a very big word, applicable to the pretentiously lofty model and to the pretended painter alike. True and false postures and the language appropriate for them, like so much else, are upside down. Marvell, toward the end of "The Last Instructions," refers to "false pretense" (969). Since pretense, by definition, is itself a false pose, a false pretense is either doubly false or a self-canceling replication which becomes unfalse. Unfalse, again by definition, affirms that which is true but does so by means of a double negative which blocks the mind from direct access. "False pretense" is less striking than "not immutable" (not-not-mutable) or "unimmortal" (not-not-mortal), the double negatives which Milton erects (*PL*, 5.234 and 10.611) as traffic signals to slow down and think, but the raveling or unraveling is not done quickly.

"False pretense" therefore will need to be reread in the context in which the phrase occurs, and an argument which maintained its own internal consistency would require examination of the ending of "The Last Instructions" as well as of "The Second Advice" and "The Third." I propose, however, to look at only the first two conclusions and reserve the third on the grounds that the consistency of "The Last Instructions" is more important than my own. "The Second Advice" and "The Third" are not to be written off, whoever the author was, but some sense of the wholeness of "The Last" really should be preserved.

V

Endings but Not Closures

Since "The Second Advice" could not end with a picture of "Madam l'Édificatresse" (340), splendid though that portrait be, it continues with an address to the "Imperial Prince, King of the seas and isles, / Dear object of our joys and Heaven's smiles" (345–46). The juxtaposition necessarily causes the prior elevation of the Madam to seem, retrospectively, even more absurd, and it probably lowers the prince as well. "Imperial" sway is attributed to him, but his smiles, while theoretically there, are not in fact visible. "Swarms of insects . . . / Our land devour and intercept our sun" (350). Devouring insects remind me of locusts, as in Deuteronomy 28.42: "All thy trees and fruit of thy land shall the locust consume." The fundamental geographical location, however, has to be Virgil's Crete as revisited by Waller. The fact is unmistakable from the allusions to Minos, to the labyrinthine maze, and to Daedalus, in lines earlier quoted for their send-up and put-down of Hyde and shortly to be requoted, in part, for what they suggest about Charles. A secondary context, especially for the "swarms," therefore may be the hives of Virgil's apiarist. That "industrious" keeper, to use Dryden's adjective (*Georgics*, 4.53), sees "a swarming Cloud arise, / That sweeps aloft, and darkens all the Skies" (83–84). The keeper allows the bees to swarm in mock-epic self-importance, but only for a time: "Two Pretenders oft for Empire strive," when "intestine Broils alarm the Hive" (92–93); "Yet all those dreadful deeds, this deadly fray, / A cast of scatter'd Dust will soon alay" (130–31).

> . . . when the swarms are eager of their play,
> And loathe their empty hives, and idly stray,
> Restrain the wanton fugitives, and take
> A timely care to bring the truants back.
> The task is easy—but to clip the wings
> Of their high-flying arbitrary kings.
>   (157–62)

The wings of Hyde, "who so near presumes" (357), need comparable treatment: "Melt the soft wax with which he imps his plumes" (358). So do the wings of others who, according to "The Last Instructions," "themselves would reign" (966). The question asked ("Second Advice," 351, 355, 357) is whether Charles is the Minos or the Sun to do it:

> Thou, like Jove's Minos, rul'st a greater Crete
>
> If thou art Minos, be a judge severe
>
> Or if our sun . . .

Lord says that the "lines give a satiric twist to Waller's comparison of Charles to Minos," but the statement misleads very seriously. The satiric twist certainly occurs, but Waller compared Charles not to Minos but to Jove, "Teaching the brawny Cyclops how to frame / His thunder mix'd with terror, wrath, and flame" (331–32). Fenton long ago spotted the passage in Virgil (8.431–32) which underlies Waller's line; it occurs as Jove descends to give directions for making the shield and as Vulcan is already at work forging Jove's thunderbolts. Vulcan's instructions to cease that work in order to begin the new task were earlier quoted for Marvell's lines about not building ships, but the immediately preceding part was skipped over as not needed then. It is helpful now not to stress again Waller's hyperbolic magnitude as he places the weapons of Jove in the hands of Charles, but to clarify what happens when Waller and Virgil are reworked in "The Second Advice." In forging the thunderbolts, the materials being reworked by Vulcan himself are these:

> Three Rays of writhen Rain, of Fire three more,
> Of winged *Southern* Winds and cloudy Store
> As many parts, the dreadful Mixture frame:
> And Fears are added, and avenging Flame.
> (Dryden, 8.567–70)

With a picture like this in the background, even a Minos-like Charles looks relatively small. When one adds a double dubiety—"If thou art Minos . . . Or if our sun"—he looks smaller still.

Before giving light, this "Imperial Prince" first needs to see more clearly himself: "having clear'd thine eyes, / Thy native sight will pierce within the skies" (361). Since the satirist has momentarily taken himself to Crete and is not entering Hell, all hope need not yet be abandoned. With restored sight, the king can

> view those kingdoms calm of joy and light,
> Where's universal triumph but not fight.
> (363–64)

This closely resembles what Lucan said of Nero, however, when the emperor ascended from a joyful earth to a joyful heaven.

> Then shall Mankind consent in sweet Accord,
> And warring Nations sheath the wrathful Sword;
> Peace shall the World in friendly Leagues compose,
> And *Janus'* dreadful Gates for ever close.

With or without irony, Lucan anticipated Nero's ascent to the heavens prior to the descent upon the world of the Peace just mentioned. "The Second Advice" envisages a reascent by Charles to his own divine origins: "Since both from Heav'n thy race and pow'r descend, / Rule by its pattern, there to reascend" (365–66). The syntax certainly seems to imply the phrase "in order to" (reascend); if so, then unless the prior condition is met ("Rule by its pattern"), the subsequent reascent in effect is ruled out. The next lines, the final couplet, look to be a threat rather than a compliment.

> Let justice only draw and battle cease;
> Kings are in war but cards: they're gods in peace.

Game cards with painted pictures of a king, even if a king of trumps, are poor substitutes for Jove. Pope's Belinda proves that much by winning the game but losing the lock. The king's divinity, moreover, is evidently not in fact divine except in a peace which at present cannot be found. Waller and Virgil cannot possibly be kept out of mind in reading this envoy. Perhaps Lucan can, but even if so, this conclusion does not offer straightforward praise.

Despite 436 lines in between, the envoy of "The Third Advice" picks up the envoy of the "Second." A repeated "Let . . . " construction is the syntactic pointer to that fact, possibly a needed one since the threat is now dropped though some of the earlier substance is repeated in varied form.

> Here needs no sword, no fleet, no foreign foe:
> Only let vice be damn'd and justice flow.
> Shake but like Jove thy locks divine and frown—
> The sceptre will suffice to guard thy crown.
>
> (443–46)

Another nice twist occurs since if vice is damned it must also be dammed, but with the kind of dam that lets justice flow. Waller is being retwisted at the same time since he had alleged, "Small were the worth of valor and of force, / If your high wisdom govern'd not their course" (323–24). In the new version, however, unless head-shaking and frowns prove effective, then England is in a perilous state. Many of the preceding 436 lines, after all, satirized the absence of a fleet due to improvident lack of frowning upon those who were not industrious keepers. At present there is scarcely anything *but* a sceptre to use for sword and fleet in case of need. A foreign foe certainly should be unnecessary as well as unwanted in any circumstances, but one of the reasons suggested here is that a domestic foe is already winning the war.

"The Third Advice" also says that the mask of pretense is being taken off. "What servants will conceal and couns'llors spare / To tell, the painter and the poet dare" (439–40). With a change of costume too fast to be seen, Charles is to slip into the role of Priam: "Hark to Cassandra's song ere Fate destroy, / By thy own navy's wooden horse, thy Troy" (447–48). This Cassandra began life in this poem as the seamstress married to the former Monck, now Albemarle. Earlier she tried hard to iron out her world and her husband and ennobled herself (though not her appearance) in the process of urging them to live up, not down, to her. She finally put on her own mask as Cassandra— "Alas, the fate / I see of England and its utmost date" (413–14)—and has not taken it off again. Her own, after all, continues to be appropriate in an uninverted way. This picture is becoming surrealistic with metamorphoses of Charles into Priam and of a seamstress into a duchess who rises to the occasion by becoming Cassandra. Enclosed in the rhyming of "destroy" and "Troy" is that which makes the verb applicable to the noun, and it is "thy"—Charles's, that is—"thy own navy's wooden horse" (448). Apelles, who could paint thunder, probably could also contrive a montage effect for the Trojan horse and one or more of England's sunk, burnt, or otherwise disabled ships, but I cannot imagine what it would look like. It would have to convey future defeat of the foe by means of a treacherous and dishonorable stratagem, indicate that Troy devised the instrument of its own downfall despite Homer's notion that its enemies did, and reflect not only the sane insanity of Cassandra but also the mad sanity of those who refused to hearken unto her. The couplet which inseparably rhymes "destroy" with "Troy" is not, however, the end of the verse paragraph. Tumult is everywhere, but shipwreck can be averted.

> Us our Apollo from the tumult's wave
> And gentle gales, though but in oars, will save.
> (449–50)

The poet doubtlessly hoped that Charles might yet save Troy and a small ship of state dependent on oars, not sails, but he did not end on this note either.

In the final verse paragraph, the satirist presents a metamorphosis of a metamorphosis by changing into "Philomel" (451) who herself had already been changed. She had no tongue wherewith to speak because her theoretical protector had first raped and then mutilated her. She created a speaking picture, true enough, but it was not a flattering one, and she regained her voice, but not until after an unsafe exit, effected by divine assistance, from this world into a different kind of reality beyond the customary reach of art or life. Accounts differ on the fate of Tereus the ravisher; he may have become the hoopoe bird or he may have destroyed himself. He did not become Jove.

> So Philomel her sad embroid'ry strung,
> And vocal silks tun'd with her needle's tongue.
> The picture dumb in colors loud reveal'd
> The tragedies of court so long conceal'd;
> But when restor'd to voice, increas'd with wings,
> To wood and groves, what once she painted, sings.

It's a lovely picture. In these circumstances its sadness is well-nigh indescribable.

6

Marvell and the Painters

I
Frameworks

Waller was not the only author of speaking pictures to suffer shrinkage under Marvell's scrutiny. William D'Avenant decided to keep the big picture in mind for *Gondibert* (1651) and thought he might as well throw in both the macrocosmic space of Homer's shield and the vast chronology on Virgil's, but since he further intended to improve upon the classics by replacing pagan fictions with biblical and historical truths, he threw out the original frame and placed his picture in a temple.[1]

This church is so ill-lit that "It seem'd the palace of eternal night" (2.6.12): "A winking lamp" (2.6.17), "This lamp was all, that here inform'd all eyes" (18). Through this pervasive gloom, "many figures by reflex were sent"—perhaps as if in some gigantic camera obscura— "instructive to the mind" (21). The painting itself presumably in-

---

1. *Gondibert* is quoted from *The Poetical Works of Sir William Davenant*, in *The Works of the British Poets*, ed. Robert Anderson (London, 1795), 4.786ff. Painter poems, including Waller's, those by "Marvell," and "The Last Instructions," are quoted from *Poems on Affairs of State*, ed. George deF. Lord, 1:1660–78 (New Haven and London, 1963). See also the References below.

cludes a wealth of pictorial details which are not, however, described; D'Avenant's purpose is to give instead a panoramic survey of momentous events without pausing to examine particulars. He begins at the beginning with "the great creation by bold pencils drawn" (53). Six days and seven quatrains later, "an universal herd appears" (60). "The painter now presents" Adam and Eve to our "view" (61), and, moving briskly along, "Deep into shades the painter leads them now; / To hide their future deeds" (65). "A noble painted vision next appears" (66); it is Noah's Ark cresting the Flood, and "This first redemption to another led" (71). Twelve lines later, in stanza 74, we come to the scene of the Ascension: "The holy mourners . . . did seem with him to rise; / So well the painter drew."

This whole picture has about as much depth to it as a thirty-five-millimeter transparency, though one has to admit that impasto technique would probably have wasted paint to no purpose; all that D'Avenant wants or here needs is a superficial effect. Before visiting the temple, we were in a library filled, apparently, with every book ever written, but there was no suggestion that we might want to read any of them. Marvell, however, was seldom content with the outsides of things and actually went into *Gondibert*'s temple to look at the picture inside. Seeking outlandish comparisons in "Upon Appleton House," he seeks help from Davenant: "Such, in the painted world, appeared / D'Avenant with the universal herd" (455–56). This irony blows up Davenant's own large canvas quite concisely, and Marvell next reduces matters with a microscope. "Such fleas, ere they approach the eye, / In multiplying glasses lie" (461–62). In "The Last Instructions," "a tall louse" (18) is looked at instead of a flea, but since the microscope continues to be useful, Marvell switches his attention to one of the enthusiasts for that kind of minute viewing.

The individual now named is Robert Hooke (1635–1703), whose claim to some renown both was and is quite reputable. He invented the spiral spring with which my venerable timepiece is wound and formulated Hooke's Law for strength of materials (stress is proportional to strain within the limits of elasticity). Since, however, satire holds little sacred, at times not even the divinity that doth hedge a king, Hooke is himself here reduced in size as having celebrated (and illustrated) many microscopic wonders, including the cellular structure of plants as well as details of fleas.[2]

2. Ernest B. Gilman calls attention to Hooke's microscope in *The Curious Perspective: Literary and Pictorial Wit in the Seventeenth Century* (New Haven and London, 1978), 46 and 208.

The name appears toward the beginning of "The Last Instructions," as Marvell is putting down groundwork for the painter's pictures to overlay: "But ere thou fall'st to work, first, Painter, see . . . " (3). This is where the ability to "paint without colors" (5) would come in handy. Or, failing that, the artist is to "daub a sign-post" (7) or "limn" not D'Avenant's darkened temple but "The aly-roof [that of an ale-house, i.e.] with snuff of candle dim" (9–10): a proper picture in a proper place to "serve this race of drunkards, pimps, and fools" (12).

> Or if to score out our compendious fame,
> With Hooke, then, through the microscope take aim.
>
> (15–16)

One of the major points here is that Marvell almost never relies on broad effects in this poem, differing quite markably and remarkably from D'Avenant in this respect among others. "Hooke" is his means, at this very early stage, of announcing that he intends to follow the more or less standard satiric procedure of subjecting human foibles to microscopic examination and that he intends to do so not in a general way but by citing nameable exemplifications from those still alive and breathing and soon to be breathing much harder. Hooke and his microscope serve another function which cannot be fully apparent until they are replaced, as the poem nears its end, by a telescope: "So his bold tube man to the sun appli'd" (949). The reference to sun "spots" in the following line indicates that the unnamed Galileo is as conspicuously absent at this late point as Hooke was earlier present. An optical framework is being completed, one which points up the need to apply Kent's advice, "See better, Lear" (1.1.159), especially since the telescope opens the concluding address "To the King." Also important is that Galileo's absence is one of the last examples of the fact that specificity regularly singles out reprehensible and/or risible individuals but not often laudable ones. The existence of praiseworthiness can be deduced at the level of conceptual thought, but it is rarely embodied. Indeed, the poem is densely populated by Iagos ("he that filches from me my good name . . . makes me poor indeed" [3.3.159–61]) but largely depopulated of individuals who really are like the one Iago pretends to be. When, therefore, an admirable exemplar appears two-thirds of the way through the poem, the vacant space on either side maximizes the effect and justifies the poet's belief and/or hope ("if my verse can propagate thy name" [694]) that genuine worth is truly memorable.

"Hooke" thus turns out to be a useful peg for two seemingly very different purposes, the topical excitement of a meaningful detail and the (necessarily partial) establishment of a broad framing device both for itself and the not-quite-innumerable particularities which are to follow. D'Avenant offers no useful models for this kind of technique, but Milton also looked at universal human history, and the eleventh book of *Paradise Lost*, however surprising that title may seem here, supplies a helpful parallel. In drawing it, however, I must avoid the appearance of trying to mislead others or of having fallen into a chronological trap myself. It is not always easy to remember that in 1667 Milton's epic was in print some months before Marvell can have finished writing "The Last Instructions," nor to recall that the epic, when Marvell first read it, was divided into ten books rather than twelve. That Marvell did read it is apparent from parodic allusions in "The Last Instructions" which are not unlike those made by Dryden in writing "MacFlecknoe." Lord and Patterson took notice of some evidence for this fact, and more will be given here quite shortly.[3] The immediate point to be conceded, however, is that "Book Eleven" did not exist in 1667 except as the first 901 lines of a longer book which was, in fact, Book 10. The fact, for very obvious reasons, must be noticed, but it is not important for my purposes. No matter which version they punctuate, lines 898–901 unmistakably give Michael a chance to catch his breath (and the reader to do likewise)

> Day and Night,
> Seed-time and Harvest, Heat and hoary Frost
> Shall hold thir course, till fire purge all things new,
> Both Heav'n and Earth, wherein the just shall dwell.[4]

This assurance of the regular starting and stopping of things is given by Michael to Adam because the universal Flood, described at much greater length than in D'Avenant, has seemed to bring almost everything to a full stop. The renewals of seed-time, harvest, and so on, signify and exemplify the specific meaning of the "triple-color'd Bow" (897) as God's "Cov'nant never to destroy / The Earth again by flood . . . nor Rain to drown the World" (892–94). These lines, whether or not a conclusion or merely a pause, require their reader to temporarily return to where the book began. Adam and Eve, about 900 lines earlier, are "in lowliest plight repentant . . . Praying" (1–2):

3. Lord, 106n; Annabel M. Patterson, *Marvell and the Civic Crown* (Princeton, 1978), 163.
4. Milton is quoted from *The Complete Poems and Major Prose*, ed. Merritt Y. Hughes (New York, 1957).

nor important less
Seem'd thir Petition, than when th' ancient Pair
In Fables old, less ancient yet than these,
Deucalion and chaste *Pyrrha* to restore
The Race of Mankind drown'd before the Shrine
Of *Themis* stood devout.

(9–14)

The book (or, in terms of the earlier version, a very large portion thereof) comes full circle from flood back to flood. Or rather it does not, since myth, the crooked image of truth, is the start whereas biblical Truth itself is the pausing place or stop. In between, of course, and this is the second point to be made, are numerous episodes, some of them invented by Milton and some based on biblical history, with chronological narrative sequence being the most basic link for them all.

If that is a fair description, admittedly superficial, of the shape of "Book 11," then Milton's procedure and Marvell's are similar for similar reasons. In writing "The Last Instructions," Marvell faced a difficulty which the author(s) of "The Second Advice" and the "Third"— possibly Marvell himself, of course—did not really have to worry about. "The Second Advice" simply must follow wherever Waller's footsteps lead; the poem is longer, 368 lines as against Waller's 336, but not by very much. The next poem expands to 456 lines and almost has to be a longer work because more history has already occurred in the intervening time, but it nonetheless is only half the length of "The Last Instructions." By the time Marvell finished "The Last Instructions," some of the early events no longer seemed worth detailed dissection because they and their badness had turned out to be merely preliminary to events so very much worse. The newer history itself is filled, however, with convoluted events and characters which cry aloud for pronounced denunciation so that Marvell has a fairly long poem to write if justice is to be done to the rampant injustice so corruptively at work. Episodic structure, basically chronological, can be controlled but not evaded entirely. With another brief sidestep over to Milton, one notices that Adam must witness all sorts of details, horrendous in this case, that D'Avenant could and did leave out. Adam is forced by Michael to view the murder of Abel by Cain, the terrors of the lazar house, the delusory bevy of fair women and amorous men, the plagues of humanity, and so on: "O Visions ill foreseen!" (763). The particularization of detail cannot be spared, however, since it is the indispensable support for the general indictment which Michael thereby approaches: "So all shall turn degenerate, all deprav'd, / Justice and Temperance, Truth and Faith forgot" (806–7). In "The Last Instructions," the situation is similar: Without the minute specificity of "Hooke" and all the rest, Marvell's sardonic outrage at similar degeneracy would seem excessive or even senseless.

Hooke, or rather his microscope, is like the flood of Deucalion and Pyrrha as a detail which also begins to establish a frame. At this point the analogy seems to have exhausted its usefulness or even to break asunder, but that is not so. In Milton, the progression is from myth to Truth but also from the murderous death of one person to nearly universal destruction; improvement occurs in one sense but degeneration in another. In Marvell, the telescope at the end does indeed allow one to see farther than the microscope and to behold that which has often been regarded as of much greater significance. This progression, more or less literally, is upward from earth to the heavens. The implications, however, are extremely disquieting to contemplate. The microscope and telescope are aimed in opposite directions at apparently very different objects, but gross details are imperceptible to the naked eye merely because they are too minutely small in the one case and too distantly high in the other. Fleas and fools, moreover, quite often have no more than nuisance value, whereas sunspots are alarming. With Hooke's lenses the painter can see "a tall louse" (18), identifiable in the text itself with "the new Comptroller" (17) and in the footnote with "the new Comptroller of the Household, Lord Clifford of Chudleigh." Through Galileo's lenses Marvell is looking at the king:

> And you, great Sir, that with him empire share,
> Sun of our world, as he the Charles is there.
> (955–56)

This flourish is wonderfully Walleresque, but its complimentary grace is undercut by the spots seen five lines earlier and by that which was seen with Hooke's help some 900 lines earlier. Lord Clifford, moreover, is a nonentity. Marvell points to his function as flunky in the text but not his nameable identity. "Clifford" is a detail not from the poem but from the note, though one recognizes the probability that this particular information might well have been superfluous in 1667. His personal insignificance becomes magnified, as it were, by the enormous number of individuals who are to be named and catalogued later on. "Charles," the name reserved for the end, towers above all the rest, but since he is the Comptroller who really counts, his sunspots are in no sense risible. Marvell is moving up, it is true, but the "progress" threatens to become disastrous.

This optical framing of names and functions obviously must remain incomplete until nearly the end of the poem, but it has been anticipated in at least two ways. First, Marvell name-drops quite shamelessly throughout the poem; he normally calls the roll not only of malfeasances but of malefactors and invites us to watch them squirm under a dissecting glass. Nor are these individuals mentioned casually or offhandedly. Ruyter, the Dutch admiral, makes a brief sneaky appearance at line 437 before sailing up the Thames not quite a hundred lines later. Waller rises in line 263 (to be put down, naturally), and he is fittingly preceded by Higgons, Waller's friend and a source for the painter device, in line 197. Hyde, the Lord Chancellor, is never far away, not nearly far enough in Marvell's opinion, and can often be glimpsed as he furtively hatches vain empires even though he wears many faces. A second anticipatory device depends on the fact that these and other figures are often grouped into scenes, sometimes plotting away in a corner of the picture, sometimes striking a public pose, and these scenes are compositionally arranged in such a way that triptychs become numerous. Once that becomes evident, then two leaves or panels alert us to the existence of a third even when we do not yet see it and can merely guess what it will actually look like when it does appear.

The painter is given three figures to paint first; next, the two parliamentary parties (of the Court and of the Country) gyrate around the Speaker; in one scene, Hyde is flanked by the Archbishop of Canterbury and Baptist May. Even that "louse" unbiologically mates at a distance with ants (the "Myrmidons" [488]) called into existence by Hyde and with the "squatted toad" (877) which Turnor, the Speaker, is revealed to be. Tripartite substructures are by no means the only kind constructed by Marvell, but there are enough of them to establish organizational context for expectable triplicity; when telescopic sight finally supplements microscopic and unaided viewing, the result is or should be a sense of fulfillment more than of total surprise. The immediately subsequent envoy "To the King"—not because of an absolute necessity but also not unexpectably—divides into three distinguishable parts as well; one of the texts, to mention at this point a single piece of suggestive evidence for the fact, presents the envoy in the form of three verse paragraphs.[5]

To see how these substructures establish expectation, one pretty

5. The three-paragraph text is Lord's, in *State Poems*. In Lord's edition of Marvell the lines are divided into six verse paragraphs; in Donno's, into five. The same basic copy text appears to have been used in each case.

well has to start at the place where Marvell begins to establish them; variations on a theme presuppose the theme, after all. The initial portraits for the painter to paint are of (Henry Jermyn, Earl of) "St. Albans," of (Anne, née Hyde) "her Highness" the Duchess of York, and of (Barbara Villiers, Countess of) "Castlemaine."

> (1) Paint then St. Albans full of soup and gold (29).
>
> (2) Paint then again her Highness to the life (49).
>
> (3) Paint Castlemaine in colors that will hold (79).
>
> (4) Draw next a pair of tables op'ning, then
> The House of Commons clatt'ring like the men.
>
> (105–6)

I quote four "openings" because the fourth clearly contrasts with and makes more visible the parallelism of those which precede: individuals against a pair of tables and a House; titles against Commons; thrice-given "Paint" against "Draw" (even though the words themselves presumably denote the same activity). In line 29, which introduces "St. Albans," the word "then" means "therefore" (the situation is as I, the poet, have indicated in the first verse paragraph; therefore paint St. Albans . . .). In line 49, the word continues to mean "therefore" but also signifies "yet" or "still" (therefore paint her yet again); the Duchess has been painted with some regularity, after all, in Waller's poem and in earlier answers to it. There is no "then" in line 79; Marvell often distorts his verse (a splendid example will be cited fairly soon), but it is too early at this point to insert "then then then" or "again still therefore then yet" (or whatever). The painter has enough of a problem merely finding durable enough colors to overlay the eroding cosmetics on Castlemaine's aging face without worrying about how many times she's been painted and/or been painting herself for whatever sexually reprehensible reasons. He needs, in fact, to get some paint down fast because at this very moment, she is in hot pursuit of what is inside "her lackey's drawers, as he ran" (81). St. Albans, as noted in the preceding chapter, is famous for the "plenipotence" (44) producible from his "breeches" (42), and the Duchess "naked can Arch'medes' self put down" (51) or, more wonderful still, "after childbirth . . . renew a maid" (54). As Chernaik rightly says, "Reality could hardly appear more base than in the character sketches of the Earl of St Albans, the Duchess of York, and the Countess of Castlemaine near the beginning of the poem."[6] Since allegory, however, can be baser still, one might add that the sketches portray, though not to the exclusion of all else, a three-headed and -titled sexual monster whose counterpart is to be the monstrosity known as the Excise Bill.

But to have a bill, one must first have a Parliament. "Next draw" the tables and the House, therefore—the fourth "opening" quoted above. "Describe the Court" Party "and Country" (107) drawn up like opposing (not chess- but) backgammon men; "the cheat Turnor," otherwise known as the Speaker of the House, "must throw" the dice (114) which determines the moves. "Excise," the bill to be moved, is "a monster worse than e're before / Frighted the midwife and the mother tore" (131–32). In lines 142–46, we learn that "Black [John] Birch," the father, was "of his brat enamour'd" and "Bugger'd in incest with the mongrel beast." Sordid sexuality thus recurs, but Milton's hellish Trinity of Satan, Sin, and Death have more horribly replaced Marvell's three earlier portraits for mock-epic purposes. Excise also presumably has 497 more heads than the composite sexual amalgam of Albans-Duchess-Castlemain since "A thousand hands she has and thousand eyes . . . With hundred rows of teeth" (133–35). She is thus equipped, in round numbers, very much like the collective body of the House with its MPs—except, obviously, for (Sir Henry) "Wood" (162) who resembles, however improbably, "Headless St. Dennis" (167). Marvell specifically compares Excise to the "cassowar" (136) or cassowary bird; it is omnivorous (as Margoliouth points out) and has as a distinguishing feature a "crown upon its head" (as Chambers's *Cyclopaedia* puts it).[7]

I think I also see here the Hydra, "a terrible monster, born of Typhon and Echidne" (to quote Chambers again, the background reference being to Hesiod); it gave Heracles a battle, one recalls, because two heads grew to replace each one lopped off. "Excise" at length "receives a total rout" (306), or that seems to be the case. What in fact occurs is that monstrosity is driven underground only to pop up again in transmogrified fashion with numerous new heads. The House decides "to land tax from the excise turn round" (331). It also takes up a bill of major economic importance which would ban the import of cattle from Ireland. Supported by the Court side, it is seen in monstrous

6. Warren L. Chernaik, *The Poet's Time: Politics and Religion in the Work of Andrew Marvell* (Cambridge, 1983), 202.

7. E. Chambers, *Cyclopaedia: Or, An Universal Dictionary . . . with the Supplement . . . by Abraham Reese*, 4 vols. (London, 1791).

terms by Country: "The Irish herd is now let loose and comes / By millions over, not by hecatombs" (351–52). One of Virgil's monsters was Fama or Rumor (*Aeneid*, 4.173–97), "A monstrous Fantom, horrible and vast" in Dryden's translation (4.260).[8] Dryden exaggerates Virgil's numbers in a triplet (with a hexameter further stretching the third line), which nonetheless is worth quoting: "Millions of opening Mouths to Fame belong; / And ev'ry Mouth is furnish'd with a Tongue: / And round with list'ning Ears the flying Plague is hung" (263–65). Fama is on the loose in Marvell's poem also: "Each day they bring the tale," in this particular case only "too true" (315); "But a fresh news the great designment nips" (397); "Fresh messengers still the sad news assure" (411).

The worst beast, however, is Hyde himself, "Blither than the hare that hath escaped the hounds" (335) and more "renewed" (338) than "decrepit Aeson, hash'd and stew'd" (337). Aeson, the father of Jason, was given a curative potion of bull's blood by Medea; Hyde's secretary was John Bulteel; "the troop of Clarendon," mentioned as being "all full" (177), consists of "Haters of fowl, to teal [duck, that is] preferring bull" (178). Hyde and his followers evidently consume themselves but somehow bloat rather than waste away, and Excise, like Milton's Sin and Death, manages to keep breeding after its own apparent demise.

The total rout of the monster, which unfortunately did not in fact occur in line 306, brings Marvell to a turning point a bit less than one-third of the way through the poem. All sorts of triads, both major and minor, fill parts of the remaining two-thirds and function, in part, as reminders of earlier portraits. Among the Lords, Hyde is to confront Buckingham ("Blasted with lightning, struck with thunder" [358]); among the House, "Next the twelve Commons" ("condemn'd to groan" [359]) are taken on. Parliament is prorogued (336), reprorogued (825–26), and reprorogued again (861).

> Captain, lieutenant, ensign, all make haste
> Ere in the fi'ry furnace they be cast.
> Three children tall, unsing'd, away they row,
> Like Shadrack, Meshack, and Abednego.
>   (645–48)

The "giant Mordaunt" (260)—sometimes known as John, Viscount Mordaunt but here another monster both dreaded and morally

8. Dryden is quoted from *The Poems*, ed. James Kinsley, 4 vols. (Oxford, 1958).

dreadful—later reappears "within his castle tow'r" to "Imprison parents and the child deflow'r" (349–50) and later still helps "mure up the gates" (420) of Windsor. Hyde, to repeat a point for a reason which will be obvious, makes up a Trinity with the Archbishop (811) and Baptist May (805), and there is a progression all the way up to three kings and all the way down to unholy ghosts and Charles's ghastly nightmares of regicide:

> While the pale ghosts his eye does fix'd admire
> Of grandsire Harry and of Charles his sire.
> Harry sits down, and in his open side
> The grisly wound reveals of which he di'd,
> And ghastly Charles, turning his collar low,
> The purple thread about his neck does show.
>
> (917–22)

Shakespeare's Richard III—this may or may not be coincidental—was visited by ghosts of murder victims on Bosworth Field. They are clearly visible to him and to the audience, but Richard internalizes them; not Fama, but "My conscience hath a thousand several tongues, / And every tongue brings in a several tale, / And every tale condemns me for a villain" (5.3.193–95). Charles, at any rate, "The wondrous night . . . revolves / And rising straight on Hyde's disgrace resolves" (925–96).

In Charles's nightmare, the triptych actually is of two kinds. In "a dead shade of night" (885), grandsire, father, and son cannot be easily separated even though two of them are deceased, but it nonetheless is true that the two ghosts are linked to another "airy picture" (904), an elusive phantasm in feminine form whom the king "divin'd" to be "England or the Peace" (906). This picture exemplifies the fact that triads are sometimes stretched into a quadrangular shape or into pentagons, and that simple numbers can and do give way to irregular multiplicities which could be added up if there were reason to do so. There can be no reason, however, why trinities, including Satanic versions, should preclude other compositional blocks in the picture, especially when three has been well established as a kind of recurrent norm (or even abnormality) against which other numbers can be compared. Doubleness, to engage in subtraction, also frequently appears, partly because duplicity is almost everywhere to be found. Saint Albans, subject of the very first portrait, is both "the new court's pattern" and "stallion of the old. / Him neither wit nor courage did exalt" (30–31). Having affirmed one doubleness and denied a second, Marvell next introduces a third factor applicable to both of the preceding: "But Fortune chose him for her pleasure salt" (32). A grimly humorous quadrangle emerges in a variation on Satan's determination to continue to fight: "What though the field be lost? All is not lost" (*PL*, 1.105–6), especially not "courage never to submit or yield" (108). Therefore, "We may with more successful hope resolve / To wage by force or guile eternal War" (120–21). "What matter where, if I be still the same" (256)? In the mock-epic version (307–10),

> Broken in courage, yet the men the same,
> Resolve henceforth upon their other game:
> Where force had fail'd with strategem to play
> And what haste lost recover with delay.

Haste led to force which now gives way to guileful stratagem, and a fourth factor therefore becomes indispensable to negate the effect of the first two. It consists, rather splendidly, of trying hard to do nothing.

Saint Albans himself, summoned back from his first appearance at line 29, now reappears in the next couplet with a duplicated "to," a "too," and two versions of *soo*: "St. Albans straight is sent *to to* forbear, / Lest the sure peace, for*soo*th, *too soo*n appear" (311–12). He will pop up twice more (at lines 365 and 427) before we have seen the last of him. The picture of Turnor, the Speaker, looks blacker with each repeated glance, and the first four—at lines 114, 236, 837 (where he has resorted to appearing "With face new bleach'd, smoothen'd and stiff with starch" [838]), and 851 ("Turnor's dress'd" [854]—prepare for the full-dress portrait which begins at line 863: "Dear Painter, draw this Speaker to the foot." Like the traditional *blazon* of a poet's beautiful beloved, this one starts at the top ("Bright hair, fair face, obscure and dull of head" [867]) and works its way down, but his foot is never actually reached because the belly and other parts immediately below take Turnor down to the "urinal" (880) and to his "Sergeant's wife," a "Pertelotte" to his unChaucerian "Chanticleer" (883–84). This turns out to be the penultimate picture. The next verse paragraph begins, "Paint last the King and a dead shade of night." Chaunticleer is replaced by Charles, and Pertelotte by "the Peace." Though "Naked as born" (893) and in the king's eyes a "coy vision" (901), and though the king "wonder'd first, then piti'd, then he lov'd" (900), sexual excitement quickly shrivels: he "soon shrunk back, chill'd with her touch so cold" (903).

II
Proper (and Improper) Names

Earl Miner, bypassing the substructures just noticed, argues that this entire poem is triadic in structure.

> [Marvell's] structural approach . . . took the form of three central narrative sections representing various confrontations, with preceding and closing sections of portraits of members of the Court. He begins with an attack on prominent members of the Court, who are pictured as debauched and politically corrupt (ll. 1–104). He closes with the satiric picture of the king attempting to force the favors of his naked vision (ll. 885–948). (To this is added a coda, "To the King" [ll. 949–90], in which the painter device is not employed.) In between he presents three narratives, or representations of action and confrontation: that of the tumultuous sitting of Parliament in the Autumn of 1666 (ll. 105–396); that of the Court's seeking frantically to obtain peace (ll. 397–522); and that of the Dutch invasion of the Thames and the Medway in the summer of 1667.[9]

The "coda" that must be added and the quadrangles and pentangles noticed above may be cause for less than total confidence on this matter, but in any case, room must be found to accommodate much larger numbers than any of those yet mentioned. The really big ones, in overtly terrorizing form, are exemplifed, of course, by the Excise monster with its thousand hands and thousand eyes and hundred rows of teeth. But Parliament, its internally divided foe and friend, is also characterized by its own swollen bulk and the multiplicity of its members. Homer catalogued ships, a listing that might have been satirically useful in "The Second Advice" or "The Third" had space and Waller's prior design permitted its inclusion. Marvell certainly could have converted that epic device into mock-epic form by further expanding one of his triplicities at line 697 or so.

> Each doleful day still with fresh loss returns:
> The *Loyal London* now a third time burns,

---

9. "The 'Poetic Picture, Painted Poetry' of *The Last Instructions to a Painter*," in *Andrew Marvell: A Collection of Critical Essays*, ed. George deF. Lord (Englewood Cliffs, NJ, 1968), 166–67; rpt. from *MP*, 63 (1966): 288–94.

> And the true *Royal Oak* and *Royal James*,
> Alli'd in fate, increase with theirs her flames.
> Of all our navy none should now survive,
> But that the ships themselves were taught to dive,
> And the kind river in its creek them hides,
> Fraughting their pierced keels with oozy tides.
>   (697–704)

He chose, however, to adopt an elegiac tone of lament for three burnings and three ships to counterpoint a sardonic tone for the culpable fools on shore, where "Confusion, folly, treach'ry, fear, neglect" (610) are the five negative factors in noncontrol. One reason is to avoid shattering the mood of the preceding scene, the death of Douglas, "the valiant Scot" (696), the only personage in the entire poem (I think this statement is true) who shines forth, immaculately unblemished in character, admirable while living and to be admired in death. Douglas must be returned to, but a second reason why Marvell dispensed with Homer's ships is that he had already imitated Milton's catalogue of demonic fallen angels.

"Say, Muse," Milton commands (1.376), "thir Names then known, who first, who last." This command itself varies an earlier one: "Say first, for Heav'n hides nothing from thy view / Nor the deep Tract of Hell" (27–28); the varied repetition occurs because the new inhabitants of the deep tract are now to be listed. "First *Moloch*" (392), "Next *Chemos*" (406), "*Thammuz* came next behind" (446), and so the call rolls on until "*Belial* came last" (490). This also is Marvell's technique when Parliament is called, but whether Milton's fallen angels or Marvell's tottering humans are worse is a question not worth asking. "Say, Muse," Marvell commands, "for nothing can escape thy sight" (147). "Of early wittals" (wittols [< "wetewolds"], cuckolds) "first the troop march'd in" (151). "Court officers . . . the next place took" (169). "Next the lawyers' mercenary band appear" (185). "Last then but one, Powell, that could not ride" (213). And, "The lords' sons, last, all these did reinforce" (217). "For never since created man, / Met such imbodied force, as nam'd with these / Could merit more than that small infantry . . ." This, as it happens, is *Milton*'s summary statement (573–75), and it certainly magnifies. But then, so in its own way does Marvell's:

> Never before, nor since, an host so steel'd
> Troop'd on to muster in the Tothill Field.
>   (219–20)

In both poems, these catalogues array the seemingly irresistible force of numbers; "But strength at last still under number bows," as Marvell puts it (277). What is unclear (to me, at least) is how readily one is supposed to recognize and respond to individual names in the two torrents which roll overwhelmingly on. These places are, thank goodness, among those where editorial footnotes are most abundant, and the notes show, by and large, with what meticulous care both Milton and Marvell selected their examples. I sometimes think, however, that if instant recognition of "Rimmon" (467), much less "Azazel" (534), was a prerequisite for entry into Milton's "fit audience . . . though few" (7.31), then it must always have been a small dress circle indeed. Pepys certainly would have pounced on Marvell's "Garr'way" (298) since, as Lord's note informs us, his accounts were examined by William Garraway, member for Chichester, on 3 October 1666. Marvell's editors, however, give us inconsistent assessments of what the names are specifically meant to suggest. Lord relies on Evelyn's diary for the statement that "Fox" (170) made a fortune, "honestly got and unenvied." Donno explains in a note to lines 105–6 that, "In the following identifications of the Members of Parliament, information derives, where possible, from the *Flagellum Parliamentarium*, a satirical roll call of 178 MPs compiled in 1671–72 and formerly attributed to Marvell." In consequence, "Fox" now is noteworthy not for an honest and unenvied fortune but for having "cheated £100,000." In the poem, "Court officers . . . follow'd Fox, but with disdainful look" (169–70). So far, so bad, but is it disdain for honesty or for fraud? Pepys probably knew one way or the other or would have gossiped around till he found out what the current opinion of Fox was rumored to be. Rimmon can be looked up in 2 Kings 5.18, for example (though not in 16.10, the reference mistakenly given by Hughes), or Acts 5.43 ("the tabernacle of Moloch, and the star of your god Remphan"); Azazel is the word translated by scapegoat in Leviticus 16.8, 10, and 26 (though not in verse 20, the one cited by Hughes, where the word is "sair," a "kid"). From those starting points, one could easily begin a search through biblical commentaries for interpretive aid. Since, however, getting behind Lord and Donno, or rather on the back side of Evelyn and the *Flagellum* does not seem feasible, "Fox," the name as given by the poem and not the man himself, probably has to be dealt with in its own terms. In some cases, at least, this procedure almost certainly is a necessity; "Talbot" (206), for example, was the name of three MP's, not one, and the *Flagellum* mentions two of them with equal disparagement: One was "a great cheat" and the other "a great cheater."

Chernaik (204–5) addressed this problem by enlisting help as found in one of the appendixes to *The Dunciad*. Since I need it too, I shall requote some of the remark which Chernaik cites but omit a part of it and also start a little earlier as well as go beyond the point where Chernaik left off. "The Publisher to the Reader" remarks that speedy publication seemed desirable "since those *Names* which are [the poem's] chief ornaments, die off daily so fast, as must render it too soon unintelligible." On the other hand,

> . . . whoever will consider the Unity of the whole design, will be sensible, that the *Poem was not made for these Authors, but these Authors for the Poem*: . . . I would not have the reader too much troubled or anxious, if he cannot *decypher* [italics added] them; since when he shall have found them out, he will probably know no more of the Persons than before.
>   Yet we judg'd it better to preserve them as they are, than to change them for *fictitious names*, . . . Had the Hero, for instance, been called *Codrus*, how many would have affirmed him to be Mr. *W*——Mr. *D*——Sir *R*——*B*——, &c. but now, all that unjust scandal is saved, by calling him *Theobald*, which by good luck happens to be the name of a real person.[10]

Marvell's characters, with similar satiric good luck, also have real names behind which there was no hiding and concerning whom, in some cases, there is no possibility of confusion about what their deficiencies actually were. "Theobald," however, really *is* Codrus, at least to some extent; the fiction has come alive or been incarnated in a specific renameable way. Looked at from the other side of the chronology, behind Theobald, despite or rather because of his palpable reality, stands Codrus, and behind Marvell's specificity stand Vice figures who are not fictional, or at least not imaginary, but grimly real.

From this point of view, the diary to cite for information about "Fox" is not Evelyn's (Lord's source) but Pepys's for 23 April 1661 (ironically, the Coronation Day of Charles): "If ever I was foxed it was now." And the *Flagellum's* information that "Fox" was a cheat has to be true even if it is totally inaccurate. Margoliouth said there were more than eighty names in the poem, a figure that Lord and Donno have subsequently taken on trust, but the only way to arrive at so

10. *The Poems*, 5: *The Dunciad*, 2d ed., ed. James Sutherland (London and New Haven, 1953), 203, 205–6.

low a total is by enumerating people rather than naming them so that "Turnor," for example, is counted only once despite recurrent use. I cannot see on what principle an accurate arithmetic could be based and doubt that Marvell had one in mind. The number of *individuals* is not so staggering as the 178 found by Donno in the *Flagellum* or, to cite an unsatiric counterpart, the enormously long list of the names of the Roman consuls which Lemprière supplies (I haven't counted these either, but they require twenty-two-and-a-half columns with approximately thirty names per column, depending on how many details are given for each name).[11] Unable to find a rationale in arithmetic, I have looked for an alternative principle of selection whereby to choose illustrative examples of Marvell's manipulative techniques. Since Marvell refers to "name" in three cases and in one of them adds the word "cypher," my choices will not, I hope, seem entirely arbitrary.

"Two letters next unto Breda are sent," one of them "in cypher" (449–50).

> The first instructs our (verse the name abhors)
> Plenipotentiary ambassadors
> To prove by Scripture treaty docs imply
> Cessation, as the look adultery,
> And that by law of arms, in martial strife,
> Who yields his sword has title to his life.
> Presbyter Holles the first point should clear,
> The second Coventry the Cavalier.
>
> (451–58)

"Hector Harry" (a.k.a. Henry *Coventry*) first shot out of sight in line 228, at that time accompanied by "Will the Wit" (his brother William), both eager "to fight a battle from all gunshot free" (230). At his next appearance, not only has brother Will disappeared but Henry's own nickname has been lost: He is one of the "two ambassadors" who "Chain'd together . . . Like slaves shall beg for peace at Holland's doors" (369–70). "Ambassadors" reappears as the rhyme in 452, and the second slave has to be Denzil *Holles* even though he is not named "Presbyter Holles" until line 457. "Coventry" recurs in 928 and 934, but it is William bobbing up again so that both Harry and Holles have now dropped out. This is not so much shuttle diplomacy as revolving-

---

11. *Lemprière's Classical Dictionary* (London, 1984; 1st ed., 1788), s.v. "Consul."

door chicanery. Letters are in cypher, the Bible is misread, the law of arms willfully distorted, cavalier and presbyter pervertedly paired. There is a peculiar kind of rhyme to it all: in *hors* and *dors* and words suggested by those suffixes; in the eye-rhyme and corrupt infolding ("im-plico") of im*ply*-adult*ery*; in the yoking of life with strife and clear with "c[ava]lier" or "C/lier." To say that there is *neither* rhyme nor reason to it all would therefore be partly untrue. With a fine distortion of verse itself, "Verse" abhors "plenipotentiary ambassadors" partly because only two words, neither of which means what it says, wipe out a whole line. "Verse" itself has to be tucked inside a parenthesis (which is metrically present even if the visible typography has been added by printer and/or editor). "Name" must also be folded in: Outside the verse and the parenthesis it keeps changing or even vanishing. Vice, of course, alters its appearance but, far from disappearing, its reality is the stable substance underlying Protean shiftiness.

"Pett," in strong constrast, is a name with commendable substance to it, possibly in fact and certainly in the poem, but it is subjected to a vicious attack which forces it into unnatural configurations. In this case, at least part of the true history evidently is both simple and unambiguously unchangeable.[12] Peter Pett "superintended the dockyard at Chatham." He was "to bear all the blame" and was "arraigned" but "set free on bail of £5000." "Marvell spoke" (in Parliament, that is, representing Hull) "against sending him to the Tower." "Impeachment proceedings were begun . . . but the matter was dropped." Peter Pett sounds much less capacious than plenipotentiary ambassadors, but since "His name alone seems fit to answer all" (768), it turned out to be stretchable.

> Whose counsel first did this mad war beget?
> Who all commands sold through the navy? *Pett.*
>
> . . . .

12. The quotations which immediately follow are from Lord's note to line 767. Pepys, however, gives a mixed account of the affair. On 19 June 1667, he wrote, "his faults to me seem only great omissions," and he adds, "Lord Arlington and Coventry were very severe against him; the former saying that, if he was not guilty, the world would think them all guilty." (Wheatley comments, "Pett was made a scapegoat. This is confirmed by Marvell." He next quotes from "The Last Instructions.") On 13 June, however, Pepys had been of the opinion that "Pett should have carried up higher by our several orders, and deserves, therefore, to be hanged for not doing it."

> Who the Dutch fleet with storms disabl'd met,
> And, rifling prizes, them neglected? *Pett.*
>
> . . . .
>
> Who all our seamen cheated of their debt,
> And all our prizes who did swallow? *Pett.*
> Who did advise no navy out to set,
> And who the forts left unrepaired? *Pett.*
> (769–70, 773–74, 777–80)

This impressive string of accomplishments couldn't possibly be managed single-handedly or -namedly. "Peter" is never mentioned, but the
rhythm of the metrics fills up the gap: first with "navy Pett" and then
with "neglected," "swallow," and "unrepairèd Pett." These are not
proper Christian names at all, however, and so—in lines deliberately
not quoted above—he becomes "Bergen Pett:"

> Who would not follow when the Dutch were beat?
> Who treated out the time at Bergen? *Pett.*
> (771–72)

Distortion of Pett's last name—or of "beat" into "bet"—is here required, but blamers of scapegoats are too busy distorting characters
and facts to let that stop them. Pett's first name is to become mis-
pronouncedly and polysyllabically worse, a veritable monster of a
name:

> Who to supply with powder did forget
> Landguard, Sheerness, Gravesend and Upnor? *Pett.*
> (781–82)

To have Landguard-Sheerness-Gravesend-and-Upnor as one's first
name is truly frightful, but since glossolalia or (though the word does
not, I think, exist) glossonomia sometimes signals religious frenzy,
one more first name is supplied.

> Who all our ships expos'd in Chatham's net?
> Who should it be but the Fanatic *Pett*?
> (783–84)

That "*Pett*'s" "name alone seems fit to answer all" is self-evidently
true, and "*Pett*" next is wrenched from terminal to initial position to
become the "first cause" of all woe and thus not only the answer to all

questions but even the reason why Parliamentary questions have to be asked. "Had he not built, none of these faults had been; / If no creation, there had been no sin" (787–88).

> . . . the Fanatic *Pett?*
> *Pett,* the sea-architect, in making ships,
> Was the first cause of all these naval slips.
>   (784–86)

This double cross, with its climactic cross-over of the placement of words and responsibilities, is name-calling which can seldom have been bettered for worse effect. Even so, Marvell has one final use for "Pett" in reserve. Slightly more than 150 lines later, Hyde is "provok'd" by his opponents to such great anger that momentarily he loses self-control and gives away the game. He

> his foaming tusk does whet,
> To prove them traitors and himself the Pett.
>   (941–42)

   Somewhere prior to line 786, Pett's name became much more significant than Pett himself. The process visible in the poem probably mirrors reality in that Peter Pett, the dockyard superintendent, may have been largely irrelevant to the Parliament enquiry itself; scapegoats, after all, are important because of their function, not their personal identities. Much the same is true of heroes, of course. Here, the idea is not to project guilt upon another and thus purge it but rather to bask in reflected glory; however, the individuals nominated for the praise to be vicariously shared almost have to assume mythic dimensions or, more accurately, to have those dimensions conferred upon them, in order to qualify for the role. When the hero is the winner of a war or a World Series (I write this in early September, but it is sometimes well to look ahead), mythopoeic activity is fairly simple. When he loses, matters are less easy. "Forth from its scabbard, pure and bright / Flashed the sword of Lee" is the way I remember, perhaps inaccurately, the beginning of some verse I was required to memorize when a child in a less than perfectly reconstructed South. I reminisce because others, for sins not yet committed, may have had to memorize Mrs. Hemans's celebrated lines:

> The boy stood on the burning deck
> Whence all but he had fled;

The flame that lit the battle's wreck
Shone round him o'er the dead.[13]

In Marvell's version of a comparable scene, it is "Fortunate boy!"; this is the Scot named "Douglas," and

If either pencil's fame,
Or if my verse can propagate a name,
When Oeta and Alcides are forgot,
Our English youth shall sing the valiant Scot.
(693–96)

"Fortunate boy" may look patronizing today or perhaps glibly insensitive, but Donno rightly points out that Marvell's model here is Virgil, and it is worth adding that Waller probably is in the background too. Waller, it may be remembered, had three particularly horrible deaths to refer to in his own "Instructions": "Three worthy persons . . . dy'd" York's "garment with their scatter'd gore" (147–48). Making the best of a truly abominable situation, Waller converted a bane to a blessing.

Happy! to whom this glorious death arrives,
More to be valu'd than a thousand lives!
(149–50)

Waller and Marvell, good Latinists both, must have known the difference between "fortunatus," a word of very high commendation, and "felix" (happy), which is higher still. Page, commenting on Virgil's "fortunati ambo" (Aeneid, 9.446), reminds us "that *fortunati* is not *felices*, 'blessed,' but a weaker adjective . . . ; it is only in a modified sense that Virgil can call even a death such as that of the two friends 'happy.' "[14]
It is tempting to suppose that Marvell, like Virgil, is willing to go as far as fortunate and that Waller, with characteristic hyperbole, is willing to go further, but this may be pressing too hard. Page cites Connington's translation ("happy pair!") despite its exaggeration, and he could have quoted Dryden too:

13. Quoted from *The Oxford Dictionary of Quotations*, 3d ed. (Oxford and New York, 1979), 244.
14. *The Aeneid* [7–12], ed. T. E. Page (London, 1900; rpt. 1956).

> O happy Friends! for, if my Verse can give
> Immortal Life, your Fame shall ever live:
> Fix'd as the Capitol's Foundation lies;
> And spread, wher e'er the *Roman* Eagle flies!
> (9.597–600)

In any case, while "Fortunate" is probably as high as Marvell would care to go, since at least some restraint is normal for him, this praise for "Douglas" is very high indeed. Or so the adjective reveals. What, however, of "boy"? Latin also is helpful here, and to see why, one needs to look at how Marvell initiates the verse paragraph which confers the praise: "Not so brave Douglas" (649). The negation looks back most immediately to the preceding line which named "Shad-rack, Meshack, and Abednego" (648) as three exemplary models whom "Captain, lieutenant, ensign, all make haste" (645) to emulate (in, of course, their own cowardly way). In the apocryphal part of Daniel, Shadrack and his companions sang a hymn which entered the liturgy with more than one title. In the Book of Common Prayer, it is (or, until recently, was) the "Benedicite" ("O all ye works of the Lord, bless ye the Lord") or "Song of the Three Children." Marvell's reference to "Three children tall" (647) probably reflects this usage, but an alternate Latin title is "Canticum trium puerorum" or "Canticle of the Three *Boys*" (italics mine). Marvell would never have been misled by these titles, however. These were young men as distinct from old ones, but they were "children of God," not adolescents. "Then Daniel requested of the king [Nebuchadnezzar], and he set Shadrach, Me-shach, and Abed-nego, over the affairs of the province of Babylon" (Daniel 2.49). Subsequently forced to choose between idolatrous worship and martyrdom—"*Turn, or burn*," as Matthew Henry puts it, commenting on Daniel 3.8–18—they elected that which Marvell's three officers are fleeing to escape: "Ere in the fi'ry furnace they be cast" (646).[15]

Of the biblical trio, Henry remarks,

> We have here such an instance of fortitude and magnanimity as is scarcely to be paralleled. We call these the *three children* (and they were indeed *young men*), but we should rather call them the three champions, the *first three* of the *worthies* of God's *kingdom among men*. . . . when they were duly called to the

---

15. For biblical commentaries, including Henry's, see the References below.

fiery trial, they acquited themselves bravely, with a conduct and courage that became sufferers for so good a cause.

"Fortunate boy!" is an accolade which is, in fact, scarcely to be paralleled elsewhere in this poem.

Even so, something is very seriously wrong with it, though not with "Douglas" himself. I have been placing quotation marks around the name because "Douglas" evidently does not totally correspond to historical reality any more than "Pett" does. Marvell's hero disdains "love's fires" (660) and "courtship" (654) whereas Archibald Douglas "left a widow, Frances, who petitioned for a prize ship as compensation" (Lord's note). That, however, is not the major problem. The difficulty, or part of it at any rate, is that the role of the "Children" has already been appropriated in wholesale fashion by three cowards, and the part of Daniel has been played as well. "The guards" themselves "Long since were fled" (629–30), but "Daniel had there adventur'd" (631). He has all the physical appearance of a warrior and none of the reality: "Paint him of person tall and big of bone" (633); "Mix a vain terror in his martial look, / And all those lines by which men are mistook" (637–38). Lord, following Margoliouth, thought the man was "probably Sir Thomas Daniel, who commanded a company of foot guards," but however that may be, this "Daniel" is rightly named only in terms of irony. Marvell picks up the story given in Daniel 6: When "He heard how the wild cannon nearer roar'd" (640), "Daniel then thought he was in lion's den" (642). And next, with a jump backwards to chapter 3, "when the frightful fireships he saw, / Pregnant with sulphur, to him nearer draw" (643–44), "away they row" so as to remain, like the Children, "unsing'd" (647) by the fire. From the point of view consistently adopted in this poem, these really *are* "three champions," to requote Matthew Henry, "the *first three* of the *worthies* of God's *kingdom among men*." They are, after all, the ones who providentially and miraculously survive. "Douglas," however, "the valiant Scot," "felt / His alt'ring form and solder'd limbs to melt" (685–86). Indeed, "The *Loyal London*" itself "now a third time burns" (698).

Simple equations are thus inadequate; the three biblical names are misappropriated by the cowards, and the biblical title—"pueri"—is reduced from plural to singular to be conferred upon "Douglas" instead. Role reversals occur so that fake imitation, numerically exact, succeeds (un)admirably whereas true emulation, with numerical discrepancy, falls short. It is no accident, therefore, that Marvell's praise occasionally strikes a note which sounds hollow. Since "Daniel" has the appearance of a hero without the substance, role reversal dictates that "Douglas" be a hero without looking like one. In this case, however, he is reminiscent of Adonis as courted by an improbably chaste Venus or possibly Narcissus as wooed by an ungarrulous Echo. "On" the "lovely chin" of "Douglas,"

> The early down but newly did begin,
> And modest beauty yet his sex did veil,
> While envious virgins hope he is a male.
> His yellow locks curl back themselves to seek,
> Nor other courtship knew but to his cheek.
>
> (649–54)

"The nymphs would rustle . . . " (658). "They sigh'd and said, 'Fond boy, why so untame, / That fli'st love's fires, reserved for other flame?' " (659–60) "Fond boy" and "Fortunate boy" ought to be worlds apart, and perhaps they are, since superficial effeminacy, like Beauty itself, may be in the eyes of the beholders. If so, however, then the coloration and tone of the painter-poet have been momentarily affected by what the nymphs actually—or would like to—see. "Like a glad lover the fierce flames he meets / And tries his first embraces in their sheets" (677–78). This is not the standard martyrdom of a virginal soul about to be wedded to the mystical Bridegroom. Martial (4.32) once marveled at the beauty of a dead bee enclosed in amber; Herrick underlined the point of how art can transform aesthetically displeasing objects by substituting a dead fly. It was "A Corps[e] as bright as burnisht gold" (6). "Not *Marshals Bee*, which in a Bead / Of *Amber* quick was buried . . . More honour had, then this same *Flie*; / Dead, and clos'd up in *Yvorie*" (11–12, 17–18).[16] Marvell retained the bee, but the fact that he does so stresses an artfulness which is evident with or without the allusion:

> His shape exact, which the bright flames enfold,
> Like the sun's statue stands of burnish'd gold.
> Round the transparent fire about him glows,
> As the clear amber on the bee does close,
> And, as on angels' heads their glories shine,
> His burning locks adorn his face divine.
>
> (679–84)

16. Herrick, "Upon a Flie," *The Complete Poetry*, ed. J. Max Patrick (Garden City, NY, 1963), 248.

As with Yeats's burning figures in Byzantium, this is, self-consciously, the artifice of eternity. But Marvell's own comparison is the self-immolation of Heracles on Mount Oeta: "When Oeta and Alcides are forgot." Like Waller in "On St. James's Park," Marvell prefers to use the name "Alcides"; it means "valiant," and "Douglas" is, explicitly, "the valiant Scot." The fiery end of a hero is finely apt, but since half of the doublet is a mountain, not a person, this is at least a slightly disconcerting replacement for either the three Children or for Virgil's "fortunati ambo," the fortunate pair of Euryalus and Nisus. It may not be amiss, therefore, to recall that Heracles burned himself as his only remedy for a burning poison administered to him by Deianara (his treacherous wife) by means of the coat not of Nisus but Nessus. "Hercules," as Lemprière (303) summarizes, "as soon as he put it on fell into a desperate distemper and found the poison of the Lernaean hydra," that many-headed monster, "penetrating through his bones." "As the distemper was incurable," Hercules "erected a large burning pile on the top of mount Oeta." He

> laid himself down upon it as on a couch, leaning his head on his club . . . and saw himself on a sudden surrounded with the flames without betraying any marks of fear or astonishment. . . . and after the mortal parts of Hercules had been consumed by the fire, he was carried up to heaven . . . and his friends, unable to find either his bones or his ashes . . . showed their sense of his glorious services, by raising an altar on the spot where the burning pile had stood.

Lemprière cites far too many sources, some still famous and some not, to quote here, especially since situational similarity, not verbal echo, is the point. And that "Douglas" is "Heraclean" is, I think, quite clear:

> But when in his immortal mind he felt
> His alt'ring form and solder'd limbs to melt,
> Down on the deck he laid himself and di'd,
> With his dear sword reposing at his side
> And on the flaming plank so rests his head
> As one that's warm'd himself and gone to bed.
> His ship burns down and with his relics sinks,
> And the sad stream beneath his ashes drinks.
> (685–92)

"I have built a monument more enduring than bronze" is the claim in Horace's ode (3.30). "If my verse can propagate a name" is Marvell's less confident equivalent. The attempt, certainly, was made, and the tribute to "Douglas" is a glowing one. If that adjective looks to be singularly ill-chosen for this fiery death, it also is important to see that "Douglas" had wedded himself not to a Frances, as Archibald had, but to a Deianara whose name had been changed to England, and she was already married to a Charles. To revert to an earlier symbolism, the fundamental reason why this whole picture seems partly out of focus is that the Children and "Douglas" cannot possibly be interchanged, and not simply because three other people have cut "Douglas" out. "When," to requote Matthew Henry, "they were duly called to the fiery trial, they acquited themselves bravely, with a conduct and courage that became sufferers for so good a cause." In 1667, however, that kind of heroism had no relevance to anything other than itself. It may be worth remembering in the future—"Our English youth shall sing the valiant Scot"—but the proposition quite literally depends on an *if*: "If my verse can propagate thy name." At present, in the context of the many "heroes" named and celebrated on either side of him, it is "Douglas" himself who is singularly ill-chosen, not by Marvell or by this poem but by the times and, from one point of view, by himself. When that which is false has become the normative standard, the "true" has to be put inside quotation marks, much as "Verse" had to be parenthetical. It no longer looks right but somehow out of place and at least slightly wrong.

Equally "wrong" is the picture of De Ruyter, the Dutch commander, sailing blithely unopposed up the Thames. Virgil was willing to balance his praise for Euryalus and Nisus, the "fortunati ambo," with a later celebration of Lausus, even though that youth was a warrior on the wrong side who was slain by Aeneas. "And here," as Dryden translates, "Heroic Youth, 'tis here I must / To thy immortal Memory be just" (10.1123–24). Ruyter, however, is explicitly "old" (532) in the poem and aged sixty in the footnote. Lord saw "a general indebtedness" in 533–40 to "the first meeting between Antony and Cleopatra in Shakespeare's play," as described by Enobarbus in the famous passage which begins, "The barge she sat on" (2.2.193ff.) Since Antony regularly is an "old" ruffian in the play, the analogy is suitable enough, but there is no Cleopatra in this scene unless it is a boy actor prepared to play "Douglas" in the scene which immediately follows. I think I see Spenser's Guyon in the background, encountering salaciously coy nymphs: "The wanton Maidens him espying, stood . . .

Abasht . . . But . . . two lily paps aloft displayd, / And all, that might his melting heart entise / To [their] delights" (2.12.66).[17]

However close or general this similarity may be, there is certainly a wrongness perversely present when an elderly preening Dutchman can begin "to shave" his beard like "am'rous victors" (533), when English maidens (526–28) become

> beauties ere this never naked seen.
> Through the vain sedge the bashful nymphs he ey'd:
> Bosoms and all which from themselves they hide,

and when "wanton boys on every rope do cling" (542). It is monstrous that this kind of pastoral idyll, a Bower of sensual Bliss, be discovered in an English setting to "swell his [Ruyter's] old veins with fresh blood, fresh delight" (532). Especially is this so when "Douglas," far from feeling a melting heart, "felt / His alt'ring form and solder'd limbs to melt."

A prominent concept in Virgil's treatment of Lausus is "vetustas" (10.792). Dryden translates with "Posterity" (1126), an almost inevitable oversimplification since a concise English rendering of the ambivalent Latin probably cannot be discovered. Virgil's double point, as Page explains, concerns "antiquity," an idea dependent on time as it extends both backward and forward. It is the ancient past that now and in the future can lend "credit for what might otherwise seem incredible; . . . At the same time 'antiquity' is also the period of heroic deeds such as later days cannot imitate; the deed of Lausus is only credible in a long past time of loftier chivalry and diviner exploits." Only crooked analogies can possibly be drawn between thinking of this kind and the prevalent standards of 1667. The young and valiant Scot is misplaced, mistimed, and dead; the opponent is not a defeated Lausus but a lecherously victorious Ruyter, either corrupting the locale through which he voyages or—even worse—discovering it to be already corrupt in its meretriciously idyllic appearance. In this topography, admirable qualities quite literally cannot and do not survive.

17. Quoted from *The Works*, ed. Edwin Greenlaw et al., 10 vols. (Baltimore, 1932–57). Spenser's own model was Tasso, and in Fairfax's translation (1600; 2d ed., 1624), the Tasso seems even closer to (though a dilated version of) Marvell's scene. See *Jerusalem Delivered*, tr. Edward Fairfax, 15.59–66 (Carbondale, IL, 1962).

III
Charles (Not Christ) the King

"Douglas" and "Pett" are not names to conjure with in 1667 because plenipotentiary ambassadors, however hollow in their lack of genuine substance, reverberate far more imposingly. For purposes of counterresonance, the name desperately needed is, of course, "Charles," and Marvell has held it back, though for a different effect, quite as carefully as Waller did. In Waller's first "Instructions," the royal presence at last was gloriously revealed, but in Marvell's "Last Instructions" glory is merely potential whereas a sense of absence continues to be strongly felt. The context provided by Marvell himself may be sufficient for the major point to be visible, but the structural parallelism between the two poems establishes this notable difference with especially great clarity.

Just prior to the envoy itself, Charles is to encapsulate within himself three of the major roles hitherto taken separately: the painter, the poet, and the model.

> Painter, adieu! How well our arts agree,
> Poetic picture, painted poetry;
> But this great work is for our Monarch fit,
> And henceforth Charles only to Charles shall sit.
> His master-hand the ancients shall outdo,
> Himself the painter and the poet too.
>
> (943–48)

Philomel at the end of "The Third Advice" was a lovely picture to behold, and this is a pretty one too, especially in its alliterative articulation of an aesthetic which underlies the idea itself of a painter poem: poetic picture, painted poetry. The tones, however, cannot assume truly idyllic coloration from the golden tints of "Douglas" nor from the dark hues which the painter and poet have earlier employed. "St Dennis" and "French martyrs" (167–68) made a brief appearance early on, as did a bit of slightly fractured French in line 494: "*banquiers banquerouts.*" "Adieu!"—shortly to be contrasted forcefully with "accurs'd" (967)—nonetheless is a curious word whereby to bid farewell to Greek, Roman, Dutch, Flemish ("Rubens," 119), or English painters, the only kind hitherto referred to. Since the word, etymologically, is a commendation "to God," its benevolence cannot be faulted, however, and the fondness of the poet is apparent. So, of course, was that of Protogenes for his sponge, dog, and canvas once they all by chance agreed. One also necessarily recalls the other models, painters, and poetry which are to be subsumed by the king: the dwarf Gibson with no colors for a blank canvas, Apelles busily undoing by night the work done by day, a freed Caspaspe handed over like a slave, the painted Castlemaine, and hundreds of lines of sardonic inversions and perversions of celebration. The third sitting of "Lady State" was happening back in the first two lines of the poem, and considerable wastage or devolution has filled up or perhaps left increasingly vacant much of the intervening space. Sometimes forced by his models to disfigure his poem as deliberately as Apelles marred his picture, Marvell parodies Waller's invitation to Charles to stand up inside the now finished picture and possibly turns inside out Pigmalion's love for the object that he himself had carved. Directly and indirectly, Charles has been responsible for bad government, bad politics, and bad life; here the suggestion is that he might as well be his own bad artist. God only knows what speaking picture the "Charles" of this poem might create by painting himself, but to be told that "His master-hand the ancients shall outdo" cannot possibly be reassuring to anyone—Marvell, for example—with admiration for "vetustas."

Perhaps, however, these encapsulating lines are to look not only back but also forward. Patterson (165) calls attention to the fact that Margoliouth, following the *State Poems* of 1689, prints "will agree" rather than "well": a reading "which is more interesting but, alas, probably not correct." Future tense, while possibly helpful here and soon to be used prophetically, is not essential for the supposition that the "great work" which is "fit" for "our Monarch" is the picture of Charles himself which next is seen. If that is the case, then Marvell has anticipated an instruction given the painter in "The Fifth Advice":

> Give a prophetic touch,
> If thou know'st how; if not, leave a great space
> For great things to be portray'd in their place.
> (78–80)

The space most obviously left vacant for great things will turn out to be the one which opens up on the other side of the poem's last line, but "To the King" is itself inadequately filled up, and the first major indication of that fact is that this is where Marvell pulls out Galileo's telescope to balance Hooke's microscope. This framing device, as earlier noted, is a magnification which diminishes, but a further detail previously omitted as not needed then is worth noticing now.

Milton also peered through this telescope in *Paradise Lost*, the first occasion being to look at Satan's shield vis-à-vis the moon:

> his ponderous shield
> Ethereal temper, massy, large and round,
> Behind him cast; the broad circumference
> Hung on his shoulders like the Moon, whose Orb
> Through Optic Glass the *Tuscan* Artist views.
> (1.284–88)

The second was to look at Satan himself vis-à-vis the Sun:

> There lands the Fiend, a spot like which perhaps
> Astronomer in the Sun's lucent Orb
> Through his glaz'd Optic Tube yet never saw.
> (3.588–90)

Satan's shield, unlike those of Achilles and Aeneas, hugely depicts nothing whatsoever, and Milton's negative dubiety ("perhaps . . . yet never saw") suggests that Satan himself is darkly invisible save to the eye of the mind. In Marvell's reworking, as "To the King" begins, it is the Sun which cannot perceive its own imperfections.

> So his bold tube man to the sun appli'd
> And spots unknown to the bright star descri'd.
> (949–50)

Earlier in the poem, it was Hyde who played Satan's part. He was of the persuasion that "Gain and revenge, revenge and gain are sweet" (363). Perhaps the reason he was untroubled by Satan's question, "But what will not Ambition and Revenge / Descend to" (9.168–69), was that he had not yet made Satan's discovery: "Revenge, at first though sweet, / Bitter ere long back on itself recoils" (171–72). In the envoy, however, it is Charles behind whom Satan's shadow looms even as Milton's lines lurk behind Marvell's. "Optic trunk" (953), echoing Milton's "Optic Tube," reinforces the allusions already made but also helps to disclose a crucial distinction. Satan *is* the malignant spot and is so unalterably, but not so with Charles. Warned of "spots unknown,"

> Through optic trunk the planet seem'd to hear,
> And hurls them off e'er since in his career.
> (953–54)

The tense sequence—"seem'd," "hurls e'er since"—is of the prophetic kind which progresses from present-past to present-future. It is bold (as in "bold tube") but corrective in purpose and thus not culpable. A second crucial distinction thus begins to open itself at this point, the one between a selfless muse who offers harsh advice and self-serving advisers who do not. "Blame not the Muse that brought those spots to sight" (957).

> She blames them only who the Court restrain
> And where all England serves, themselves would reign.
>
> (965–66)

But

> Bold and accurs'd are they that all this while
> Have strove to isle our Monarch from his isle.
> And to improve themselves, on false pretense,
> About the common Prince have raised a fence.
>
> (967–70)

The enisled isle should be unenisled, and the fence, because not a defense against attack but a barrier against goodness, should be dismantled. These first and third negations affect the one in between by suggesting that false pretense, in theory at least, could be made to cancel out its own double negativity to reveal an inner positive force. And, by implication, if the face of truth were revealed behind pretense, then satiric masks to counter governmental charades could also be removed as no longer needed or appropriate. "Bold tube" thus counterbalances "Bold and accurs'd" since the existence of both is mutually dependent; elimination of the latter renders the former superfluous.

By eminently reasonable extension, if the muse has hindered rather than helped the furtherance of this goal, then she herself should be banished rather than invoked. Jonson (Epigram 65, "To My Muse") once vented displeasure on his muse for having offered unmerited praise:

> Away, and leave me, thou thing most abhorred,
> Thou hast betrayed me to a worthless lord.[18]

18. Quoted from *Poems*, ed. Ian Donaldson (London, Oxford, and New York, 1975), 35.

Marvell, turning the idea upside down, indicates that if the muse were to be wrong in its *dis*praise ("Would she the unattended throne reduce" [961]) and thus be guilty of "Banishing love, trust, ornament, and use" (962), then

> Better it were to live in cloister's lock,
> Or in fair fields to rule the easy flock.
> (963–64)

Sacred song and pastoral poetry perhaps are suggested here as fitter subjects than satiric painting for a muse which mistakes its object. In any case the muse can gracefully though no doubt shamefacedly retire from the field of action to rule the easy flock, but that option is by no means available to the king. Indeed, if he hears but refuses to listen, then the muse has not in fact erred even if misunderstood and wrongly interpreted as placing blame on the sun for its own spots. In that case, in fact, no misunderstanding actually occurs since the false interpretation in effect is self-verifying whatever the original intent of the warning may have been. This is as close to the power of positive thinking as Marvell comes in this envoy, and it is by no means close enough to be comforting. A redeemable and redeeming monarch certainly should be distinct from damnable counsellors, but good reason exists for skepticism about the wisdom of maintaining the distinction unless the monarch himself not only observes and preserves that difference but also translates it into decisive action. The potentially remedial strategies of Deuteronomy can be replicated unto the "Fifth Advice to a Painter" or even beyond, but the old law, like the old guard, will remain perdurably in force, unless and until the good news of the gospel is heard. In this case neither Marvell nor a muse, whether errant or true, can proclaim it.

Nor does it seem likely that the name of Charles will be the potent force required. Part of the evidence is that Jove's thunder fitfully returns at this point as a power which significantly does not in fact exist, and Marvell has to reforge it before revealing its absence. Two inversions of Waller—Jove's descent to Vulcan's workshop and a navy with no ships—were made in the envoy of previous poems and have been used earlier in this "Last" one. In the middle, Hyde already replaces both Jove and Charles when "among his Cyclops he retires / To forge new thunder and inspect their fires" (371–72); Hyde also "march'd our whole militia's force / (As if, indeed, we [had] ships or Dutch had horse")) (481–82). To vary these jibes rather than merely repeat them still again, Marvell chooses these lines of Waller to undermine and detonate:

> Those which inhabit the celestial bower
> Painters express with emblems of their power:
> His club Alcides, Phoebus has his bow,
> Jove has his thunder, and your navy you.
>
> (313–16)

Marvell's corresponding lines wear an innocent-looking face despite the lowering to less resonant mythic names:

> But Ceres corn, and Flora is the spring,
> Bacchus is wine, the country is the king.
>
> (973–74)

Myths always evoke multiple associations, and I am therefore unsure whether a visible progression occurs through three-fourths of this couplet. "Ceres" and "Flora," for whatever it is worth, do not look explosive to me whereas riotous "Bacchus" may be suspect by name alone, apart from his wine and deplorable jokes about Dutch courage. There can be little doubt, however, that word order has been carefully contrived. Since Ceres (is) corn, Flora is spring, and Bacchus is wine, the fourth clause surely should be "king is country." The reversal actually presented by "the country is the king," while clearly a rehandling of Waller's syntax ("and your navy you"), here points up the further inversion that if all of these equations do hold true, then the status of the king as well as of the country has diminished to an alarming degree. The country's condition would scarcely bear thinking about if its sorry condition did not force one to do so. The further suggestion is that if priority of causes is to be examined, then Charles's decline has lowered the country rather than the reverse: As Charles goes, so goes England, and in consequence both seriously need to be redirected by a different director, preferably a more powerfully thunderous one than any of the divinities just named.

Instead of power, one discovers a tumbled series of debilitating metaphors through much of this envoy. The sun's spots that "seem his courtiers, are but his disease" (952); "those spots" now brought "to sight" ("which in your splendor hid") do "corrode your light" (957–58). "Not so does rust insinuating wear, / . . . As scratching courtiers undermine a realm / And through the palace's foundations bore" (975, 978–79). Depending on which of these images one chooses to trace out, the regal foundations are termite-ridden or the armor of Justice is rusty or the body of the kingdom-king is diseased or proper light-sight is obscured. These personal and interior deteriorations and de-lapidations are not easily acknowledged, much less remedied.

The last lines, moreover, indicate that external malefactors are dangerously numerous and that benevolent assistance is in exceptionally short supply. The palace guard may be mere "vermin" or, alternatively, a breeding "warren" of rodents, but at present they infest the court and, if not exterminated, will surely cause further ruination. "The smallest vermin make the greatest waste, / And a poor warren once a city ras'd" (981–82). Such creatures ought to be beneath contempt, no doubt, but they cannot and must not be ignored. The admirable substitutes for "scratching courtiers" (978) are easily visible, but a major reason why is that there are not very many of them. "Where few the number, choice is there less hard" (989). In the much earlier parliamentary backgammon game, an "unknown reserve" (perhaps in inverted anticipation of "spots unknown")

> still remain'd,
> A gross of English gentry, nobly born,
> Of clear estates, and to no faction sworn;
> Dear lovers of their king, and death to meet,
> For country's cause, that glorious think and sweet;
> To speak not forward, but in action brave,
> In givir g gen'rous, but in counsel grave.
>
> (286–92)

In a satiric context where value systems often are upside down, to speak of something "gross" which "remain'd" may be an especially apt way to signify twelve times twelve, and to find 144 good men and true in this particular Parliament might be considered rather encouraging. One would have to multiply twelve by twelve thousand, however, to arrive at the number of the blessed in Saint John's mystical arithmetic (Rev. 14.1), and 144,000 is taken to be symbolic of the "remnant" that shall be saved. It is, Poole says,

> A small number in comparison of such as [it] should be . . . a number made up of twelve times twelve, by which is signified that they . . . should answer the Israelites indeed of the Old Testament, that remnant of the twelve tribes whom God had chosen, who adhere to the doctrine and precepts of the twelve apostles.

If Marvell's "gross" suggests numbers of this kind and if his "remain'd" has the same force as Poole's "remnant," then the future is disconcerting or even terrifying to contemplate. The article on "Remnant" in Bauer cites the major biblical texts for this concept as it developed in Hebraic thought and continued into Christian thinking.[19] Two of those texts, however, can here serve to illustrate since Romans 9.27 restates Isaiah 10.22: "Esaias also crieth concerning Israel, Though the number of the children of Israel be as the sand of the sea," only "a remnant shall be saved." Marvell's "unknown reserve" was not numerous even in line 286, and their number has been lessened in later lines by various treacheries, most notably in the example of the valiant Scot. However small the band now may be, they reappear to end the poem.

> But they whom, born to virtue and to wealth,
> Nor guilt to flatt'ry binds, nor want to stealth;
> Whose gen'rous conscience and whose courage high
> Does with clear counsels their large souls supply;
> That serve the King with their estates and care,
> And as in love on Parliaments can stare,
> Where few the number, choice is there less hard:
> Give us this Court and rule without a guard.
>
> (983–90)

Juvenal (6.348–49) wanted to know, "Quis custodiet ipsos / custodes," variously translatable as "who will watch the watchers" or "who shall keep those keepers" (Dryden 6.465) or "who will guard the guards themselves?" Marvell, preparing to introduce "Douglas," has already said that "The guards . . . Long since were fled on many a feign'd pretence" (629–30). "Feigned pretence" prepared for "false pretense" even as fleeing guards anticipated "rule without a guard." The uselessness, indeed the damaging presence, of unguarded guards is apparent. But those who are virtuously loyal, while few and thus both conspicuous and easily chosen, are also conspicuously anonymous. John Wallace believed that "there is not a word to suggest who the actual men were that Marvell considered to be the best candidates for high office, because the choice was wholly the King's."[20]

19. *Encyclopedia of Biblical Knowledge: The Complete Sacramentum Verbi*, ed. Johannes B. Bauer (New York, 1981) (a translation of *Bibeltheologisches Wörterbuch*, 3d ed. [Graz-Vienna-Cologne, 1967]).

20. *Destiny His Choice: The Loyalism of Andrew Marvell* (Cambridge, 1968), 177.

There can be no dispute about this regal prerogative, but Wallace himself indicates that candidates might be proposed by observing in his next sentence that "Buckingham was the man of the hour . . . and his views on toleration make it easily conceivable that Marvell approved of his bid for power." "Buckingham" is not, however, a name found here, nor does it seem likely, in this case, that absence reveals implicit presence. If anything, the many names which are actually mentioned in the course of the poem must surely affect adversely one's assessment of the forcefulness of an anonymous few. They appear, moreover, in nearly terminal and thus emphatic position so that one ends the poem with anonymity capped by a final recommendation about what *not* to do: "rule without a guard." And since we have previously seen that "strength at last still under number bows" (277), these final lines cannot seem strongly positive in their effect. Satire seldom *is* positive, of course, except by negative, sometimes devious, implication, and yet a very obvious question here is how, exactly, does one manage to rule without a guard? Especially if there remains only a remnant that does not need extremely close watching for nefarious treachery? And the most obvious question and by all odds the most important one is this: What choice, if any at all, will Charles actually choose? Or in terms of satiric masking and unmasking, what is the face behind the royal mask?

"The ending is clearly abrupt: we are not even told how Caesar was affected." Thus Duff comments on Lucan's inconclusive ending. "But we can guess," he adds. Earlier readers had a guess incorporated in Lucan's text since sixteenth- and seventeenth-century editions regularly included a finale tacked on by Sulpitius. Rowe omits naming his source but adds sixty-five lines inspired by "Some looser Muse" who "lightly treads / The devious Paths where wanton Fancy leads" (10.861–62). With this apology for translating earlier guesswork, Rowe is able to finish with a resonant, rolling hexameter. "*Nemesis* the Shield of Safety spreads" (869) to save Caesar for a later death at "avenging *Brutus'* Hand" (873). And Caesar's

> Friends, unknowing what the Gods decree,
> With Joy receive him from the swelling Sea;
> In Peals on Peals their Shouts triumphant rise,
> Roll o'er the distant Flood, and thunder to the Skies.

Since this glorious triumph is explicitly based on ignorance of what the gods decree, Rowe takes away with one hand what he gives with the other. His last line is a marvelous example, in fact, of self-

conscious pretense. Marvell refused to offer anything remotely comparable, and he therefore stopped but did not conclude. So far as I can
tell, unless and until Charles made a move of his own, there was
nowhere for Marvell to go except sideways or backwards. And since
Charles, from a Marvellian point of view, became increasingly like
Lady Castlemaine in making cosmetic changes but not cosmic ones,
Marvell himself sidestepped to lampoons and backstepped to the
grimly factual prose of *An Account of the Growth of Popery and Arbitrary Government in England*. There is some evidence that he also
doffed the mask of satire and donned that of a secret agent working in
behalf of interests which finally brought William of Orange to the
throne, but Marvell did not live to see that day.

7

Waller, Marvell, and Dryden

Marvell did not stop writing in 1667, but what he produced in subsequent years is not satisfying to contemplate. The portrait of "Douglas" was extracted from "The Last Instructions" and touched up to become the centerpiece of "The Loyal Scot"; the attack on Hyde was renewed in "Clarendon's House Warming"; two prose works, both of substantial length, controverted religious and political matters; and letters were faithfully sent to the parliamentary constituency of Hull. One can add a few other pieces, including some verse satires by "Marvell," possibly genuine and possibly not, but it is quite clear that by the end of "The Last Instructions," Marvell had painted himself into a corner. It was the same one Waller had backed himself into, though from a different direction, with roughly comparable results. Waller also seems to have written comparatively little verse after celebrating Lowestoft, and unless one is disposed to look favorably on the pious poems because of their content, he had more or less reached a dead end some years before he died.

The possibly surprising fact of the matter is that the two authors, quite without knowing it, had long been converging on opposite sides of a meeting point even though they arrived there by antithetical methods which appear to be mutually exclusive. Marvell's eye for the telling detail, the particularities of specific experiences, ran counter to Waller's broader strokes even in lyric verse; the glue appropriated to the mistress would never have suited the lovely rose at all. The minutiae required by Marvell's satiric explosions of puffed-up appearances intensified this difference between the two poets when they instructed the painters, and in this respect, "The Last Instructions" is as characteristic of Marvell's mind as the first "Instructions" is of Waller's. And yet there was very little that either one could continue to do as an author of poetry to accomplish the goals of reform which both thought desirable. Marvell fought gamely on, in Parliament and out, but it is unimaginable that he could ever have returned to lyric forms even if he had not unexpectedly died, and the later verse satires are very minor skirmishes when compared to the anti-epic substance of "The Last Instructions." Waller also continued to struggle until nearly the end, and it may be worthwhile to notice briefly three examples which show effortful strain not customarily found in Waller's seemingly fluent productions. One of these will enable a final comparison to "Marvell" and a last glance back at Statius, the Roman poet cited in examining Waller's poem for Lady Rich and Marvell's poem for Hastings. The other two point in the direction of Dryden.

Statius (*Sylvae*, 1.2) had been able to celebrate "The Great Equestrian Statue of the Emperor Domitian" in the emperor's own lifetime, and Waller might have seized a similar opportunity in 1672 when Sir Robert Viner erected a statue of Charles II in Stocks Market. The statue had originally shown a king of Poland triumphant over a Turk but had been reworked to represent Charles II lording it over Cromwell. Statius (vv. 84–86) refers to an older equestrian statue in the Forum, originally of Alexander the Great but with its head replaced by that of Julius Caesar, and at one time Waller might well have viewed such material as heaven-sent for celebratory analogies of varying kinds. Evidently, however, this was not, in Waller's opinion, another perfect occasion for a complimentary poem; he made no use of it at all. For this omission to seem in any way significant, one must quickly add three further facts. First, another statue, this one of Charles I on horseback, had been cast in 1633 but not erected at the time; it was finally placed at Charing Cross in 1675. Second, "Marvell" wrote satiric verse for both statues, "On the Statue Erected by Sir Robert Viner," and "The Statue at Charing Cross," while another wit managed to manufacture "A Dialogue between the Two Horses."[1]

---

1. All three poems are given in Lord's *State Poems*, and those by "Marvell" are included in his edition of Marvell; Donno lists the titles among "Other Attributions" but does not print them.

And third, Waller did write a poem for the statue of Charles I though not one for the effigy of Charles II.

Statius was not completely reduplicated by any one of the satires but was parceled out, as it were, for various purposes. Domitian's horse, we are told, is preferable to the Trojan horse, among other reasons because "that one . . . was harmful" (as the Loeb translates) "and contained fierce Achaeans." At Charing Cross in 1675, a temporary return is made to the Great Fire of 1666 and rumors concerning its cause: "The Trojan Horse . . . Had within it an army that burn'd up the town." This point is genuinely fearful, as is the statement by one of the horses in the "Dialogue" that as the lesser of two evils it would "rather bear Nero than Sardanapalus." Other barbs, while horrific in implication, replace grandeur with grandiose absurdity. Placement was important for Statius: "Well suited to the work," he says, "are its surroundings."

> But a market, they say, does suit the King well
> Who the Parliament buys and revenues does sell,
> And others to make the similitude hold,
> Say his Majesty himself is bought too and sold.

Domitian's statue was completed and erected with such remarkable speed that Statius wonders, "Did it glide down, a completed work, from heaven?" The one of Charles I causes the satirist to ask, "But why is the work then so long at a stand? / Such things you should never, or suddenly, do." "What can be the mystery why Charing Cross / This five months continues still blinded with board?" The suggestion made is that not Charles but "Pulchinello is to be restor'd." Viner's statue, after being unveiled, was reveiled for further work, and "Marvell" explains why. "Each one that passes finds fault with the horse, / Yet all do affirm that the King is much worse." The pejorative comparison involves much more than artistic representation, of course, and "To see him so disguis'd" by being reveiled also is double-edged. For Statius, the noble horseman bestrides his steed in awesome fashion: "Not more loftily does the Bistonian steed bear Mars." Charles II evokes a notably different comparison: "So loose is his seat that all men agree / That Sir William Peeke" (London's mayor in 1667 [Lord's note]) "sits much firmer than he."

Domitian was to be the last of the twelve Caesars, but Statius hopes that the Emperor will not soon forsake Rome for heaven. "Keep thy affections fixed on earth . . . may'st thou joyously see thy grandsons offer incense." This is the point of gravest importance when transferred to England since Charles II had a brother but no legitimate sons who could succeed him. The satirist turns Statius around, therefore, in two ways. On the one hand, Charles II, while far worse than Charles I, is himself not so bad as James would be. The poem for Viner's statue thus concludes with the bitter hope that Charles, more or less like Domitian, will continue to reign:

> But with all his faults pray restore us our King,
> If ever you hope in December for spring;
> For though the whole world can't show such another,
> Yet we'd better by far have him than his brother.

On the other hand, one of the talking horses wants to know "when things will be mended?" The question has to do with artwork but also with England itself, and the answer is that no genuine improvement can be expected until the last of the Caesars has gone: "When the reign of the line of the Stuarts is ended."

These statue poems do not score points from Waller as the painter poems did, but the fact that Waller wrote up only one of the statues is only part of the reason. Also important is that Waller himself has shifted ground in two significant ways and thus is much less open to satiric response. First, "On the STATUE of King CHARLES the First, at CHARING-CROSS" (*Works*, 206), mentions the "reign" of "his Son" but in no way celebrates it; unlike Statius, Waller attributes no loftiness to the current monarch to be lowered. Second, the poem preaches against rebellion not so much because revolt is wrong but because it never actually works.

> . . . heav'n this lasting monument has wrought,
> That mortals may eternally be taught,
> Rebellion, though successful, is but vain;
> And Kings so kill'd rise conquerors again.
> This truth the royal image does proclaim,
> Loud as the trumpet of surviving FAME.

Charles II is living proof of this fact even as the recovered and newly erected statue of his father proclaims it. There can be no ongoing dialogue here as in the painter poems because both sides, like the talking horses themselves, are in substantial agreement on at least two fundamental issues, the undesirable present reality and the undesirableness of regicide as a means to remedy matters. "Marvell," after all, was not proposing that rebellion be raised, nor does the "Dialogue" suggest that the reign of the Stuarts be brought to a violent end. The Glorious Revolution, when it did arrive, was glorious, in part at least, precisely because it took another form.

In the meantime, the sometime hope existed that a foreign war might unify the country behind its monarch, perhaps after the manner of Henry V long ago, but with Turks instead of the French as the enemy. In 1683, the Turks besieged Vienna in July and did not retreat until September, when the city was relieved by a force commanded by King John III (surnamed Sobieski, 1624–96) of Poland. He had earlier defeated the Turks at Choczim in 1673 and been elected king the following year. An astounding fact is that it was his statue that Robert Viner had caused to be altered in 1675 so that it represented Charles II trampling on Cromwell. By 1683, the associations and origins of the previous decade's artifact were evidently less in the public eye and therefore less grotesque, yet Waller not only left that statue alone but suppressed the name(s) of the Polish hero in a bifurcated poem which celebrates that hero's second victory over the Turks as a model which Charles might emulate and even overgo without having to resort to force. In structure, "Of the Invasion and Defeat of the TURKS, In the Year 1683" (*Works*, 134–37) is rather like "Upon the Death of my Lady Rich," the poem from 1638 which was cited above in the first chapter to illustrate some of Waller's characteristic strategies. That they are still thought useful forty-five years later is not necessarily to Waller's discredit; Statius, after all, was writing in about A.D. 90. But Waller now has insuperable difficulty in achieving a match between his two structural halves.

At Vienna, the Turk was driven back by a strong counterattack but also, at least in Waller's poem, had invited his own defeat. He "Would Christians chase, and sacrifice to fame." "Breaking truce, he so unjustly fought" that the debacle

> seems to cry aloud,
> To warn the mighty, and instruct the proud;
> That of the great, neglecting to be just,
> Heav'n in a moment makes an heap of dust.

Waller, forsaking universal brotherhood in this poem, urges that the moment be seized "their present ruin to complete / Before another SOLYMAN they get." In their present confusion and disarray, the Turks evidently could be subdued without mounting a costly military crusade, and Waller is confident that this plan would have the further advantage of causing "timely union" between "Christians . . . by themselves opprest." It is this second point, in fact, that becomes the principal substance for the poem's domestic application. If Charles would engage in "such a glorious task," English Christians doubtless would unite behind him, especially since the task might be accomplished "Without a Tax upon his subjects laid, / Their peace disturb'd, their plenty, or their trade." Mercantile heroism may be a notable comedown from one point of view, but for a moment or two it can seem to have the unarguable force of practical, even hardheaded reality behind it.

> What THESEUS did, or THEBAN HERCULES,
> Holds no compare with this victorious peace:
> Which on the TURKS shall greater honor gain,
> Than all their giants, and their monsters, slain.
> Those are bold tales, in fabulous ages told;
> This glorious act the living do behold.

Among the obvious problems, however, is that peaceful domination headed by Charles presupposes martial victory over the "Solyman" by the unnamed "Sobieski"; a second is that the only way English pragmatism could substitute for the heroism of antiquity would be by displacing rather than fulfilling it. Waller's advice may have been eminently suitable and sensible, had Charles been the sort of monarch to heed it, but Waller must reject a substantially important part of his own customary presuppositions in order to offer it. Equally obvious, or so one would think, is the futility of an attempt to accomodate oneself to a monarch whose statue in Stocks Market was a travesty of a statue of a Polish hero. In 1683, however, Waller was thrashing around, and lest one patronize old Waller too much, it is worth remembering that Dryden, nearly five years later, was to work with similar "Turkish" material in a poem for James II (to be noticed quite shortly) which is at least as futile as Waller's for Charles.

One also might want to recall that Waller wrote no poem for the death of Charles, though Dryden—and Flatman and a few others— did. Instead, Waller returned to a theme important in his poem of 1683 and reworked it for

> A Presage of the Ruin of the TURKISH Empire: presented to his Majesty King JAMES II. on his Birth-Day.

Fenton totally bypassed this poem in his "Observations" but may have made a silent comment by printing it (*Works*, 172–74) immediately following "Instructions to a Painter" despite the existence of other poems written in the intervening years. The ironies are manifest and, depending on point of view, either painful or ludicrous to behold. In either case, there is some genuine pathos to the Latin line which Waller appends at the end. "Haec ego longaevus cecini tibi, maxime regum!" (These things I in my old age have sung to thee, O greatest of kings!) I personally can see no pathos in Dryden's "Britannia Rediviva: A Poem on the Prince [son of James II], Born on the Tenth of June, 1688," but the title and the fact that June 10 was Trinity Sunday (a point which Dryden chooses to stress) are fully as ironic now as Waller's heading for his birthday poem to the king, and Dryden's references to the Turkish crescent soon to be surely defeated by an English Constantine are no less preposterous.

I make these comparisons with no intent of denigrating Dryden but to lead up to a fact which I take to be of considerable importance. Dryden boxed himself in quite as badly, or so it seems, as Waller and Marvell did, but Dryden was able to escape as they were not. Not only that, but even before 1688 he had been facing precisely the same difficulties that his elders did and had handled them with seemingly consummate ease. Dryden had been on the periphery of the painter poems since he wrote up part of the battle of Lowestoft as a compliment to the Duchess of York:

> Verses to Her Highness the Dutchess, on the memorable Victory gain'd by the Duke against the Hollanders, June the 3. 1665. and on Her Journey afterwards into the North.[2]

And while "Marvell" was thinking of Nero, Dryden had turned the Great Fire of 1666 to panegyric ends in *Annus Mirabilis*. Already, therefore, he was repolishing Waller's praise and later would write the funeral poem for Charles that Waller declined to produce. He also would refine and aim in a different direction the satire of Marvell and "Marvell"; the notable instance for comparative purposes here is "The Medal," a glittering performance which makes most productions look underrehearsed.

The truly remarkable poem, however, is of course *Absalom and Achitophel*. The fact is obvious in any context but especially so in the one described here because polished praise and forceful satire unite

2. Dryden is quoted from *The Poems*, ed. James Kinsley, 4 vols. (Oxford, 1958).

with one another, as if both Waller and Marvell had jointly resolved to surpass their own separate work by judicious amalgamation of the superior elements from each. Or that can appear to be the case if one considers only the broad aims and general effects. In actuality, Dryden's poem could not possibly have resulted from even an improbable combination of the talents of Waller and Marvell, and the reason Dryden could and did handle problems that baffled the two older authors is that he was able to alter perspectives which were fundamental for both. Dryden is sometimes approached by means of inverse chronology from the direction of Pope's satire, but to see where Dryden stands in relation to Waller and Marvell—more accurately, where they stood in relation to him—a backward jump in time is helpful instead.

Quintus Curtius Rufus, in his antagonistic *History* of Alexander the Great (3.1), records that after the Gordian knot was cut, what was left was merely a rope. In the 1640s, an antiroyalist work appeared under the title, "The King's Cabinet Opened," and the writer of "A Satyr, Occasioned by the Author's Survey of a Scandalous Pamphlet, intituled The King's Cabinet Opened" was responsively outraged. This pair presents attack prior to defense but in other ways is not unlike royalist painting and antiroyalist repainting. At the end of the loyal side in this debate, "The Close" picks up Alexander and the knot and also includes a myth which the painter poems were later to employ, the maze of Minos on Crete.

> No *winding* Characters, no *secret* Maze,
> Could so *perplex*, but they have found their wayes.
> They *thred* the Labyrinth, and what to do?
> Whe'r *tends* the Guide? what *purchase* in this Clew?
> Rash *Alexander* forc't King *Gordius* Knot,
> And so in hand found he a *Rope* had got.[3]

Tracing these images out against their background is not profitable unless one is interested in seeing that they probably work to cross-purposes. Escaping the maze presumably is a desirable end, after all, and a rope would be far more useful than a knot in doing so. The author, however, is less interested in consistency than in condemning malicious confusion of the king's two bodies, those of the merely mortal man and the sacred monarch. The position thus taken here is

---

3. *Rump: or an Exact Collection Of the Choycest Poems and Songs Relating to the Late Times . . . 1639, to Anno 1661* (London, 1662; rpt. 1874), 178.

that some cabinets are best left closed. More specifically, to discover that the ruler is himself governed by fleshly demands is to relearn an obvious but irrelevant and pointlessly demeaning fact and to unlearn a valuable truth.

Waller unquestionably approved of this distinction and adopted it wholesale for much of his active life as a writer of complimentary verse. Fenton (cliii) hands down a report that Waller "employ'd the greatest part of a summer in composing, and correcting" a ten-line poem about Tasso to be "writ in the TASSO of her ROYAL HIGHNESS" (that is, of Mary, the second Duchess of York and consort of James). For his collection of eminent Beauties, to repeat a phrase from Fenton's observations on Lady Rich, Waller continued to entertain the idea that "The Hero's race excels the Poet's thought," but the thought in this case is expressly bookish in origin and use: a poem to be written at the front of an earlier poem which itself celebrated a heroism of the past. And when, rightly or not, the cabinet of the king himself was opened instead of the book of the duchess, either emptiness or a corroded image was discovered as that which existed behind the pretentious display. This fact was resisted by Waller for very understandable reasons since it undermined the foundations of his art and his nationalistic fervor, but he made his resistance with decreasing vigor and greater infrequency not wholly attributable to his own advancing years.

Marvell and "Marvell" were suspicious of Charles when the painter poems were being written, but at that time it was hard to be sure and even harder to accept that the fundamental problem was the king rather than corrupt ministers. Marvell, by the time he died, was convinced that a tyrannical papist controlled the show, but by then he was writing prose, not poetry, to prove it. Waller was still trying to keep the king's cabinet from being opened too far. Dryden evidently decided that it could not be kept shut and also was able to see the usefulness and even praiseworthiness of a rope in preference to a Gordian knot.

At the outset of *Absalom and Achitophel*, the doors are deliberately pried apart to show an imperfect monarch who closely resembles King David in his lapses but not very closely at all in his redemptive role as a prefiguration of Christ.

> *Israel*'s Monarch, after Heaven's own heart,
> His vigorous warmth did, variously, impart
> To Wives and Slaves: And, wide as his Command,
> Scatter'd his Maker's Image through the Land.
>
> (7–10)

In terms of rhetorical strategy, the lines concede that which cannot successfully be denied, and they attempt to convert moral weakness into genial behavior. It seems likely that Waller would never have admitted, much less conceded, this point about the king's notorious profligacy, and "Marvell," of course, had earlier been bluntly coarse in satirizing it. What Marvell needed at the end of "The Last Instructions" was Christ the King, but he was nowhere to be found. What Waller hoped and urged was that his king might embody Christian values in a Jovian form to raise Eden in England and turn the world itself around. Dryden made do without needs and hopes of that kind and stood both of his elders on their heads by appropriating Christian and classical heroism for the culpable side. Achitophel thus plays a Virgilian Satan to Absalom's Miltonic Christ, and the role of Charles as rightful ruler is confirmed, in large measure, not by what he is but by what those on the other side both are and are not.[4] Unlike Marvell, therefore, Dryden does not inflate in order to deflate unheroic treachery but rather to indicate the serious magnitude of the threat and the genuinely preferable worth, however genially flawed, of the king.

Since Dryden's marvelous poem needs no praise from me, the point to be made here is that Marvell might easily have lived long enough to read it and that Waller in fact was still alive and still writing when it appeared, but they could never have written anything quite like it themselves, either separately or jointly. Nor would they have tried. Their minds and art were of a different kind.

4. I gave some evidence for this statement in "Absalom and Achitophel: Christ and Satan," *MLN*, 74 (1959): 592–96.

Appendixes

I.
"Upon the Death of my Lady RICH."

MAY those already curst ESSEXIAN plains,
Where hasty death, and pining sickness, reigns,
Prove all a desart! and none there make stay,
But savage beasts, or men as wild as they!
There the fair light, which all our island grac'd,   5
Like HERO's taper in the window plac'd,
Such fate from the malignant air did find,
As that exposed to the boist'rous wind.
Ah cruel heav'n! to snatch so soon away
Her, for whose life had we had time to pray,   10
With thousand vows, and tears, we should have sought
That sad decree's suspension to have wrought.
But we, alas, no whisper of her pain
Heard, 'till 'twas sin to wish her here again.
That horrid word at once, like lightning spread,   15
Strook all our ears—the Lady RICH is dead!
Heart-rending news! and dreadful to those few
Who her resemble, and her steps persue:
That Death should license have to rage among
The fair, the wise, the virtuous, and the young!   20

The *PAPHIAN Queen from that fierce battel born,
With goared hand, and veil so rudely torn,
Like terror did among th'Immortals breed;
Taught by her wound that Goddesses may bleed.
All stand amazed! but beyond the rest   25
Th' †heroic dame whose happy womb she blest,
Mov'd with just grief, expostulates with heav'n;
Urging the promise to th' obsequious giv'n,
Of longer life: for ne'er was pious soul
More apt t' obey, more worthy to controul.   30
A skilful eye at once might read the race
Of CALEDONIAN Monarchs in her face,
And sweet humility: her look and mind
At once were lofty, and at once were kind.
There dwelt the scorn of vice, and pity too,   35
For those that did what she disdain'd to do:
So gentle and severe, that what was bad
At once her hatred, and her pardon had.
Gracious to all; but where her love was due,
So fast, so faithful, loyal, and so true,   40
That a bold hand as soon might hope to force
The rowling lights of heav'n, as change her course.
Some happy Angel, that beholds her there,
Instruct us to record what she was here!
And when this cloud of sorrow's over-blown,   45
Through the wide world we'll make her graces known.
So fresh the wound is, and the grief so vast,
That all our art, and pow'r of speech, is waste.
Here passion sways, but there the Muse shall raise
Eternal monuments of louder praise.   50
There our delight, complying with her fame,
Shall have occasion to recite thy name,
Fair SACHARISSA!—and now only fair!
To sacred friendship we'll an altar rear;
(Such as the ROMANS did erect of old.)   55
Where, on a marble pillar, shall be told
The lovely passion each to other bare,
With the resemblance of that matchless Pair.
NARCISSUS to the thing for which he pin'd

*Venus.
†Christian Countess of Devonshire.

Was not more like, that yours to her fair mind: 60
Save that she grac'd the sev'ral parts of life,
A spotless virgin, and a faultless wife:
Such was the sweet converse 'twixt her and you,
As that she holds with her associates now.
How false is hope, and how regardless fate,   65
That such a love should have so short a date!
Lately I saw her sighing part from thee;
(Alas that That the last farewell should be!)
So look'd ASTRAEA, her remove design'd,
On those distressed friends she left behind.   70
Consent in virtue knit your hearts so fast,
That still the knot, in spight of death, does last:
For, as your tears, and sorrow-wounded soul,
Prove well that on your part this bond is whole:
So, all we know of what they do above,   75
Is, that they happy are, and that they love.
Let dark oblivion, and the hollow grave,
Content themselves our frailer thoughts to have:
Well chosen love is never taught to die,
But with our nobler part invades the sky.   80
Then grieve no more, that one so heav'nly shap'd
The crooked hand of trembling age escap'd.
Rather, since we beheld her not decay,
But that she vanish'd so entire away,
Her wond'rous beauty, and her goodness, merit   85
We should suppose, that some propitious spirit
In that coelestial form frequented here;
And is not dead, but ceases to appear.

From *The Works of Edmund Waller, Esq; In Verse and Prose*. Published by Mr. Fenton. London: Printed for J. and R. Tonson and S. Draper in the *Strand*. MDCCXLIV. [Line numbers have been added.]

II. The Textual Crux in Marvell's "Coy Mistress"

The celebrated crux in Marvell's "To his Coy Mistress" now exists and has long been provocative partly for textual reasons but also—perhaps more importantly, in fact—because "glue" has not been thought a word that a poet so polished as Marvell would use, at least not in so elegant a poem. The vehement spokesman for this view is Adams, Marvell's editor for the Norton Anthology. In earlier editions, "glew" was "an odious reading"; as of 1986, despite "efforts . . . to salvage 'glew' by declaring it a dialectal form of 'glow,' " it is "a reading as odious in Marvell's time as in ours."[1] The "efforts" here mentioned are those of Martz (1963) and Lord (1968), who do indeed give *glew* but only with a very firm understanding that it does not mean glue but glow. While, therefore, the three editors differ on what to print, they nonetheless share a strong belief about the impropriety of glue itself. The hostility, moreover, goes back at least as far as 1927, when Margoliouth, the founder of modern texts of Marvell, stated, "I cannot believe that Marvell wrote 'glew,' " and it may date from as early as 1726, when Cooke silently emended to *dew*, the reading that Margoliouth, Adams, and many others subsequently came to prefer.[2] Because of Cooke's silence, however, caution is needed lest a hasty conclusion be reached, for what repels can also attract, a fact made abundantly clear by Clayton (1972) when he asserts that *glew* is more "appropriately sensuous *and* grotesque" than "tepid 'morning dew' " (369). About evaluations of this kind there may seem little to be said since, after all, *chacun à son goût*. In this case, however, the better maxim to cite may be *La goût est fait de mille dégoûts* since distaste for gluing, despite what Adams says, is in fact a phenomenon dating from times later than Marvell's own. The second chapter of this study gives the evidence for that point, but the textual problem itself is very tangled.

For many years the prime authority for the majority of Marvell's poems, including "To his Coy Mistress," was the posthumous Folio, *Miscellaneous Poems*, published in 1681 by a "Mary Marvell" masquer-

1. *The Norton Anthology of English Literature*, 5th ed. (New York, 1986), 1.1388, and 4th ed. (1979), 1.1361. Frequently cited authorities on Marvell— including Clayton, Lord, Margoliouth, and Martz, all mentioned in this paragraph—are listed in the References.

2. For Cooke's edition—and also Thompson's of 1776—I have relied on the apparatus included by more recent editors. Among others who have adopted Cooke's emendation in recent years are the following: John Hollander and Frank Kermode, *The Oxford Anthology of English Literature* (New York, 1973); John Broadbent, *Signet Classic Poets of the Seventeenth Century* (New York, 1974); Herschel Baker, *The Later Renaissance in England* (Boston, 1975); Mario Di Cesare, *George Herbert and the Seventeenth-Century Religious Poets* (New York, 1978; a Norton Critical Edition which, despite the title, includes Marvell's lyrics); T. G. S. Cain, *Jacobean and Caroline Poetry* (London and New York, 1981).

ading as the poet's nonexistent widow. The work supplies what even now appears to be a basically sound text, despite the imposture behind it, but in any case it had to be the only source with substantive, as distinct from editorial, authority because there simply was none other. The situation might have changed in the 1940s when the Bodley acquired a book-manuscript catalogued as *Eng. poet. d. 49*, but since those interested in Marvell did not know of the acquisition until some years later, the effect was not immediate. This volume consists of sheets from the 1681 Folio with inked-in "corrections" (which resemble print), along with manuscript additions in an unidentified hand. While the original provenance is not provable, the work *may* derive from William Popple, Marvell's nephew and sometime associate, and despite general agreement about the necessity of consulting the volume, its reliability has been variously assessed. Craze reflects the spread of opinion in writing, "I have not accepted half the corrections that E. S. Donno did . . . but I accept more than Legouis."[3] Both 1681 and *Eng. poet. d. 49* testify to the presence of the word "glew" in Marvell's "To his Coy Mistress." Unfortunately, as Lord observes, "the Bod. MS. compounds the difficulty" rather than simplifying it "by emending *hew* to *glew* and *glew* to *dew*." In 1726, Cooke might have adopted *dew* from this source directly or indirectly, but the point can only be speculative.[4]

3. Craze, 10. This entire matter continues to be thorny. Legouis made substantial use of the Bodleian volume but in many cases preferred "to suspend judgement" (1.235). Donno—chiding Legouis—wrote, "It is to be hoped that the textual notes included in this edition," her own, i.e., "will make any further suspension of judgement unnecessary" (10 n.). Di Cesare (see preceding note) asserts, "In many ways more important than 1681 is a volume in the Bodleian Library . . ." (213). Chernaik—concerned, however, primarily with poems other than the lyrics—maintains that the volume's "authority is by no means as absolute and unquestionable as some recent scholars have claimed" (206).

4. This possibility exists because Thompson in 1776 claimed to have used two manuscript books, one of them a compilation by Popple, to which Cooke therefore conceivably had access fifty years earlier. Lord read the Bodleian volume against Thompson's text of the poems on Cromwell and other post-Restoration satires and concluded (xxxi) that the "comparison proves beyond question that the MS described by Thompson . . . had been recovered." Conceding that "Thompson was wrong about the hand" and that the manuscript was the work of a commercial scribe rather than Popple himself, Lord nonetheless believed that it "was undoubtedly compiled under Popple's direction." Chernaik has vigorously challenged Lord's conclusions about canon and text, but the details of this part of the dispute are not relevant here.

Another manuscript has also been reexamined in recent years. Catalogued in the Bodley as *Don b. 8*, but usually referred to as "Haward,"
it is a miscellaneous collection compiled from various authors by Sir
William Haward sometime after 1667. Thorn Drury read it long ago
on Margoliouth's behalf (see Margoliouth 1.208), but only to collate
the satires, not the lyrics. He may not have noticed the presence of
"To his Coy Mistress" or, if he did, just possibly may have chosen to
ignore it since this version appears to be hopelessly corrupt. In either
case, it was freshly recovered by Conrad Kelliher, who described and
transcribed it in *NQ* and had it photographically reproduced in the
book which documents an exhibition held at the British Library to
commemorate the tercentenary of Marvell's death.[5] Among the many
deficiencies in Haward is the omission of entire couplets for a total
loss of ten lines, a high proportion indeed in a forty-six-line poem.
Even so, as Kelliher points out in the British Library volume, the
year of compilation, "almost certainly 1672" but in any case well
before 1681, means that "this is the only known text of Marvell's most
famous lyric that is totally independent of the 1681 Folio," and it
therefore must not be ignored. Kelliher himself advances the theory
that "some of the readings here may survive from an earlier stage in
the composition of the poem" and in the *NQ* publication singles out
the final couplet as a particular case in point. The lines, as given in
1681,

> Thus, though we cannot make our Sun
> Stand still, yet we will make him run,

in Haward take this form:

> And synce Wee cannot make the Sun
> Goe backe, nor stand, wee'l make him run.

Kelliher (again in *NQ*) comments:

> The only other defensible variant in this part of the poem is, I
> suggest, in the last line, where "Goe backe" reverses the normal
> process of corruption by introducing a wholly new idea. The
> Folio reading, not without some loss of compactness, balances
> "stand" more pointedly against "run." Marvell must have de-

---

5. In what follows I specify, sometimes parenthetically, which of these publications is being quoted.

cided [note the presumption of revision] that a backward glance of this kind was foreign to the spirit of the poem.

Overlooked in this remark is that running actually can be in either direction, as in Milton's Nativity poem ("Time will run back, and fetch the age of gold," 135),[6] but there may be some attractiveness to the possibility that retrograde motion at one stage was explicitly present. More to the immediate point, however, is that Haward does give *glew* and does so, moreover, in a way that bolsters belief that the word means "glue" since "Sits on thy skin" (1681) is replaced by "*Stickes* on thy Cheeke" (my italics).

Weighing this inconsistent and inconclusive evidence naturally has led to very different conclusions. In the hope of some much-needed clarity, I now give a summary view of three of the couplet's forms:

1681 (followed by Martz and Lord, endorsed by Clayton):

Now therefore, while the youthful hew
Sits on thy skin like morning glew.

1681 as "corrected" by *Eng. poet. d. 49* and supported by Haward (adopted by Donno, Craze, and Wilcher and endorsed by Kelliher's remark in the British Library volume that the "natural position" of *glew* "is as the first rhyme"):

Now therefore, while the youthful ~~hew~~ glew
Sits on thy skin like morning ~~glew~~ dew,

Cooke (and followers, including Adams, Margoliouth in his second edition, Broadbent, and Legouis):

Now therefore, while the youthful hew
Sits on thy skin like morning dew.

(A fourth form requires only parenthetical inclusion. In 1927, Margoliouth observed that the 1681 printer duplicated *st* in line 42 of "The Gallery" so as to produce "do*st st*ore" from "do store." He also pro-

6. Milton is quoted from *Complete Poems and Major Prose*, ed. Merritt Y. Hughes (New York, 1957).

posed that a similar dittography of *g* brought forth "morning glew" from "morning lew." "Lew," meaning "warmth," was dialectal—though not more so and possibly less than *glew: glow*—as well as obsolete, and the conjecture failed for want of adherents. Margoliouth himself, "by no means confident" even at first, in effect abandoned the theory in his second edition to "return to Cooke's commonplace but probably correct emendation.")

This summary view makes clear, I think, not only editorial divergence but also the reason why modern claims on behalf of one or another of the competing forms so often rests on an understanding of the couplet and its context. A reliable control on probable or even permissible details cannot be established on textual evidence alone. As it happens, Martz, Lord, and Clayton are able to eliminate one cause of uncertainty by taking the presence of *hew* for granted. Lord briefly comments that "the youthful *hue* of the lady is compared with the tints of the sky at dawn," and Clayton (370) states that "the 'youthful hew' is the conventional rosy glow of youth." Martz makes a comparable assumption to argue for "glow":

> Here *glew* can only means *glow* in the sense for which OED cites a Shakespearean example: "Brightness and warmth [note that "lew," "warmth" in effect has been subsumed] of colour; a state of glowing brightness, a flush" (OED "glow" *sb*. 2). Most important, *glew: glow* makes better sense in the context than *dew*. The speaker is talking about a *hue*, a color; and what could be more appropriate than to compare his lady's hue with the morning-glow of sunrise? The next couplet [not quoted by Martz:
>
> > And while thy willing Soul transpires
> > At every pore with instant Fires,]
>
> may contain a suggestion of moisture; and yet even here it is the *Fires* that transpire through the pores: *Fires* and *glow* fit well together.

Wilcher argues against modernizing "glew" to "glue" precisely because the former spelling "makes apparent the possibility that Marvell, a Yorkshireman, had in mind . . . a homophonic northern dialect form of 'glow' current in fourteenth- and fifteenth-century texts."[7]

---

7. In fairness to Wilcher, I should add that he also proposes the possibility that Marvell had in mind "the modern meaning of 'glue' "; he further argues, "From its presence in the three earliest texts . . . it looks as if the word 'glew' or 'glue' figured in Marvell's poem at some stage of its composition."

Broadbent, on the other hand, thought *Fires* fitted well not with "glow" but with *dew*:

> *dew . . . fires*   youth is like a liquid bloom or sweat; her soul breathes out of her pores like air; then burns with quick heat—three elements arising from the fourth, earth.

In the British Library volume, however, Kelliher associates the pores with "*glew*—the moisture that 'transpires / At every pore.' " Donno begs some of these questions in her annotation:

> It is to be noted that the reading *glue* (in this much debated couplet) appears in rhyme position in both *Eng. poet. d. 49* and in *F*. In the Folio, however, its transposition to 1. 34 resulted in a reading editors have almost invariably emended.

Also to be noted is that Donno is vague about which line is being emended in what way and with what result. Indeed, she comes close to omitting *hew* altogether, mentioning the word only once in a brief textual note and with no comment on why it can or should be so summarily dismissed. Instead, she proceeds to argue in a way reminiscent of Martz but to a completely different conclusion:

> Moreover, the sense of *youthful glue* is entirely consonant with the theme of the poem as the following quotation makes clear: 'Life is nothing else but as it were a glue, which in man fasteneth the soul and body together' (William Baldwin, *Moral Philosophy*, 1547, cited in the *OED*).

Craze at least acknowledges the existence and possible claims of *hew* when he asserts that "this 'glue-dew' combination is far better than the Folio's 'hew-glew', better too than the 'hew-dew' of Cooke's alteration." Fully confident that Haward is indeed a draft, he further states,

> The 'glue' or 'glew' which . . . 'sits on thy skin' is youthful perspiration; in the Haward MS. it 'stickes on your Cheeke'. The Folio then goes on and adds 'Soul transpires' to 'Body perspires', with 'every pore' as the logical connection.

Comments of this kind, though they certainly make excellent sense in their own terms, leave one in a quandary. Martz and Donno are the most obvious examples of those who invoke historical precedent about usage in much the same way to arrive at mutually exclusive conclusions; they thereby indicate—however unintentionally—that not even the *OED*, massively and thoroughly historic though it is, in this case seems to be enough. Lacking further textual authorities of a more conclusive kind, I can see no way of resolving the problem except to go on a fishing expedition outside as well as inside the already large confines of the *OED* in the hope that something worthwhile will be caught. That, in effect, is the strategy adopted above in the chapter on "Glue and Marvell's Mistress." The information given there, even in my own opinion, does not provide as many answers as one would like, but it probably obviates some of the questions by showing that they need not be asked and possibly enables a better understanding than hitherto of the implications of those that remain.

Since Margoliouth himself abandoned "lew," the dittography needed to account for it can be passed over as well. But he never retracted his statement that glue "had its modern sense in" Marvell's "day and would therefore be inadmissible in this context." This remark seems to me demonstrably upside down, though not because a "modern" and an older "sense" notably diverge in denotative significance. Margoliouth was discounting the possibility, proposed to him by "the late Henry Bradley" (presumably the well-known bibliophile), "that '*glew*' might be right in the sense of 'glow.' " This is the translation, of course, re-proposed by Martz and Lord, apparently without noticing Bradley and certainly without meeting Margoliouth's objection to it. But the translation is not necessary; "glew" *qua* "glue" works quite well indeed. The reason, however, has nothing to do with whether the word was favorably grotesque or unfavorably odious. This last point, moreover, is supported by the facts that "dew," in physiological contexts, turns out to have been no better, though definitely not worse, than "glue" as a lustrous word and that even "hue" at times has had no more intrinsic loveliness than an animal's or a varlet's "hide."

If *glew* is admissible in the sense of "glue" and without prejudice either way about its being in some sense bizarre, then the next question might be in which line the word should appear. I can see no way of addressing this problem, however, apart from the closely related question of what the rhyme ought to be and therefore shall temporarily postulate that the word is *dew*. On that basis, it can be observed that Kelliher may have been hasty in supposing that the "natural position" of *glew* "is as the first rhyme." Part of the evidence given above in my second chapter suggests that if anything, this statement ought to be reversed. From the point of view of physiological chronology, dew necessarily precedes glue, since the first—to requote Aquinas—is "at the beginning of its transformation," whereas the second "has already reached its ultimate perfection." Because of the developmental process, *youthful* "dew" is more accurate than "youthful" *glue*. "Morning," on the other hand, while it certainly can connote youth, also can be a more elastic word, perhaps especially so if one is thinking Hebraically. In that case, after all, every "day"—especially the Sabbath for purposes of ritual—"begins" with the evening; morning comes afterwards, not before. Milton reflects this fact by scrupulously punctuating Raphael's account of the several days of creation with variant statements of "when first Ev'ning was, and when first Morn" (*PL*, 7.260; cf. 275, 338, 386, 448, and 550). This particular point, moreover, probably is not affected one way or the other by Donno's argument that "the sense of *youthful glue* is entirely consonant with the theme of the poem," among other reasons because her evidence at best is inconclusive. Her quotation from Baldwin, "life is nothing else but as it were a glue," says nothing of literal or figurative age. Browne, quoted above in connection with the requisites for vitality, refers specifically to the ages of thirty and seventy in making a comparable metaphoric point.

The existence of "hew," however, ought not be forgotten. Despite Donno's near silence on this matter, the word does have considerable authority, both substantive and editorial. Fortunately, if it is to be in the poem in either line, there probably can be no question but what it must appear first. *Mutatis mutandis*, all of the arguments make it nearly inconceivable that either dew *or* glue could precede hue. Since "hew" must come first, if at all, Marvell could have begun by thinking of skin and its hue, either in the general sense of external form and appearance or in the specific sense of tint, complexion, *color*. A relatively general condition of skin could have led on to dew, not merely as a word with traditionally reverberant connotation but as a fairly precise term of physiological moisture, of humidity as "radical humour" or as "leshad," that very best oily moisture of life itself. Dew of that kind might have been refined still further to *glew* as perfected fluid and the superlative bond of unity. The *dew: hew* of Hosea vi.4–5, quoted above, thus might be a step toward *hew: glew*, but a more important point is that, of the three words, glue is the one with greatest force in terms of ultimate comparative values. No physiological fluid could have been more close to ideal stasis, nor could any term have signified a bonding unity more complete. Since it is difficult to see how Marvell could have praised the lady more highly than by commending the integrative perfection of her glue, it might be argued that the word is not only more forceful but more climactic than the others and therefore should appear last. Donno may be correct, of course, in presupposing that it is the Folio wherein a transposition, unfortunately, has been made. Equally possible, however, is that the "correction" made in the Bodleian volume is itself an unintentional transposition and that its *glew*: *dew* actually should be *dew*: *glew*. If, at least, *hew* is indeed the word to be discarded and if, moreover, "glue" is climactic, then the couplet would have to be this:

> Now therefore, while the youthful dew
> Sits on thy skin like morning glew.

This proposition is not, I think, extravagant, but any stronger claim might be.

Legouis decided to leave the problem "until fresh evidence turns up" (1.235). From a purely textual perspective, that seems to me to be the only sensible thing to do. In the meantime, however, as I have tried to indicate both here and in the chapter above, some misconceptions can be cleared away.

References

Extremely frequent citation of reference materials has often been necessary. A system therefore had to be devised which permitted the inclusion of many references as unobtrusively as possible since footnotes otherwise would threaten to overwhelm the text and continually disrupt discussion to no useful purpose. I explain here the system adopted and the rationale for it. There are four sections: (1) texts for Waller; (2) texts for Marvell; (3) dictionaries and similar books of reference; and (4) biblical commentaries.

1. Waller: No modern text for Waller is yet available, although Philip R. Wikelund has been preparing one for some years. Earl Miner received permission to print Wikelund's text of "On St. James's Park" as an appendix to *The Cavalier Mode from Jonson to Cotton* (Princeton, 1971); uncertain about proprieties, I asked Professor Wikelund's permission to use it here and would like to express thanks for his kind reply. The poem is also given in *Ben Jonson and the Cavalier Poets* (A Norton Critical Edition), ed. Hugh Maclean (New York, 1974). "Instructions to a Painter" was included in *Poems on Affairs of State*, ed. George deF. Lord, 1: 1660–78 (New Haven and London, 1963). (I also quote from this volume for subsequent painter poems, including Marvell's "Last Instructions"; there seemed little point in changing texts for poems so closely related to one another.) For other poems by Waller, the text quoted is *The Works*, ed. Elijah Fenton (London, 1744); Fenton includes plates for the medals struck for the birth and coronation of Charles II (referred to in my

discussion of "On St. James's Park"), and his "Observations" (i–clxviii) continue to be indispensable. See also *The Poems*, ed. G. Thorn-Drury (London, 1893).

2. Marvell: Painter poems, as just indicated, are quoted from Lord. The Scolar Press published in 1969 a facsimile of the 1681 Folio: *Miscellaneous Poems* (London, 1681). It was reproduced in original size from the British Museum (now the British Library) copy "except for a number of pages reproduced in the Appendix" from Bod. MS. *Eng. poet. d. 49* (concerning which, see Appendix II above, "The Textual Crux"); "the last two leaves (missing in all known copies [of the printed folio]) are also reproduced from the Bodleian MS. after page 144." "To his Coy Mistress" is quoted from the facsimile; an unedited text seemed appropriate here since one of the questions raised about the poem concerns editorial decisions. Otherwise, the poems are quoted from *The Complete Poems*, ed. Elizabeth Story Donno (Middlesex and New York, 1972; rpt. 1976, 1978). Standard authorities on Marvell are referred to only by name, without footnote. Most of the comment is keyed to the text itself so that the location of quoted matter is usually obvious; when needed, a reference is parenthetically incorporated wherever the name is mentioned. Occasionally, to prevent confusion, I depart from this general rule and give a conventional footnote. Additional authorities (in alphabetical order) are as follows:

Chernaik: Warren L. Chernaik, "Appendix: Manuscript evidence for the canon of Marvell's poems," in *The Poet's Time*: *Politics and Religion in the Work of Andrew Marvell* (Cambridge, 1983), 206–15.

Clayton: Thomas Clayton, " 'Morning Glew' and Other Sweat Leaves in the Folio Text of Marvell's Major Pre-Restoration Poems," *ELR*, 2 (1972): 356–75.

Craze: Michael Craze, *The Life and Lyrics of Andrew Marvell* (London, 1979); in effect an edition since full texts, with discussion of important variants, are given.

Haward: See Conrad Kelliher, "A New Text of Marvell's 'To his Coy Mistress,' " *NQ*, 215 (July 1970): 254–55; and *Andrew Marvell*: *Poet and Politician* (The British Library, 1978).

Legouis: *The Poems and Letters*, ed. H. M. Margoliouth, 3d ed. rev. Pierre Legouis "with the collaboration of E. E. Duncan-Jones," 2 vols. (Oxford, 1971).

Lord: *The Complete Poetry*, ed. George deF. Lord (New York, 1968).

Margoliouth: *The Poems and Letters*, ed. H. M. Margoliouth, 2d ed., 2 vols. (Oxford, 1952).

Martz: *The Meditative Poem*, ed. Louis Martz (New York, 1963).

Wilcher: *Selected Poetry and Prose*, ed. Robert Wilcher (London and New York, 1986).

3. Standard scholarly practice allows that footnotes be omitted for references to the *Oxford English Dictionary* (the *OED*), the *Dictionary of National*

Biography (the *DNB*), the Bible, and volumes in the Loeb Classical Library (translations taken from the Loeb are so identified but otherwise are my own). The same practice is here extended to the following:

OLD: *The Oxford Latin Dictionary*, 8 fasc. (Oxford, 1968–82).
Lewis and Short: *A Latin Dictionary* (Oxford, 1879, repr. 1955).
Liddell and Scott: *A Greek-English Lexicon*, rev. Jones and McKensie (Oxford, 1940; rpt. 1961).
OCD: *The Oxford Classical Dictionary*, 2d. ed. (Oxford, 1970).
Young: Robert Young, *Analytical Concordance to the Bible* (innumerable editions.)

Three dictionaries, despite the customary alphabetical order which makes footnotes pointless, need special notice.

Leigh: Edward Leigh (1602–71), *Critica Sacra . . . Observations On all the Radices, or Primitive Hebrew Words of the Old Testament . . . Philologicall and Theologicall Observations upon All the Greek Words of the New Testament*, 3d ed. (London, 1650) (combining the two parts from earlier publication). This work of necessity is keyed not to an English alphabet but to Hebrew and Greek. Leigh gives no transliterations, a practice I invert by giving only transliterated forms of the words under which the entries are to be found. The entries themselves are macaronics of Hebrew, Greek, Latin, and English; where possible, I quote only the English, eliding the rest. When elision is impossible, I supply translations.

Young: William Young, *A New English-Latin Dictionary . . . A New Dictionary, Latin and English*, 8th ed. (London, 1792). The "8th" is misleading since it counts earlier editions not only of Young but also of the *Thesaurus* of Robert Ainsworth, London, 1736 et seq., on which Young largely based his own work. (For a discussion of Young, Ainsworth, and their predecessors, see DeWitt T. Starnes, *Renaissance Dictionaries* [Austin, 1954].) I have used Young repeatedly in devising translations of Latin, partly because of the date and ancestry, partly because the translations from both sides serve as a double check on translatable meaning.

Wilson: Thomas Wilson (1563–1622), *A Christian Dictionary* (London, 1622); separately paginated are supplements for words "specially" used in Apocalypse or Revelation, Canticles or Song of Songs, and Hebrews. I have used Wilson, like Young, with some frequency, in this case as another authority for usage of biblical words in English.

4. Since biblical commentary also is keyed to specific texts, I also can cite it by naming the author and identifying the verse being explained, again without footnote. In this case, however, further comment is in order since the reason for selecting the particular works used here (listed below) may not be obvious. The aim has been to limit the enormous amount of possibly pertinent material to manageable proportions and yet to "bracket" Marvell and Waller by including representative authorities, historically well established

and well known, on the usage of biblical words in times prior to, concurrent with, and somewhat later than Marvell and Waller themselves. Lapide's massive commentary is especially valuable as a survey of traditional views from the Fathers on down; a reference to "Lapide" sometimes means, in fact, only that he is reporting, not necessarily expressing, an opinion, but for my purposes it has not always seemed worthwhile to make a distinction. Evelyn Simpson documented Donne's use of Lapide's earlier volumes (some of them were not published during Donne's lifetime and others not until after Lapide's own death, eight years later). She asserted, in what may be a pardonable exaggeration, that Lapide was "immensely popular." See *The Sermons*, ed. George R. Potter and Evelyn M. Simpson, 10 vols. (Berkeley and Los Angeles, 1953–62), 8.393–96 and 10.366–74 (the quoted phrase is from 10.370). Lapide was saving Psalms for last and died too soon. As a result, the slightly earlier commentary of Cardinal Bellarmine was widely used as a supplement and sometimes printed uniformly with Lapide's own work. A twenty-four-volume edition appeared at Paris, 1857–63, rpt. 1865. "Poole" ambivalently refers to two works, but since they are in different languages (and for different audiences), there is no confusion about which one is being quoted. The gargantuan Latin *Synopsis* is more philological in its attention to Hebrew and Greek and thus more "up-to-date" than Lapide. Poole began work on an English commentary, less formidable in length, in which he adapted a selection from the Latin materials in combination with glosses already available to many English readers. Those divines who completed the work after Poole's death explicitly acknowledge debts to the following:

> "the Geneva Notes" (*i.e.*, those incorporated in the English Bible first published at Geneva, 1560 and not completely displaced even by the Authorized Version; see the facsimile, with introduction by Lloyd Berry [Madison, 1969]) "those of famous Diodate" (*i.e.*, John Diodati, translator of the Bible into Italian, uncle of Milton's friend Charles; *Pious and Learned Annotations* reached a 4th edition "Corrected, and much Augmented, with Additional Notes of the same Authour . . . And The Analysis . . . now fully completed" [London, 1664])
>
> "the Dutch Annotations" (*i.e.*, a translation made by Theodore Haak, at the request of the Westminster Assembly of Divines, from the Dutch annotated Bible authorized at the Synod of Dort, 1618–19; published as *The Dutch Annotations*, 2 vols. [London, 1657])
>
> "and those of our own divines" (*i.e.*, the commentary, again published for the Westminster Assembly, attributed to John Downame *et al.*, indifferently referred to as "the Assembly annotations" or "the English annotations" as distinct from the "Dutch"; printed as *Annotations upon all the books of the Old and New Testament* [London, 1645])

With "all their shoulders to stand upon," Poole's posthumous collaborators modestly claim "little" for themselves, but the usefulness of the work as a guide to earlier interpretation is at least as obvious as that of the more erudite Latin "Poole" and the more traditional "Lapide." Henry Ainsworth is used primarily as a safeguard against possible idiosyncracies in other "scholarly" sources and Matthew Henry as an example, more "pious" in orientation, of continuity into times immediately after the deaths of Marvell and Waller. Tenuous biographical links exist among Marvell, Poole, and Henry (and are noticed toward the end of the chapter on "Glue and Marvell's Mistress"), but I know of none which involve Waller. The dictionaries of Leigh and Wilson described above should be rementioned here since their content, in effect, is that of biblical commentary. Further bibliographical details (in alphabetical order):

Ainsworth: Henry Ainsworth (1571–1622?), *Annotations Upon . . . Genesis . . . Exodus . . . Numbers . . . Deuteronomie . . . Psalmes . . . Solomons Song of Songs in English Metre, with Annotations* (London, 1639).
Bellarmine: Robert Bellarmine, Cardinal, S. J. (1542–1621), *Explanatio in Psalmos, editio novissima* (Venice, 1759).
Lapide: Cornelius à Lapide (Cornelis Cornelissen van den Steen), S. J. (1567–1637), *Commentaria*, 10 vols., published at Antwerp as follows: *In Pentateuch* (1616); *quatuor Prophetas maiores* (1634); *omnes divi Pauli Epistolas* (1635); *Ecclesiasten . . . Canticum canticorum . . . librum Sapientiae* (1638); *quatuor Evangelia* (1639); *Iosue, Iudicum, Ruth, IV libros Regum, et II Paralipomenon* (1642); *Ecclesiasticum* (1643); *Salamonis Proverbia* (1645); *Acta Apostolorum, Epistolas canonicas, et Apocalypsin* (1647); *duodecim Prophetas minores* (1655).
Henry: Matthew Henry (1662–1714), *Commentary on the Whole Bible*, 5 vols. (London, 1710) reprinted in 6 (Scottdale, Pa., n.d., ca. 1935).
Poole: Matthew Poole (1624–79), *Synopsis criticorum aliorumque Sacrae Scripturae interpretum et commentarorum*, 5 vols. (Utrecht, 1684–86).
———: *A Commentary on the Holy Bible*, 3 vols. (London, 1683–85; rpt. 1962).

Index

Some names are deliberately omitted: those of Marvell and Waller, for example, as well as the nearly innumerable names of those who briefly appear in the Painter poems.